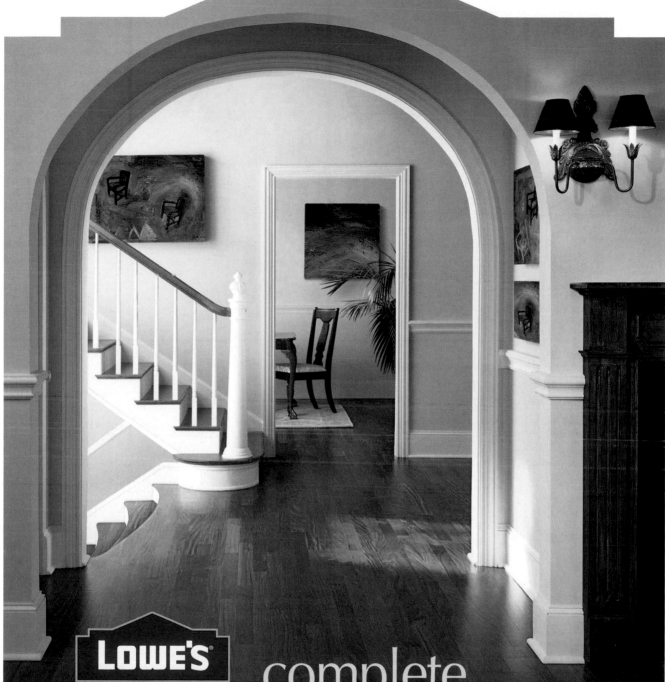

LOWE'S
Improving Home Improvement

complete
tile & flooring

tile and flooring know-how

A NEW FLOOR HAS A TRANSFORMING EFFECT. NOT ONLY DOES IT DRAMATICALLY change the look of a room, it can enhance comfort, versatility, and ease of maintenance. And that transformation can be quick. In some cases, you can install a new floor in less time than it takes to paint a room. Tile—on floors, walls, or countertops—takes a bit more time, but results in a high-quality, low-maintenance surface that will be a beautiful addition to your home.

This book will equip you to make an informed decision about the type of tile or flooring you need, letting you weigh such important factors as durability, ease of installation, and cost. It gives you complete instructions for installation, including tips that will aid you in doing a professional-looking job. You'll also learn how to make repairs and how to maintain the materials you install.

Lowe's Complete Tile & Flooring joins our growing series: **Complete Home Improvement & Repair, Complete Landscaping, Complete Home Decorating, Complete Kitchen, Complete Bathroom, Decorating with Paint & Color,** and **Complete Patio & Deck Book.** They're all part of our commitment to providing you with ideas, information, and inspiration, along with the right tools, materials, fixtures, and finishes, for any home improvement project.

Lowe's specialists are eager to assist you with purchasing decisions and ready with advice on installation. A Lowe's sales associate will work with installers to ensure a successful outcome. If you're going to do the work on your own, our in-store classes or the wealth of information in our How-To Library on www.lowes.com can help you tackle the project with confidence.

Lowe's has a long tradition of helping customers create beautiful homes. For tile and flooring you can be proud of, let us be your guide.

Lowe's Companies, Inc.

Bob Tillman
CHAIRMAN AND CEO

Robert Niblock
PRESIDENT

Melissa S. Birdsong
DIRECTOR, TREND
FORECASTING & DESIGN

Bob Gfeller
SENIOR VP, MARKETING

Jean Melton
VP, MERCHANDISING

Mike Menser
SENIOR VP, GENERAL
MERCHANDISE MANAGER

Zach Miller
MERCHANDISER

Dale Pond
SENIOR EXECUTIVE VP,
MERCHANDISING

Ann Serafin
MERCHANDISING DIRECTOR

LOWE'S®
Improving Home Improvement®

table of contents

6   **how to use this book**

8   **tile and flooring options**
10   today's choices
14   ceramic and stone tile
16   glazed ceramic tile
18   terra-cotta tiles
20   porcelain tile
21   quarry tile
22   polished stone tile
24   mosaics
26   tumbled-stone tile
28   rough stone tile
30   resilient flooring
36   wood flooring
40   wood parquet tiles
42   laminate flooring
44   decorative concrete flooring
46   carpeting
50   baseboards and thresholds
52   getting practical
56   choosing flooring
59   tools you'll need

66   **wall and counter tiles**
68   preparing a wall for tiling
72   laying out for wall tile
74   tiling a wall
80   tiling a tub surround
88   countertop & sink design options

96   **preparing for flooring**
98   inspecting a floor
100   firming a floor
102   removing fixtures and other obstacles
104   removing mouldings
106   removing flooring
109   creating a level surface
110   laying cement backerboard
112   installing plywood underlayment
114   preparing a concrete slab
116   expansion joints and membranes

118   **ceramic and stone floor tile**
120   laying out for a tile installation
124   marking tiles for cutting
126   cutting ceramic and stone tiles
129   mixing and applying mortar
130   laying floor tiles
134   tile base pieces and cove base
136   floating ceramic tiles
140   choosing and installing thresholds
142   installing stone tile
144   setting a patterned floor
146   tiling a hearth and fireplace surround

150   **vinyl flooring**
152   installing tiles
158   installing vinyl sheet flooring

164 strip flooring

166 floor designs

168 installing parquet wood flooring

172 installing a solid wood strip floor

178 installing wood baseboard

184 creating a striped floor

185 finishing options

186 engineered flooring options

188 stapling an engineered wood floor

191 gluing down engineered flooring

194 floating engineered or laminate flooring

198 combining wood with tile

200 repairs and maintenance

202 sanding and refinishing a hardwood floor

206 repairing tongue-and-groove flooring

208 caring for flooring and tile surfaces

210 replacing tiles

213 repairing grout

214 re-caulking

215 laminate floor repair

216 carpet maintenance

218 glossary

220 credits

221 index

Lowe's Series

PROJECT DIRECTOR René Klein

SENIOR EDITOR Sally W. Smith

Staff for Lowe's Complete Tile & Flooring

EDITOR David Toht

WRITER Steve Cory

GRAPHIC DESIGN
Rebecca Anderson

EDITORIAL/DESIGN ASSISTANT
Sarah Tibbot

PREPRESS COORDINATOR
Danielle Javier

COPY EDITOR Barbara Webb

PAGE PRODUCTION
Linda M. Bouchard

PROOFREADER Alicia Eckley

INDEXER Nanette Cardon

PRODUCTION DIRECTOR
Lory Day

DIGITAL PRODUCTION
Jeff Curtis/Leisure Arts

On the cover

TOP LEFT
Photo by Thomas J. Story
Design: Neal Schwartz, Architect

BOTTOM LEFT
Photo by Laura Dunkin-Hubby
Tiles from Lowe's

COVER DESIGN Vasken Guiragossian

TOP RIGHT
Photo courtesy of
Wicanders Cork Flooring

BOTTOM RIGHT
Photo by Thomas J. Story
Design: L. Kershner Design

Page 1: Armstrong/Bruce Hardwood

Page 2: Photo by Dominique Vorillon

10 9 8 7 6 5 4 3 2 1
First printing August 2004
Copyright © 2004
Sunset Publishing Corporation, Menlo Park, CA 94025.
First edition. All rights reserved, including the right of reproduction
in whole or in part in any form.
ISBN 0-376-00921-7
Library of Congress Control Number: 2004110357
Printed in the United States.

how to use this book

ARE YOU LOOKING FOR INSPIRATION as you consider replacing a tired-looking floor? Perhaps you want to transform a run-down bathroom with a new tile floor and tub surround. Or maybe you are seeking advice on repairing and refinishing a floor. If you are planning such a project, this book is at your service.

Almost any type of tile or flooring can fit within a modest budget, especially if you install it yourself. A reasonably handy person can learn the skills needed to install any of these products. While some flooring projects can certainly disrupt a household, they are nowhere near as time-consuming as a kitchen or a bathroom remodel. Yet the results are nearly as dramatic.

When choosing tile or flooring, check the first chapter of this book, but also read through the installation instructions for the material you are considering. That way, you'll know what to expect when you prepare the subsurface and install it. In some cases, choosing a different type of material will save you a lot of work.

flooring options

This showcase of flooring will help you begin your planning. You'll explore some general style considerations as well as glean detailed information about specific tile and flooring possibilities. The chapter also helps you assess your practical needs, so you can choose a flooring that will be right for the room you plan to transform. It includes a chart that will be a ready reference for comparing types of flooring. You'll also learn what installation tools you'll need for your project and what features to look for.

wall and counter tiles

This chapter tells you all you need to know in order to install ceramic or stone tiles on a wall or a countertop. It takes you step by step through the entire process: preparing a solid substrate, planning and laying out for the tiles, installing the tiles, grouting, and adding the finishing touches. Four projects are described in detail: tiling a wall, tiling a bathtub surround, tiling a countertop, and installing a hearth surround. In addition, you'll find tips for tiling around a window and tiling a countertop backsplash.

preparing for flooring

It's essential that your new floor rest on a subsurface that is strong and smooth enough for the flooring material you have chosen. This chapter starts by outlining the work that may need to be done, no matter which type of flooring you choose. You'll learn how to silence squeaks, patch damaged substrate, remove obstacles, tear up old flooring, and pry off mouldings.

You'll also find details on material-specific preparations. For instance, if you decide to install vinyl tiles or sheet flooring, you may need to put down plywood underlayment. To

More than 40 projects offer a wealth of choices for adding tile and flooring to your home. See pages 144–145 for instructions on creating this patterned tile floor.

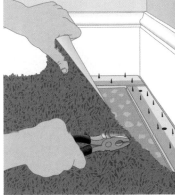

Throughout the book, step-by-step directions, illustrations, and photos help you learn each technique.

prepare for ceramic or stone tile, you will likely need to install cement backerboard. Other prep techniques, such as applying self-leveling compound, patching concrete, or using membranes, are also described.

ceramic and stone **floor tile**

Here you'll learn how to install tiles made of ceramic or natural stone. While these tiles come in a wide array of sizes and materials, their installation methods are very similar. This chapter begins with laying out the job and cutting the tiles to achieve a symmetrical appearance. You'll learn how to mix the mortar and install such materials as mosaics, "floating" tiles, and tiles for special projects such as a hearth or a patterned floor.

vinyl flooring

Sheets and tiles made of vinyl (often called resilient flooring) are quick to install and also inexpensive, yet the results can be both beautiful and durable. This chapter covers how to install a vinyl floor that is symmetrically laid out, firmly affixed, and free of flaws. In addition, you'll learn about other resilient materials, like linoleum and rubber.

strip flooring

Though many of these floors have a similar appearance (at least at first glance), there are important differences among the various types of solid hardwood, engineered, and laminate flooring. This chapter offers specific instructions on installing every type of strip flooring, including parquet. You'll learn how to sand and finish a floor, even how to paint decorative stripes.

repairs and maintenance

No one enjoys sanding and refinishing an older hardwood floor, but this chapter will explain how to do it with maximum professionalism and minimum mess. The result can be a gorgeous new-looking floor for a fraction of the cost of a new installation. Here you'll also find out how to maintain and repair almost any material that you find on a floor, including carpet.

Throughout the book, you'll find clear and helpful graphic presentations that guide you through each project. In addition to the step-by-step instructions, Lowe's Quick Tips, located in the margins, are loaded with professional advice for streamlining the job.

LOWE'S QUICK TIP

Tip boxes in the margins offer time-savers and helpful ideas.

tile and flooring options

THE LARGEST SURFACE IN A ROOM, A FLOOR CALLS FOR A thoughtfully chosen, carefully installed covering. Installing new flooring is possibly the most satisfying of all renovation projects because it quickly makes a dramatic change.

If you haven't begun to decorate, the flooring will serve as a style-setter for the room. In fact, many people select their flooring first because it's easier to coordinate other decorating details, such as furnishings or window treatments, once the flooring has been decided on.

In addition to its strong impact on the feel of a room, flooring has two other qualities: it is relatively costly, and it is something you'll probably be living with for a long time. It is well worth learning all you can about your options before making a decision. That's what this chapter is all about.

Keep in mind that the look you want often can be achieved equally well with several different types of flooring. For example, if you like the warm simplicity of wood, you can choose hardwood, parquet, engineered flooring, or even laminate. Each material has its trade-offs in ease of installation, cost, maintenance, and durability (see chart, pages 56–58).

This chapter will also introduce you to the tools you'll need should you decide to install the flooring that you select. You'll learn which will help make the job go easier, what to look for in a quality tool, and which ones are best rented.

Lowe's installation services can arrange for professional installation of every type of flooring shown in this chapter. Once you request professional services, a Lowe's-approved contractor comes to your home, takes measurements, and presents an all-inclusive bid for the work and materials. There is a modest charge for this bid; the charge will be deducted from the installation cost if you decide to hire the contractor. The bid is binding: the contractor will not add extra costs unless you agree. Lowe's guarantees that the work will be done to your satisfaction and in a timely manner.

today's choices

AS RECENTLY AS THE SEVENTIES, WALL-TO-WALL CARPETING (INCLUDING SHAG carpeting) was a standard choice for homeowners who were purchasing new homes or new flooring. Linoleum was popular in the kitchen, and bathrooms were often covered with inexpensive vinyl tiles. These choices are still available, of course. In fact, linoleum has been rediscovered in recent years as an attractive low-maintenance option, and vinyl tiles have exploded in colors that, creatively arranged, can add a light, whimsical touch to a room. But nowadays natural materials, including hardwood and ceramic or stone tile, are more often the materials of choice.

many **materials**

It used to be that granite and marble surfaces were found only in banks and office lobbies. By the same token, rougher, more rustic stone materials were seen only in vacation cabins or backyard patios. Now homeowners who like the formal appeal

of marble, perhaps in an entryway or bathroom, can install the tiles themselves. And those who prefer a casual or naturalistic decor can cover their floors with just about any material previously reserved for outdoor spaces, including limestone. Often, strongly contrasting types of material are combined in the same house—perhaps even in the same room.

For decades hardwood flooring meant strips of oak or maple installed in the traditional labor-intensive way—including the time-consuming process of sanding and applying multiple coats of protective finish. Now engineered-wood or laminate products (plastic that resembles wood) remove much of the hassle of installing a wood or wood-look floor. They come already stained and finished and are easy to maintain.

With so many choices, it can be hard to decide on a flooring product. Of course you want a floor that looks good and adds the right style for your home. But you also want to consider its durability, cleanability, comfort, and ease of installation.

For a quick survey of products, see the chart on pages 56–58. It lists and describes a wide range of flooring products, maintenance and installation requirements, and approximate cost.

The warm color of unstained wood lightens a room and complements more textured materials such as the slate tiles and jute rug in this living room.

Left: Polished granite tiles are set in a grid of oak strips that match the doors, for a clean-lined modern look.

Below: A stenciled pine plank floor will enhance a colonial or cottage-style room.

Take your time as you make this important choice. Leaf through the pages of this book and visit Lowe's to review the available products. Check out the manufacturer's recommendations for usage. For example, how resistant is the material to stains or moisture? Is it durable enough for the level of traffic that the room will handle?

Your home is a special space. You'll want to make a choice that not only suits your style but will be durable and easy to maintain so you can enjoy your new flooring for years to come.

choosing a style

The flooring you select should be compatible with the style of your house, whether it is contemporary, country, Victorian, or eclectic. Hardwood floors are a suitable choice in an old-fashioned kitchen,

for example, while laminate strip flooring would work well in a contemporary family room. Slate could be stunning in a modern foyer. If your home has a southwestern look, you might consider using terra-cotta tiles for the floor. Or, if your home has old world–style elements, then you might choose handpainted Italian floor tiles to accent the dining room floor.

scale

Many people believe large-scale flooring belongs in big rooms and small rooms call for more delicacy. Often this is true. Large tiles in a small room can overwhelm and create grout lines that aren't gentle on the eye. And a large room loaded with mosaic tiles can seem to almost vibrate. Still, it is worth experimenting by buying a few tiles and laying them in place to gauge their effect.

Above: Set diagonally to the main entrance, these 24-inch-tiles create a dramatic grid, adding to the spacious feel of this room. They were installed right up to the fireplace; no hearth is needed.

Right: Small tiles are often the best choice when you're faced with limited space. These 4-inch ceramic tiles are right in scale with this narrow bathroom.

texture

Contrasting textures adds interest to a room. In tile flooring, texture can be expressed through glazes and finishes. Stone can be honed, tumbled, or polished for varied appeal. And carpets offer a world of texture choices: closed or cut loops, or sheared or carved pile, for instance.

design **extras**

Each type of flooring material comes with its own set of coordinating design accoutrements. Borders, medallions, and inlays now come premade for wood, tile, and stone floors. And the grout between stone or ceramic tiles is very much a design element. Grout joints can be narrow or wide, plain or colored, depending on the look you want. Design elements can be used to break up the expanse of a large floor, to highlight a focal point, or to define one area of a room. In a multipurpose room, a good design plan may use different types of flooring to define two or more areas.

Remember, too, that square tiles can always be placed on the diagonal to open up a space. One rule holds true: a lengthwise pattern adds depth to a room, while a pattern running the width of a room makes it look shorter and wider.

Left: Tiles of various patterns add a personal touch and make this solid-color floor more interesting.

Below left: For texture and variety, leaf-shaped tiles were interspersed among these rough-cut flagstones. The wide • grout joints will be cleanable if they are protected with sealer.

Below: A tile medallion like this can be set into an existing wood floor, as long as you measure and cut carefully. Where the tiles abut the wood, caulk rather than grout should fill the joints.

ceramic and stone tile

LOWE'S CARRIES A VAST ASSORTMENT OF CERAMIC AND STONE TILES FOR WALLS, floors, and countertops. In addition to the tiles on display in the aisles, ask a salesperson to show you catalogs from which you can special-order tiles of just about any available color and style.

Traditionally, ceramic and stone tiles have been of five distinct types: glazed, quarry, polished stone, rough stone, and terra-cotta. Newer varieties of ceramic and porcelain tiles can now be manufactured to resemble any of these.

durability

Choose ceramic or stone tiles that are rated durable enough to do the job you have in mind. Floor tiles must be stronger than wall tiles to bear the weight of foot traffic; tiles for countertops must be nearly as strong as floor tiles. (See pages 52–53 for other practical considerations of floor tile selection.)

Because they do not need to be sturdy enough for walking on, wall tiles are often less expensive, and come in a wider choice of colors. Traditionally, these tiles have been about 4 inches square. Today, however, people install just about any size and type of tile on a wall.

While baseboards and thresholds finish off the edges of floor tiles, the unfinished edges of walls require trim. When selecting tile, be sure to think through the types of trim you'll need.

ratings

You may find tiles that have been rated by the Porcelain Enamel Institute. The ratings can confirm that you've selected the right tile for your situation.

- Group I, Light Traffic: This type of tile is especially suitable for a bathroom, which is often walked on with bare feet but otherwise doesn't face a lot of wear.

- Group II, Medium Traffic: This tile is appropriate for home interiors where little abrasion occurs, such as a living room or dining room. However, don't use these tiles in kitchens or entryways.

- Group III, Medium-Heavy Traffic: This rating indicates tile strong enough for any home interior.

- Group IV, Heavy Traffic: Tile with this rating is intended for homes or commercial areas such as restaurants.

- Group V: Extra-Heavy Traffic: This tile is strong enough for heavily used areas, such as building entrances.

There's a wide range of choices in floor tiles. A floor like this may be genuine stone or a handsome imitation.

porosity

Unglazed tiles that have been fired at relatively low temperatures are porous, so water can soak into—and sometimes even through—them. Tiles that have been fired at higher temperatures are denser and more water-resistant. "Nonvitreous" ceramic tiles (such as terra-cotta) and rough stone (for instance, tumbled marble) are the most absorbent. "Semi-vitreous" tiles are a bit less porous, but still have trouble drying out if they often get wet. "Vitreous" tiles absorb very little water. "Impervious" tiles repel just about all moisture.

The longer a tile stays wet, the greater the chance that bacteria and mildew will build up. An application of sealer to tiles will increase their resistance to moisture. Be sure to consider the likely exposure to water when you choose your tiles.

Above left: The same tiles used in the colorful backsplash make decorative accents on the white ceramic floor.

Above: Subtle accents and rectangular tiles provide an understated originality in this bathroom.

Left: A kitchen floor must put up with a remarkable amount of traffic. In addition, it has to withstand scuffing, spills, and the occasional dropped cooking utensil. Impervious tiles in colors and textures that hide grime are ideal for a hard-working area like this.

glazed ceramic tile

CERAMIC GLAZE IS A GLASSLIKE MATERIAL THAT IS BAKED ONTO THE TILE SO that it bonds firmly to give the tile a hard, protective shell. Glazing makes possible a dazzling variety of color choices, especially in the case of wall tiles.

floor tiles

A custom pattern like this is produced by combining ceramic mosaic sheets, which contain the smaller black and white tiles, with individual yellow tiles. See pages 24–25 for information on mosaics.

A common misconception is that glazed tiles are too slippery for wet areas. Some are, but manufacturers of floor tiles often employ techniques that add skid resistance to the glazed surface. The tile body may be textured, or the glaze itself may have a bumpy surface. In addition, if a floor is made up of small tiles, the closely spaced grout lines will provide plenty of skid resistance.

wall tiles

The most common glazed ceramic wall tile has a soft, nonvitreous body covered with glaze. The glaze on wall tile is not as tough as that on floor tile, but it effectively seals out moisture. If an area will be subject to scratches, choose a tile with a glaze that is hard enough for countertops. Don't install wall tile on a floor or countertop.

A rainbow of colors is available. In addition to solid-colored tiles with a smooth, glossy surface, wall tiles may be textured to resemble rough stone; crackled, with a crazed pattern of tiny cracks; variegated in color; or glazed to appear as if they were hand-painted with a brush. Most wall tiles are stocked with border and bullnose trim pieces to match (see pages 73 and 76).

The lush colors invite experimentation with mixing and matching. If you choose to create your own design, it's a good idea to buy tiles from the same manufacturer to be certain they will be exactly the same size. Most ceramic wall tiles are self-spacing: small nubs (called lugs) along each side ensure that the tiles, when butted together, will have gaps of about $\frac{1}{4}$ inch. Installing tiles that are not self-spacing requires spacers—small plastic devices that fit between tiles and assure consistent grout lines—and a bit more time and patience.

CHOOSING GROUT

The grout you choose has a lot to do with a floor's appearance. Contrasting grout lines stand out and create a geometric effect that emphasizes the shape of the tiles. If grout nearly matches the tile's color, the floor will look more like a unified whole. Ask to see either grout samples or a grout color chart so you can decide which effect you like best with your tile.

If you choose a contrasting grout, you'll need to be exacting with the installation. Lines must be consistent, and corners crisp. This can be difficult, if not impossible, if the tiles are at all irregular. Of course, if you're aiming for a rustic appearance, imperfect grout lines may not be a problem.

Grout lines may be as narrow as $1/16$ inch or as wide as $1/2$ inch. Before planning your layout, place loose tiles on a surface that is nearly the same color as the grout, and experiment with different spacing to see what looks best.

To avoid grout failure later, be sure that you choose the type suited to the thickness of the grout line. Use unsanded grout for lines $1/8$ inch wide or narrower, and sanded grout for lines wider than $1/8$ inch.

Coat the grout with grout sealer within a week or two of installation, or it will be easily stained. If you apply penetrating sealer to the entire floor, it will protect the grout as well as the tiles.

terra-cotta tiles

UNGLAZED TILES IN EARTHY COLORS ARE GENERALLY REFERRED TO AS TERRA-COTTA.
Most are a light reddish brown, but some are much darker. Others take on yellow and
gray tones. Unless the surface has been tinted, the color runs through the body of the tile.

Terra-cotta means "baked earth," which neatly sums up the simple way these tiles are
made. A tile's hue depends on the clay from which it was made. Tiles from different
countries, such as Mexico, France, Italy, or Portugal, have distinctive coloring. But you
may find significant color variation among tiles from the same area—even tiles packed
in the same box. This natural variability adds to the charm of a terra-cotta floor.

Terra-cotta tiles are nonvitreous—they readily soak up water. They must be sealed
to protect against staining. They should not be used outdoors in freezing climates.

varied shapes

You'll find terra-cotta tiles in many shapes:
square, octagonal, hexagonal, and rectangular with pointed ends. They are often laid
in interlocking patterns that use tiles of two
or more shapes and sizes. Small pieces of
different-colored tile—even art tiles—can
be incorporated into the design.

Some terra-cotta tiles are machine-
made, and can be laid in the same way as

most other ceramic tiles. Many, however,
are handmade and have irregular shapes.
Lay out for these tiles using the grid system (see page 123).

Handmade Mexican Saltillo tiles are
particularly rough-textured and uneven in
shape; you can expect chips at the edges
and small craters in the surface. Some
Saltillos come coated with a thin clear
"glaze." However, don't trust the glaze
alone to protect the tile.

This ruglike decorative area is composed of terra-cotta tiles in muted shades of red, gray, and yellow.

Left: These rectangular tiles are laid in a pattern reminiscent of a brick wall, for an outdoorsy feel.

Below: Rectangular Mexican Saltillos imitate the look of adobe blocks. Sealing and regular application of floor wax make this floor easy to wipe clean.

porcelain tile

PORCELAIN IS MADE FROM A FINE, WHITE CLAY FIRED AT AN EXTREMELY HIGH temperature. It is amazingly tough—either impervious or at least vitreous (see page 15)—and nearly impossible to stain.

Many older bathroom floors were tiled with 1-inch-wide hexagonal porcelain tiles. (You can find mosaic sheets of these tiles today.) Until recently, it was not practical to make large porcelain tiles, but now improved manufacturing methods have made large porcelain tiles widely available at a cost similar to that of glazed ceramic tiles.

Beautiful deceivers, these porcelain tiles offer the color and texture of stone with a uniformity that makes them easier than stone to install. Even homeowners who dislike materials that pretend to be something they really aren't find porcelain's versatility welcome. Decorative as well as tough, it makes an ideal choice for a bathroom.

just about any look

Because porcelain starts out pure white, it can be tinted to almost any color. And because the tiles are produced in a press, they can take on nearly any texture. That means they come in an amazing variety of colors and textures. Porcelain tiles can be manufactured to resemble tumbled or polished marble, travertine, quarry tile, limestone, ceramic tile, or even terra-cotta. At first or even second glance, many people cannot tell the difference between porcelain and the real thing. Others, however, regard these replicas as a poor substitute for the true texture and natural beauty of stone or ceramic tile. However, nearly everyone who has a porcelain tile floor will swear by its tremendous ease of cleaning and excellent stain resistance. Because the material is so strong, porcelain tiles are typically thinner than ceramic tiles. This can make them the right choice if you are concerned that your floor will be too high. And because porcelain is so strong, it is recommended if you suspect that your subfloor is not quite firm enough for ceramic or stone tile.

chips and color

Some porcelain tiles are colored on the surface only; any chips will reveal a different underlying color and texture. Through-body porcelain tiles have a uniform color that runs all the way through, so any chips are far less obvious. Make your choice based on the amount of wear you expect the tile to get.

quarry tile

QUARRY TILES WERE ORIGINALLY MADE OF CUT STONE, BUT TODAY'S TILES OF
that name are made using an extrusion process, which produces a ribbed pattern on
the back. Quarry tiles are unglazed, so they bear a resemblance to tiles cut from stone.
Because quarry tiles are made from red clay, color choices are more limited than for
porcelain tiles. Earth tones, grays, off-whites, and pastels are the usual options.

the choice for **floors**

Unglazed tiles like these are often recommended for floors because they do not get slippery when wet; even when sealer has been applied, a small amount of moisture spilled on quarry tiles will soak in, rather than bead up. Special nonskid quarry tiles have a pattern of raised dots.

Because they aren't glazed, quarry tiles may be prone to staining. Vitreous types are more stain-resistant than semi-vitreous tiles (see page 15). Applying a penetrating sealer can solve this problem.

Mosaic quarry tiles are doubly slip-resistant: the tiles themselves are unglazed and slightly rough, and numerous grout lines add further traction.

polished stone tile

WITH THE EXCEPTION OF POLISHED GRANITE, NATURAL STONE TILES WILL ACCEPT stains with distressing ease, and can be difficult to clean. But for many people, nothing else quite matches the variegated patterns and deep beauty of real stone. And with regular care, even the most porous stone can last for generations.

Most stone tiles are cut as precisely as ceramic tiles and are uniform in size. But because they are natural products, they vary in color—no two are exactly alike. For a uniform appearance, make sure all your tiles are from the same color lot, and buy extra tiles. Even tiles from the same box may vary significantly in color.

marble

Characterized by deep or light veins that can vary dramatically from one tile to another, marble has long been associated with wealth and luxury. Today, however, many marble tiles are reasonably priced.

Not all marble tile is created equal. Some types are very soft and easy to scratch or stain. Others are fairly hard and easier to keep clean, but all marble should be sealed if you expect it to be subjected to spills or scuffs. To test a scrap piece of marble tile for softness, run a key or other piece of pointed metal lightly across it to see if a scratch results.

granite

Granite is much harder and denser than marble, and usually speckled or mottled rather than veined. Commonly rated as vitreous, it can be used for countertops and areas that are subject to prolonged exposure to moisture.

Some types are a versatile gray with flecks of black and white. Others display almost whimsical red and brown specks of color against a cream background, while darker granite tiles may have a somber, European-style look.

Black and marble tiles combine for a look that is modern and geometric, yet softened by the natural swirls and variations in the individual tiles.

AGGLOMERATED STONE TILE

You may find inexpensive stone tiles with a jumbled appearance, as if a variety of stones have been mashed together. These are sometimes labeled "marble," but they are actually agglomerate tiles, made by recycling leftover stone materials. The result is an attractively complex appearance for a modest price. Most are fairly soft, like marble.

Left: Polished stone is a cool, mellow choice for a bathroom.

Below: Marble is a workable material that can be readily shaped—as in the marble tiles on this tub surround. With some practice and the careful use of templates, shaping gentle curves with a wet saw is within the reach of most do-it-yourselfers. Careful grinding and buffing finish the job.

onyx

Tiles that are made of onyx display swirls and clouds of light and dark browns. They are both expensive and soft, so choose them only if you fall in love with the look.

quartzite

Notable for their pebbly surface, quartzite tiles are nearly as hard and stain-resistant as granite, making them a good choice for floors. However, they are expensive and often difficult to find.

travertine

In addition to fine veins and mottled color, travertine is characterized by small, scattered pits on the surface. The tiles tend to be fairly soft, and the pits soak up moisture and stains. But the warm, tan hues and soft feel may make it worth the extra maintenance. Some travertine tiles are sold with the pits filled with similar-colored grout, for somewhat easier maintenance. Their pitted, absorbent texture makes them a better choice for walls than for floors or countertops, where spills may occur.

mosaics

WHEN YOU SEE A FLOOR OR WALL TILED WITH HUNDREDS OF LITTLE SQUARES or hexagons, chances are that the installation was easier than it looks. Some artistic professionals actually install the tiny tiles one at a time, just as ancient peoples did. But most pros and homeowners use flats of mosaic tile—sets of small tiles that are bonded together on a mesh backing that can be laid directly into thinset mortar.

characteristics

Mosaics may be made of almost any tile material—ceramic, polished stone, rough stone, or porcelain. The tiles may be all the same color, or several complementary shades scattered more or less at random. A mosaic tile floor is slip-resistant even if the tiles are glazed, because the closely spaced grout lines add traction.

Most mosaics come in rectangular sheets, often 12 inches square. Individual tiles may be as small as ¾ inch square or as large as 4 inches square. If you need to remove some of the tiles from a sheet, simply slice through the backing with a knife. Sheets can be laid next to each other for a seamless appearance, even if the individual tiles are not rectangular.

A border composed of 1-inch mosaic tiles fits nicely into a floor of 2-inch tiles. Such custom patterns are fairly easy to create from mosaic sheets.

variety

Mosaic tiles are available in a multiplicity of colors and shapes. In addition to arrays of squares and hexagons, mosaics may combine

GLASS AND METAL TILES

Correctly installed, glass tiles (below) are strong enough for most wall installations; some types are even installed on floors. They can be nearly transparent, almost totally opaque, milky, or smoky. Colors may be pastel or bright. Textures include glassy, pebbly, and craggy. Glass by its nature is impervious to moisture, so these tiles are ideal for areas that get wet. Depending on the glass tiles' texture, you may be able to install them using organic mastic, latex-reinforced thinset mortar, or epoxy thinset. Whichever adhesive you choose, make sure it's white; anything else will muddy the color.

Metal tiles (right) don't simply have a metallic finish; they're actually made out of copper, stainless steel, brass, or even iron. Expensive and difficult to cut, they are usually installed just as occasional accents. Some types of metal tiles may rust or discolor if exposed to moisture.

several splashy colors, or have crazy-quilt designs.

Mosaics are a good choice when you want to tile over a curved surface. The smaller the individual tile, the neater the job will look.

With just a bit of extra work, you can add a stunning focal point to your floor with a mosaic medallion. The cost per square foot is high, but a small area can add a great deal of visual interest. Some medallions are made of cut and polished pebbles, for a hand-laid look. Borders can also be created with mosaics. See pages 144–145 for an example of combining mosaics with standard floor tiles.

If you are adventurous and don't mind extra work, consider making your own mosaic pattern, using shards of broken tile. Wrap standard tiles in a canvas bag or drop cloth, and use a hammer to break them into pieces.

Above: There is an undeniable elegance to a mosaic-tile bathroom or entryway. Not only do mosaics have nostalgic appeal, they offer possibilities for patterns that can be a stunning focal point for a room.

Left: In addition to geometric patterns, mosaics are also available in free-form arrangements. This neutral combination of pattern and color will mesh well with a variety of decorating schemes.

tumbled-stone tile

TRADITIONALLY, STONE TILE HAS BEEN POLISHED TO A SMOOTH, SHINY SURFACE for a clean, formal appearance. Recently, "tumbled" marble and granite, which are nearly spongelike in texture, have become popular. The stone may be re-split, honed, or even sandblasted to create a variegated, highly textured surface. Inspired by antique stone-tiled floors and walls in Italy and Spain, tumbled tiles produce an ambiance that is elegant but visually rich—an ideal foil to sleek cabinets and bathroom fixtures.

hard stone with a **soft feel**

Some tumbled tiles are suitable for use only on walls or backsplashes, while others are sturdy enough for foot traffic. Small tumbled tiles, often arranged on mosaic sheets, are popularly used as accents on a floor.

Because they are deeply textured, tumbled tiles not only are slip-resistant; they also feel pleasant when walked on with bare or slippered feet. Because they are porous, they need to be sealed, especially those made of marble.

Most tumbled stone tiles should be installed using white thinset mortar (for a floor) or organic mastic (for a wall). When you are choosing a grout color, it's best to avoid gray or brown adhesive because it will subtly show through and muddy the appearance of the tile.

Tumbled stone makes an ideal accent material when combined with wood.

Tumbled mosaic stone tile makes an unusual but striking countertop.

LOWE'S QUICK TIP

If a floor will be subject to heavy use or occasional wetness, consider purchasing porcelain or ceramic tiles that mimic the look of tumbled stone.

Left: This tumbled stone countertop and backsplash have the appeal of an old wine cellar.

Below left: Its slip-resistant texture makes tumbled stone ideal for bathrooms. It also contrasts nicely with ceramic tile.

Below: The naturalistic color and texture of tumbled stone are shown to full advantage in this bathroom.

rough stone tile

UNTIL RECENTLY, PEOPLE WOULDN'T HAVE CONSIDERED INSTALLING ROUGH, open-grained stone anywhere but outside. But new techniques, like tumbling and sand-blasting (see pages 26–27), seek to mimic the appearance of rough-cut stone. So why not install the real thing?

limestone

Limestone tiles tend to be large, thick slabs, which may or may not be precisely cut. Colors range from cream to brown—sometimes even with blushes of pink—and are often spiced with flecks of darker material. To emphasize the rustic charm of the material, limestone installations may include exposed rough tile edges, a bit of surface unevenness, and grout lines of inconsistent widths.

Limestone is the most porous of all stone tiles. Sealing is mandatory because unsealed limestone will almost certainly develop hard-to-remove stains.

Green, gray, and red slate tiles face the range hood and line the back wall.

slate

Traditionally, slate has been produced by splitting rather than cutting the stone, followed by polishing the surface. The result is a highly textured surface that is also resistant to moisture. Harder than limestone and darker in color, slate has long been a popular choice for hallways and vestibules.

Slate tiles from exotic locations, including India, Africa, and Mexico, come in a stunning array of hues, including purple, gray, brown, yellow, and red. The texture is usually bumpy yet smooth; a single tile may be matte in some spots and shiny in others. "Vermont slate" comes as a kit, with a group of variously sized square and rectangular tiles that fit together in a defined pattern like a jigsaw puzzle.

Some types of slate are very hard and strong, while others are easily cracked; check with a Lowe's tiling expert to be sure the slate you choose will survive in your installation. Recently, slate that has been cut and left unpolished has gained in popularity. These tiles are almost as porous as limestone, so seal them to protect against moisture and stains.

bluestone

Bluestone, which is mined from quarries in New York and Pennsylvania, has a rich blue-gray color unmatched by any other product. Some of these tiles are imbued with tinges of green, rust, yellow, and purple. Bluestone has a hard, fine-grained surface.

Above: Patterns can be sandblasted into stone tiles. Although the technique is pricey, a few pieces will have a big impact on a room.

Right: Stone tiles are cut precisely enough that they can be set in patterns. This pleasing arrangement combines 3-inch tiles with 12-inch tiles.

resilient flooring

TILE THAT "GIVES" A LITTLE MAY NOT BE AS SOLID AS CERAMIC OR STONE TILE, but it has advantages: if you drop a plate on a resilient floor, it has a chance of surviving unchipped, and your legs may appreciate a bit of cushioning underfoot. Resilient tile does not require a rock-solid subsurface—only one that is smooth—and it adds only about ¼ inch of thickness to a floor, making it in many cases the easiest tile to install.

Though the word "resilient" sometimes refers to any flooring that is a bit flexible—including wood parquet, cork, and carpeting, for instance—it more commonly refers to vinyl tiles and sheets, which are covered on this and the next five pages.

vinyl **commercial** tile

Most resilient tile is made of vinyl mixed with tiny stones and other resins). "Solid vinyl commercial" tiles are actually about 90 percent vinyl, which makes them more durable and resilient than surface-printed self-stick tiles.

Most commercial tile has flecks of various colors, to hide dirt. The color runs all

the way through the tile. These tiles must be sealed regularly to prevent dirt and grime from working their way deep into the tiles. Some come pre-waxed. Single-color tiles can be difficult to keep clean-looking and scuff-free.

This product is called commercial tile because it is commonly used in grocery stores, schools, and other nonresidential settings.

This floor employs a random pattern of commercial tiles, with tan tiles interspersed among white ones.

Left: These commercial vinyl tiles not only have a pleasingly retro look, but offer a durability that Mom would be sure to approve of.

Below left: The durability and water-resistance of vinyl tile make the material an ideal choice for an entryway or mud-room.

LOWE'S QUICK TIP

Rubber tile is very durable yet resilient, making it a good choice for an entry-way, game room, or workshop. Some tiles have raised patterns or textures that add slip resis-tance. Tiles are commonly either 12 or 18 inches square, and they install just like vinyl tiles (see pages 152–157).

Even subtle differences in color make a pleasing floor pattern. These commercial tiles provide a durable and easily maintained surface.

surface-printed
self-stick vinyl tile

These tiles have a pattern or design that is printed on a hard protective surface layer; the color does not run through the thickness of the tile as it does with commercial tile (see pages 30–31). Most of these tiles are also embossed, meaning that they have a raised texture. They may mimic brick, wood, slate, or grouted ceramic tile, or they may display floral or geometric patterns.

Surface-printed tiles vary greatly in quality. The cheap ones have a very thin protective layer that is easily ripped and scratched. Avoid tiles that are so thin that you can easily bend them in half. High-

quality tiles have a thicker protective layer and are stiffer.

Almost all surface-printed tiles are self-stick. Installing them is easy. For best results, the floor should be painted with a special flooring primer. Layout is the same as for any square tile (see pages 120–122); installation is similar to that of commercial tile (see pages 154–157).

Most surface-printed tiles have a no-wax finish, which resists moisture and dirt effectively. However, the finish won't last forever. When the no-wax surface wears out, apply a special no-wax conditioner.

High-quality surface-printed tiles can stand up to heavy traffic for many years.

LOWE'S QUICK TIP

Cushioned surface-printed tiles have a foam backing. Avoid these, because they can be damaged when you move an appliance or even if you slide a chair while sitting in it.

Far from the "poor relation" of flooring materials, these self-stick tiles add a stylish touch to a cooking area. They are durable, comfortable for the feet, and easy to maintain.

LEATHER TILE

Here's an interesting new product: tiles made of cowhide. They make for a rich-looking, luxurious floor. Of course, they are not suitable for an area that gets wet or that receives heavy foot traffic. Colors include tan, brown, olive, burgundy, and black. Some types must be kept supple with regular applications of leather conditioner; others can be maintained with a weekly vacuuming, a monthly damp mopping (with plain water), and waxing once a year.

LOWE'S QUICK TIP
Tiles with small, pronounced patterns work well for a small floor—a bathroom for instance—but in a larger space they will create a monotonous effect.

vinyl **sheet** flooring

Vinyl sheet flooring is made of the same material as self-stick vinyl tiles (see pages 32–33). Sheets have a pattern printed on a thin protective layer. Patterns may be strictly geometric, or they may imitate slightly irregular ceramic or stone tile with grout lines. Some patterns are crackled or random-looking; others plausibly imitate wood planks or parquet tiles. You can even buy sheets that look like woven rugs. Sheets are usually 12 feet wide, which eliminates the need for seams in most installations.

On the plus side, a seamless floor is sure to repel all moisture and be a snap to keep clean, as long as the surface does not get torn or deeply scratched. On the downside, any damage is difficult to repair.

One of the strong points of vinyl sheet flooring is its ability to create a smooth, uninterrupted stretch of color and texture.

Better-grade vinyl sheet flooring successfully mimics stone and ceramic tile while offering comfort and easy maintenance.

LINOLEUM

True linoleum is a natural product, composed of elements like linseed oil, wood fibers, and ground stone that have been pressed onto a jute backing. Colors range from muted to vibrant, and patterns may be swirled or speckled. Linoleum is naturally resistant to bacteria and also has antistatic properties that help it repel dust and grime.

Do-it-yourselfers can install single sheets of linoleum by preparing the subfloor and using a template, much as is done with vinyl flooring (see pages 158–163). Linoleum's composition makes it an ideal material for combining different colors and designs into patterns—linoleum seams can be permanently heat-sealed. However, this requires special equipment and the expertise of a professional.

Sheet vinyl is a comfortable and utilitarian surface that is ideal for the rigors of a kitchen. Another advantage of this flooring is that it can be replaced with relative ease should you choose to update the look of your living space.

wood flooring

NATURAL WOOD IS A POPULAR FLOORING CHOICE BECAUSE IT IS VERSATILE AND durable. It can be stunning visually, yet not draw undue attention to itself. It exudes a homey warmth and offers a resilient walking surface, yet it is hardy enough to withstand almost any abuse a family can dish out.

Wood flooring does require some attention. It must be kept protected against water damage with a coating of polyurethane or wax. If it gets scratched or otherwise damaged, you may need to sand and refinish it; see pages 202–204.

At Lowe's you can choose among a good number of wood flooring options; the major types are presented on this and the following three pages.

solid hardwood

Classic hardwood flooring is composed of random-length strips of hardwood, usually 2¼ inch wide and ¾ inch thick. The strips of wood lock tightly together via tongues and grooves. Nails (or staples) are driven through the tongues so that virtually no fastener heads are visible. Once installed, the floor must be sanded and finished—a messy process that can take a week or so.

At Lowe's you can purchase solid oak flooring that has been stained and coated with a polyurethane finish—a major time-saver. However, the pieces have grooves where they meet, so the floor will not be quite as smooth as one that is sanded and finished.

Oak is the most common choice for living rooms, bedrooms, and dining rooms.

One of the wonders of wood is its versatility. As much as it suits a formal living or dining room, it also works well for informal settings where durability is as important as beauty.

Left: Light-toned birch strip flooring creates a dramatic setting for dark-wood furnishings and accents. Hardwood's natural tone can be enhanced by staining or lightened by a wash.

Below: A dramatic geometric pattern can be created as you install strip flooring, or you can purchase ready-made ornamental medallions.

Oak flooring labeled "select" is uniform in color and grain lines, and has no knots. Less expensive grades such as Number One Common contain small knots, and the boards differ from each other in color and grain lines. Many people prefer the interesting variation of a floor made from less-expensive boards.

Other species of wood are also available. Maple is classic for a kitchen; it often comes in strips that are 1½ inches wide. Species such as walnut and cherry are stunning but expensive.

WOOD FINISHES

Choose your finish when you choose the flooring. Stain is optional; at least two coats of polyurethane or wax are mandatory. If you do not stain the wood and you do apply oil-based polyurethane (which is outlawed in some areas), the floor will turn somewhat yellow in a few years. If you apply stain first, the yellowing will not be as apparent. Water-based polyurethane does not turn yellow, but it is not as durable as oil-based. Floor wax has a fine, subtle sheen but must be stripped and reapplied every year or so.

engineered wood flooring

Engineered flooring has several layers. It is made by laminating a top ply of hardwood over two or more plies of softwood. Most of the time, the top layer is stained and coated with a hard urethane finish. You'll find a wide selection of wood species and finishes to choose from at Lowe's.

Some types are installed by either stapling or setting in adhesive, while others can be "floated," using virtually no fasteners (see pages 194–197). This product has several advantages over solid wood.

■ Engineered flooring does not need to be sanded and finished, so it can be installed and walked on the same day.

■ Though only the top ply is made of hardwood, the appearance of the finished floor is actually very similar to a solid hardwood floor.

■ Plywood is extremely stable—virtually free of warps and other imperfections—easing installation.

■ Engineered flooring is typically only ³⁄₈ inch thick (solid wood is ³⁄₄ inch thick); depending on the height of an adjacent floor, this may save you the work of removing existing flooring.

However, engineered flooring has some limitations as well. For example, because of its relatively thin top layer of veneer, it generally can be sanded and refinished only once (solid hardwood usually can be sanded three times). If you need to resand every 12 years, an engineered floor will last only 24 years; a solid floor will last 48 years. In addition, most engineered flooring has a small V-shaped groove where the strips meet. Some people find this makes the floor slightly more difficult to sweep and mop.

Because the surface of engineered wood flooring is a real wood veneer, it is handsome enough to hold its own in an elegantly styled setting like this kitchen.

Like laminate, some engineered flooring is available in strips that are wider than those available with hardwood flooring. The result is a rich, contemporary look.

BAMBOO AND CORK FLOORING

Bamboo (shown at right) is actually a grass rather than a tree. At first glance, bamboo flooring looks like wood, but a closer look reveals a reedy pattern. It comes prestained and prefinished in a variety of tones. Bamboo flooring strips are installed much like either engineered or laminate flooring.

Flooring made from cork forms a soft, slightly springy walking surface that many people find very comfortable in working areas such as a kitchen. Cork has long been available in tiles, which are set in a special cork adhesive. Cork tiles are sometimes stained in colors that range from muted to vivid, so you can mix and match combinations to produce either elegant or playful effects. Cork is also available in planks that are "floated" much like laminate flooring.

wood parquet tiles

FOR CENTURIES, WOOD PARQUET FLOORS COMPOSED OF HUNDREDS OR EVEN thousands of small pieces were proudly displayed in the homes of the wealthy. Creating these floors required painstaking labor by skilled craftsmen. Today, a homeowner can easily install inexpensive machine-made parquet tiles that achieve a very similar look.

a variety of tones

At Lowe's you will find parquet tiles in a range of materials and shades. Most parquet tiles are made of oak, maple, or birch. Inexpensive tiles described as "hardwood" are likely ash or poplar. The wood used in parquet tiles may be stained lightly, or given a dark, mahoganylike appearance. Because parquet is made of interlocking strips, the juxtaposition of wood grain makes the effect even richer.

ease of installation

The tiles are laid in special parquet flooring adhesive. Parquet tongues and grooves interlock firmly so the floor's seams have no gaps. See pages 168–171 for parquet installation instructions.

Most parquet tiles have a durable no-wax finish. High-quality tiles fit together so well that there is no need to seal the joints; once installed, the floor only needs to be wiped clean.

Set on point, the rich pattern of parquet flooring is even more pronounced. Like most wood floors, parquet is interesting enough that it doesn't require the additional decoration of an area rug.

LOWE'S QUICK TIP

Before you buy parquet tiles, pull out a few and check them for quality. Each tile should hold together well—usually via a mesh backing. If the tiles fall apart easily, installing them may be difficult.

Left: Because it is made from interlocking strips, parquet has a rich texture that goes well with formal decorating styles. Although an affordable manufactured flooring, it hints of old-world craftsmanship and time lavished on detailed work.

Below: Parquet is available in several different shades of oak, maple, birch, ash, and poplar, including rich, dark tones like these.

laminate flooring

LAMINATE FLOORING IS A POPULAR CHOICE BECAUSE IT IS INEXPENSIVE, EASY TO install, and a breeze to keep clean. It has a hard surface composed of resin and melamine, made in much the same way as a laminate countertop. Most laminate flooring mimics the appearance of wood, but you can also find laminates that resemble marble, granite, and tile. The hard surface repels moisture and grime, so cleaning is usually a matter of either sweeping or damp-mopping. There is no need to apply a finish of any kind.

choosing the location

The laminate flooring that you will find at Lowe's offers excellent durability, attested by manufacturer warranties that extend for as long as 25 years. Still, it may not be a good choice for a room that receives heavy foot traffic and often gets dirty. It is possible (though certainly not easy) to scratch the surface, and scratches in it cannot be repaired. Also avoid using laminate flooring in a room where the floor often gets wet, such as in an oft-used bathroom or a hard-working kitchen.

ease of installation

Laminate flooring is installed by floating—meaning that strips are joined to each other but not to the subfloor. In older systems, the strips were joined together with glue; today's laminate flooring products simply snap together for an amazingly easy installation. The flooring rests on a pad of foam underlayment, which makes the floor subtly springy and easy to walk on.

Some laminate flooring has the rich patchwork look of various grains of wood.

LAMINATE TILE

Recently, manufacturers have been making laminate flooring in tile form. Tiles are typically 18 inches square, and often feature designs that imitate the look of ceramic or stone tile. The tiles fit together via tongues and grooves, much like wood parquet tiles, but they are floated over a foam pad rather than being glued to the floor.

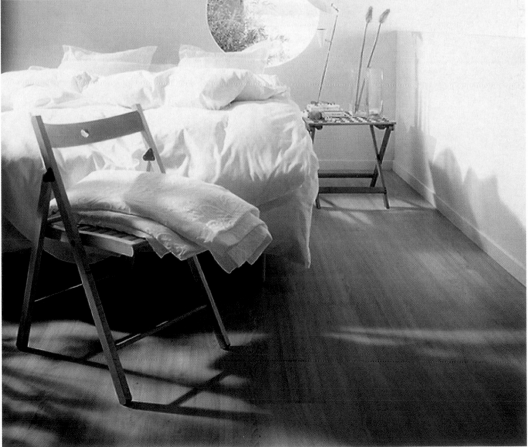

Above left: Laminates are available in a variety of wood tones that ably mimic the real thing. The subtle give of a floating laminate floor is easy on the feet, making it ideal anywhere you will be standing a lot.

Left: Laminate flooring is an economical choice for bedrooms, where traffic is minimal. As long as the flooring is not deeply scratched, a simple wipe with a damp cloth is all that's needed to maintain the sheen.

decorative concrete flooring

IN RECENT YEARS CONCRETE HAS BEEN DISCOVERED BY INTERIOR DESIGNERS, who have developed several appealing decorative uses. For instance, concrete countertops have become popular in high-end kitchens because they can be shaped, colored, and decorated to create one-of-a-kind designs. Concrete floors can be similarly fashioned to add a touch of individuality to a room. Most decorative concrete is used for outdoor patios, but interior concrete floors are increasingly popular.

effects for new concrete

There are two alternative processes used to make a beautifully pigmented concrete floor. One involves casting the new concrete and adding decorative effects while the concrete is wet. The other option is to stain an existing concrete slab. Many concrete companies now specialize in both.

Casting a new concrete floor is definitely a job for professionals; it involves special skills and equipment beyond the reach of most homeowners. In addition, it requires a team of workers to quickly consolidate and smooth the concrete.

A new concrete floor can be tinted with a wide range of colors. It can also be inlaid with items such as pebbles, seashells, or metal strips.

Cast in place, these irregular segments of colored concrete complement the unusual curve of a great room hearth.

beautifying old concrete

An old concrete slab, perhaps in a basement or an enclosed porch, can be spruced up by first cleaning it thoroughly, then applying an acid stain. The floor can be stained to a single color, or you can create faux finishes that look like marble or travertine stone. By using stencils, stamps, or simple masking tape, you can create geometric designs as well.

Simple porch and floor paint is another method worth considering because it can be fairly durable. Two-part epoxy paint meant for use on garage floors stands up to abuse and lasts a long time.

Above: Bands of colored concrete cut across a kitchen floor. A lighted toe-kick highlights the mottled texture.

Left: A cast-concrete floor in a sunroom mimics the look of vintage terra-cotta tiles while providing a more hardy, easy-to-maintain floor.

LOWE'S QUICK TIP
Acid staining requires that the concrete be cleaned thoroughly, and the stain must be applied systematically. Some people approach this technique casually, often with disappointing results. If you do not have the time to practice on another slab or in an inconspicuous area, you may be better off hiring a pro to acid-stain a slab for you.

carpeting

CARPET PROVIDES A WELCOME CUSHION UNDERFOOT, DEADENS SOUND, AND
adds to the comfort of a room. It can be installed over a floor that is less than perfect;
indeed, one of its great advantages is that it hides a multitude of flaws. It will not quiet
squeaks or mask serious unevenness, however; see pages 98–101 for fixing these problems.
With carpeting, you usually get what you pay for. In most cases, the more expensive
the carpet, the longer it will wear and the easier it will be to keep clean.

Carpeting's warmth,
softness, and acous-
tical qualities have
long made it popular
for living areas. And
because it needs no
substrate preparation,
it can be an ideal
cover-up for an other-
wise unsightly floor.

carpet **fiber**

If you choose a high-quality product that
is appropriate for the amount of traffic
in the room, it can last a very long time.
Carpet care usually means nothing more
than regular vacuuming and occasional
cleaning; see pages 216–217 for more serious maintenance. In general, the darker
the carpeting, the cozier a room will feel;
light-colored carpeting makes a room
seem larger. But even within those guidelines, you can select from a huge range
of colors and patterns.

When making your final selection it is
helpful to match the characteristics of the
common types of carpet fiber to the type
of room where you plan to install it.

nylon is currently the most common carpet material. Though inexpensive, it is the strongest of all the fibers. Nylon is easy to clean and maintain and is naturally stain-resistant and nonallergenic. If the air in the room is dry, it does tend to produce static electricity.

olefin, which is made of polypropylene, is used for indoor-outdoor carpeting and for damp areas such as basements because it has excellent resistance to moisture and mildew. It also limits static electricity; of all carpet materials, it handles stains the best. However, sometimes olefin can fade or flatten if exposed to direct sunlight for prolonged periods. "UV-stabilized olefin" does not have this problem.

Above: Carpeting is a surprisingly durable flooring that can handle furnishings that would mar other less resilient materials.

Left: An ideal choice for a bedroom, carpet will help sound-insulate the room. A neutral shade like this doesn't get in the way of a bold color scheme, and it will look just as good when the next round of decorating is in place.

olefin/nylon blend has many of the best qualities of both fibers. It is resistant to static, staining, fading, and flattening.

polyester is not as strong as nylon but is fairly durable. With wear, it may be prone to pilling and shedding, but it cleans easily.

sisal is an attractively coarse natural fiber that resists static and doesn't trap dust.

wool is soft yet strong and is available in a wide range of colors. However, it is expensive and must be cleaned carefully. It also needs to be mothproofed.

carpet **pile**

When choosing carpet, give thought to its pile—the heft, depth, and springiness of

weave. Some carpet pile wears better in high-traffic areas such as hallways; others have a luxuriant depth welcome in bedrooms and other quiet areas of the house.

cut pile carpeting has its loops trimmed off so the yarn ends stand upward. There are three basic types. Saxony cut pile has closely packed loops about $\frac{1}{2}$ inch thick. A very smooth Saxony carpet is sometimes called "plush." Textured cut pile is typically less dense than Saxony, and its fibers are cut at two or more levels to create a pattern. Frieze carpeting is made with short fibers twisted together for greater hardness and durability.

loop pile carpeting is made with fibers that are looped, so they are fastened to the backing at two points. Berber carpet, which is usually made of olefin fiber, has

Below: Sisal carpeting combines rich color and texture with a utilitarian hardiness. Use a fiber sealer in areas of wet spills.

Below right: Neutral doesn't have to mean boring. This pebble-toned carpet holds its own in a handsomely decorated dining area while providing a surface that will hide stains.

loops of various sizes, some of them quite large. Level loop carpet features small loops that are all the same size. It is less plush and more durable than Berber carpet.

cut and loop carpet combines both types of pile. The cut ends stand taller than the loops for a textured look. Cut and loop can also be sculpted.

carpet and padding
quality

The denser a carpet's fiber, the softer it will feel and the longer it will last. Simply running your fingers through the fibers will enable you to tell cheap carpeting from the better carpeting. Also pay attention to how tightly each yarn is wound; the tighter, the better.

The padding that you install under the carpet contributes to its luxurious feel and improves its longevity. As with carpet, you usually get what you pay for. More expensive padding will likely retain its sponginess longer than cheaper versions, which may pack down and even crumble with age.

d-i-y or pro installation?

You can install carpeting yourself, but do consider hiring a professional through Lowe's installation services. Professionals have the specialized stretching and fastening tools to do the job quickly—usually, in a day—and they can guarantee that the job is done right. A properly installed carpet will last longer than one that is stretched too tight or not tight enough.

Below left: Informal living areas benefit from carpeting's hardiness and comfort.

Below: Not only does carpeting suit any decorating style from informal to formal, it is relatively affordable and quick to install. In most cases, a living room and family room or three bedrooms and a hallway can be completed in a day.

baseboards and thresholds

ATTRACTIVE BASEBOARDS AND THRESHOLDS DO A LOT TO ENHANCE THE FINAL appearance of a floor. Thresholds make a safe and finished-looking transition between one type of flooring and another; baseboards cover expansion gaps between the flooring and the wall and protect the wall surface from damage.

trim options

Trim exists to cover up any gaps between varying types of material, but it also contributes to the style of a room. A few decades ago you would have been hard-pressed to find many options other than "modern" and "colonial" trim. However, these days you'll find plenty of stylish options for trimming off your floor. And you have varying trim materials to choose from. Lowe's carries these basic types.

Trim functions to make an elegant transition between the floor and the wall. Increasingly, homeowners have returned to the rich look of generous baseboards.

- Softwood moulding, generally made of pine or poplar, is moderately priced. Its wide grain lines, if carefully stained, can be made to look similar to (but not identical to) hardwood flooring. It can also be painted. This material is fairly easy to dent, however.

- Primed softwood moulding uses short pieces that have been joined together with "finger joints," which grip like clasped hands to make a knotless material. The moulding has a coat of white primer paint, so you can often get away with one coat of finish paint.

- Moulding made of medium-density fiberboard (MDF) is more resistant to denting than softwood. Do not use this product in a room that is likely to get wet; MDF absorbs moisture and swells unattractively if it gets soaked. MDF is sold primed.

- Foam moulding is usually covered with a layer of plastic that replicates wood grain. This product is sometimes called "prefinished" moulding. It is inexpensive and very easy to cut and install, and may be a good choice if its finish is the right color for your room.

- Hardwood moulding, usually available in oak, is highly resistant to dents. It can be stained to blend with a hardwood floor. Hardwood is challenging to cut with hand tools, but you'll have no problems if you use a power miter saw.

Even as you begin to pick out your flooring, anticipate the type of baseboard moulding that would look best. In this case, the visual weight of the window sills and trim called for something substantial to balance it.

baseboard options

Wood baseboard is frequently composed of two parts—the baseboard itself, and a base shoe, which is a small rounded moulding at the bottom. To trim out a floor with minimal effort, reinstall the base moulding or the base shoe that was previously attached to the wall. You may want to paint the wood base before reattaching it. If the old moulding is damaged, it may look shabby next to your new floor. In that case, install new moulding (see pages 180–183)

For a more substantial look, consider creating a wall base using bullnose tile. For a seamless look, install tiles the same color as the floor. To add definition to the room, use tiles in a contrasting color. Pieces of granite or marble can also make a handsome base. Make sure that the top edge of the tile or stone base is finished, because it will be highly visible and will need frequent cleaning.

Vinyl base cove moulding is inexpensive, is fairly easy to install, and is easy to clean (see page 135).

thresholds

If your new tiled floor comes in at the same height as an adjoining hardwood or carpeted floor, you may not need to install a threshold. You could simply cut the tiles to form a perfectly straight line parallel to the edge of the adjacent floor, then fill the gap with grout. However, if you need to resolve a difference in height between two abutting floors, or if your flooring will not cut to a clean finished edge (as is the case with carpeting, for example), you'll need to install a threshold.

Try to select a threshold that harmonizes with both the new flooring and the adjacent surface. A metal threshold that sits on top of the two floors is easy to install and covers up imperfections, but it will also collect dirt and may be a tripping hazard. A wood or marble threshold installed on the same subsurface as both types of flooring is much more attractive and easier to clean. However, it won't work with thinner types of flooring, and you must cut the abutting materials very precisely, because their edges will be visible. See pages 140–141 for instructions on installing the various types of thresholds.

Thresholds are all about safe, good-looking transitions between different types of flooring that may be at slightly different levels. A threshold like this one can be purchased at Lowe's prefinished in a range of tones to suit your floor.

getting practical

LET YOUR IMAGINATION RUN WILD WHEN IT COMES TO CHOOSING COLORS AND styles, but don't neglect the practicalities: a floor should suit both your lifestyle and your budget. Choose flooring materials that not only look good when they are first installed, but will stay looking good, with a minimum of maintenance, for many years to come.

cost

In most cases, you'll thank yourself later if you spend a little more for the flooring than you had intended, rather than settling for a ho-hum option. Better-quality tiles, wood flooring, or resilient flooring is almost certain to last longer and be easier to keep clean.

Factor in not only the cost of the materials, but the difficulty of the installation. Depending on your circumstances, certain

Brick-style ceramic tile with well-sealed grout lines makes this solarium easy to keep clean and copes well with moisture.

types of flooring may require that you remove old flooring and perhaps even beef up the subflooring—either of which can add to the expense.

durability

Consider how the room will be used, and choose a kind of flooring that will survive without a great deal of maintenance. High-traffic areas are best served by ceramic tile. Stone tile, vinyl tile or sheet goods, and hardwood flooring are good choices for areas that receive moderate to high traffic. Carpet and laminate flooring are appropriate for areas that will not be heavily used.

cleanability

Be clear on how your flooring will need to be maintained. Carpeting needs to be vacuumed regularly, and will grow dingy if it often gets dirty. Hardwood floors must be kept well protected with polyurethane or wax. Laminate flooring should be protected from scratches. Even vinyl flooring eventually requires regular applications of an appropriate finish.

comfort

Many people find very hard flooring, such as ceramic or stone tile, uncomfortable or even painful to walk and stand on; others see no problem, as long as they wear shoes. Wood flooring is slightly softer, vinyl tiles and sheet goods are softer yet, and carpeting is downright cushy. Of course, you can always add comfort to a room by putting down a throw rug or two. Radiant heat (see page 117) can make the hardest floor feel cozy on winter days.

Left: This slate tile is more than decorative. It is positioned where people enter the house from the outside, and thus helps keep dirt and mud off the wood floor, which is more prone to scratching.

Below: For the family that enjoys entertaining, cork provides a soft surface underfoot and minimizes the sound of footsteps. A patchwork of brightly colored cork tiles provides a springboard for the simple furnishings.

Lightly textured tiles
are slip-resistant, while
the clever insertion of
wood strips between
the tiles melds this area
with the hardwood
flooring.

safety

All the flooring in a home should be slip-resistant. Take special care when choosing ceramic and polished stone tiles to make sure they will not create a slick surface.

If the floor in one room is more than 1/2 inch higher than the floor in an adjacent room, the transition between the two can create a tripping hazard, especially for elderly folks or young children. A flush threshold that slopes down to the lower floor (see pages 140–141) will lessen the danger, but the best solution is to install flooring that is nearer the height of the adjacent floor.

air quality

Homeowners are increasingly concerned about indoor air pollution. Underlayment and the adhesives that are used to install some types of flooring—and indeed some types of flooring themselves—emit volatile organic compounds (VOCs) into the air.

If you are concerned about VOCs in a particular product, ask a Lowe's flooring expert, who can contact the manufacturer for specific information. (This can often be handled by a phone call made during business hours.)

Particleboard typically contains the highest amounts of VOCs; plywood usually contains somewhat less. Laminate and engineered flooring may use either plywood or particleboard, so check for VOC levels. Plywood used for underlayment or subflooring will probably contain some VOCs.

Ceramic and stone tile are generally free of pollutants, but the adhesives used to install them likely will contain some VOCs. Solid hardwood is basically VOC-free, but the stain and finish—and the adhesive, if you glue the hardwood down—may contain them.

Unless you or a family member are particularly sensitive to pollutants, simple solutions are usually all that's needed to solve the problem. Consider buying low-emitting adhesives. Ventilate your home well during the installation and for two or three days afterward.

sound dampening and enhancing

If you want to soften the sound of footsteps as well as music or the television, opt for a soft flooring material—the softer it is, the more noise it will dampen. Carpet is the most effective noise reducer; rubber, cork, and vinyl have moderate dampening properties. An area rug can work almost as well. On the other hand, you may want to brighten the sound in a room that features a stereo or entertainment system. In that case, consider hardwood or ceramic tile.

If you plan to have a floated laminate or engineered floor, consider installing a layer of soundproofing foam under the flooring. That way, the room itself can have bright sound, yet the sound will not transfer readily to the room below or to adjacent rooms.

minimizing disruption during installation

Before you purchase flooring products, look through the relevant portions of this book to get a realistic notion of how long it will take to prepare the substrate and install the floor. If your floor is in sound condition, you may be able to install some materials—such as laminate flooring, engineered wood flooring, or floating ceramic tiles—in one day. Solid hardwood can take more than a week to install, sand, and finish. Most other products can be installed in a few days.

You will need to clear the room of all furniture and perhaps appliances during construction. If space in your home is limited, consider using a storage container drop-off service to stow your stuff out of the way for a week or so.

In addition to the practical job of dealing with muddy shoes and boots, the terra-cotta tile of this mudroom floor beautifully complements the hardwood of the great room beyond. The two flooring materials, each carefully chosen for the room in which it is installed, make a simple nose-to-nose transition in the doorway.

TYPE AND CHARACTERISTICS	INSTALLATION AND CARE
Bamboo Made by laminating strips of split bamboo onto plywood planks, bamboo flooring is a stable and reliable flooring material with a pleasingly exotic appearance. Colors range from blonde to medium-dark brown. Because bamboo grows quickly, it is an easily renewable, environmentally friendly product.	The subfloor need not be very strong or very smooth. Prefinished tongue-and-groove strips are stapled or glued down. Cut the pieces with a power saw. If the floor will get wet, apply an extra coat of polyurethane or wax after installing. Reapply finish after a few years if it gets worn or scratched. Bamboo cannot be sanded.
Carpeting Carpet cushions the feet like no other flooring, and helps keep a room quiet. It is usually most practical for living areas that receive light traffic and rarely get wet, but tightly woven types can work well even in a bathroom. Carpeting is available in a wide variety of styles and materials.	The subfloor need not be very strong or very smooth for carpeting. Professional installers have specialized tools and experience, so they can install carpeting quickly. Padding is usually stapled to the subfloor, and tack strips are nailed around the perimeter. The carpet is stretched, attached to the strips, and trimmed. A high-quality carpet with stain protection is usually easy to keep clean. Ground-in soil and other stains require spot or steam cleaning.
Ceramic tile Glazing gives tiles a hard surface that is impervious to water. Wall tiles are fairly soft and available in almost any color; floor tiles are much harder, but tend toward more muted colors. The glazing can be slippery, so for floors, choose tiles with a bit of texture.	The substrate must be smooth and extremely strong; at least one layer of cement backerboard is recommended. Tiles are set in thinset mortar (for floors) or organic mastic (for walls). Cut the tiles with a snap cutter, wet saw, or nibbling tool. Joints must be filled with grout. The tiles themselves are virtually maintenance free and easy to clean, but grout must be kept sealed.
Ceramic tile—porcelain This product is extremely durable and resistant to stains. Many colors and styles are available. Porcelain can be manufactured to resemble ceramic tile and natural stone.	The substrate must be smooth and extremely strong. Tiles are set in thinset mortar, and are cut using a wet saw. Joints are filled with grout, which must be kept sealed.
Ceramic tile—quarry These tiles are not glazed, so they are not slippery when wet. Quarry tiles have muted, natural colors that usually run toward grays and browns.	The substrate must be smooth and extremely strong. Set the tiles in thinset mortar; cut them with a snap cutter, wet saw, or nibbling tool. Grouted joints must be kept sealed. Vitreous types are fairly resistant to stains; semi-vitreous types are easily stained. Regular application of a sealer will make staining less likely.
Ceramic tile—terra-cotta These are the softest of the ceramic tiles. Tiles vary slightly in color. Most are tan, brown, or reddish brown, their color reflecting the clay from which they were made. Some types are regular in shape, while some handmade types (such as Mexican Saltillos) are uneven in shape and irregular in size.	The substrate must be smooth and extremely strong. Set the tiles in a thick bed of thinset mortar; irregular tiles may need to be back-buttered as well. Make all cuts using a wet saw. Terra-cotta tiles definitely need to be sealed.

CHOOSING FLOORING

TYPE AND CHARACTERISTICS	INSTALLATION AND CARE
Cork Cork has a natural springiness that holds up for decades, as long as the floor is well maintained. It creates a comfortable, warm surface and is hypoallergenic. It also has sound-deadening qualities. Cork is usually sold in plank form, unstained or lightly stained. Tiles 12 inches square are less common and may be natural in color or stained with muted to bold color.	Like laminate flooring, cork planks are typically floated over a soft, rolled-out subsurface. Cut the pieces using a power saw. Most types snap together, so no glue is needed. Cork tiles require a very smooth subfloor. They can be cut with a knife, and are set in cork flooring adhesive. Cork comes prefinished; you may need to reapply polyurethane every year or so.
Hardwood flooring—engineered Made by laminating a layer of hardwood onto a plywood strip, this product offers the warm look of natural wood but is much easier to install than a solid hardwood floor. Many wood species and stains are available.	The subfloor need not be very strong or very smooth. Most types are stapled onto the subfloor; some are floated over a sheet of underlayment. Cut the strips using a power miter saw. Engineered flooring comes with a durable polyurethane finish. It can be sanded only once.
Hardwood flooring—solid This popular flooring material is available in random lengths with tongue-and-groove edges that fit tightly together. Oak strips are usually ¾ inch thick and 2¼ inches wide; maple is usually 1½ inches wide; other species are available in various widths.	The subfloor need not be very strong or very smooth. Strips are fastened to the subfloor using a special tongue-and-groove stapler or nailer. Cut the strips using a power miter saw. Once installed, the floor must be sanded, perhaps stained, and then sealed with at least two coats of polyurethane or wax. Solid hardwood flooring can be sanded up to three times.
Laminate strips or tiles This product has a laminate top coat that is far more durable than the type used on a typical laminate countertop. Available patterns often imitate hardwood or ceramic or stone tile. Some people object to the faux appearance, but others appreciate its ease of maintenance. Though the surface is hardy, it can be scratched, so area rugs are recommended if traffic will be heavy.	The subfloor need not be very strong or very smooth. Laminate flooring is floated atop a layer of sheet underlayment. Cut the pieces using a power saw. Pieces snap together, making for a very easy installation. The surface is impervious to water, but standing water could seep into the seams and damage it.
Linoleum Unlike vinyl sheet flooring, linoleum is a natural product made from oils, wood fiber, and bits of stone. This makes it environmentally friendly, and lends a subtle organic feel. Many colors and patterns are available.	The subfloor need not be very strong, but it must be smooth. Install linoleum much as you would vinyl sheet flooring, but use special linoleum adhesive. Keep the floor covered with coats of acrylic sealer. Tears and other damage can be repaired.
Mosaic tile Made by adhering small pieces to a mesh backing, mosaic tile may be composed of ceramic or natural stone tile. An excellent range of colors and textures is available. Mosaics can be used on walls or floors. Because of the many grout lines, a mosaic floor is usually not slippery when wet.	The substrate must be smooth and extremely strong. Set the sheets of tiles in thinset mortar. Cut the sheets using a utility knife. Cut individual tiles using a nibbling tool or a handheld snap cutter. Grouting is demanding because there are so many grout lines. Apply tile or grout sealer regularly.

TYPE AND CHARACTERISTICS	INSTALLATION AND CARE

Stone tile—polished

Gleaming, smooth natural stone has an elegant and stately appearance. The tiles are cut precisely, but they will naturally vary from each other in color and pattern. Marble tiles tend to be veined. Granite is usually speckled. Travertine is mottled and veined. Inexpensive agglomerated tiles, composed of stone fragments held together with resin, have a rich pattern that includes several colors. Although it is a popular choice for bathroom floors, polished stone can be slippery when wet.

The substrate must be smooth and extremely strong. Set the tiles in white thinset mortar; make sure they are level with each other. Cut the tiles using a wet saw. Typically, grout lines are narrow. Marble, travertine, and other soft stone must be kept well sealed or it will be prone to stains. Apply a sealer made for natural stone. Granite is extremely hard and resistant to stains.

Stone tile—tumbled or rough

Marble that is tumbled has an entirely different appearance from the polished version. These tiles have a porous—sometimes even spongelike—texture. There are variations in color, but veins and other patterns are generally absent. The result is a floor that feels relaxed yet sumptuous. Rough-cut stones such as limestone and slate have similar properties and appearance.

The substrate must be smooth and extremely strong. Set the tiles in white thinset mortar. The tiles may be somewhat irregular in shape, leading to grout lines of varying width, but this adds to the charm of the floor. Cut the tiles using a wet saw. Apply an acrylic sealer to the tiles before grouting so the grout does not soak into them. Left unsealed, these tiles will readily soak up stains, so keep them well protected with regular coats of sealer.

Vinyl sheet flooring

Sometimes mistakenly referred to as "linoleum," vinyl sheet flooring has a tough but flexible top layer with a pattern that is usually embossed. Patterns include wood tones, brick, tile, and geometric designs. The pattern is coated with a tough, shiny, no-wax coating. Because it is a continuous sheet rather than individual tiles, this product is excellent at repelling water.

The subfloor need not be very strong, but it must be smooth. Make a paper template of the floor, lay it on top of the sheet, and cut the sheet with a knife. For many types, spread adhesive over the entire floor; lay the sheet while the adhesive is wet. "Loose-lay" sheets are installed without adhesive; you apply double-sided tape along the perimeter. The no-wax coating will last for some years, after which you will need to apply a sealer made for no-wax floors.

Vinyl tile—commercial

These 12-inch-square tiles are made of vinyl and other materials. Flecks of color, which run through the thickness of the tile, help hide dirt. Commercial tiles are a great value, offering durability and resilience for a small cost. Two or more colors can be combined in a pattern.

The subfloor need not be very firm, but it must be smooth. Spread vinyl adhesive, allow it to dry, then set the tiles. Cut the tiles with a knife. Cover the tiles with acrylic finish or wax (even if they come prefinished), because bare tiles will stain easily.

Vinyl tile—self-stick

This is essentially the same material as vinyl sheet flooring in the form of individual tiles. Better-quality tiles are stiff, have a thick top layer, and are well protected with a solid no-wax coating.

The subfloor need not be very firm, but it must be smooth. The tiles are self-stick, so you need apply no adhesive; simply peel off the paper backing and press the tile in place. Cut tiles using a knife. The no-wax coating will likely last for some years, after which you will need to apply a sealer made for no-wax floors.

tools you'll need

NO MATTER WHAT KIND OF FLOORING YOU INSTALL, TO ACHIEVE PROFESSIONAL-looking results, you must use the right tools. For instance, if you apply the right adhesive using a properly sized notched trowel, you'll find it easy to make tiles or resilient flooring stick and to form a smooth surface. When you are installing strip flooring, a good-quality power miter saw, equipped with a sharp blade, can make all the difference.

Avoid bargain-bin tools, which are often uncomfortable and awkward to work with. At Lowe's you will find plenty of high-quality tools that won't break your budget.

tools for preparing the **substrate**

Before laying tiles, it is often necessary to install an underlayment of cement backerboard (for ceramic and stone tile) or plywood (for resilient flooring). Less often, the structure of a floor or wall needs to be strengthened. A modest collection of carpentry tools will enable you to handle most of this work.

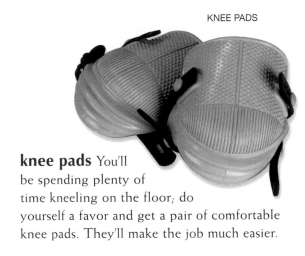

KNEE PADS

knee pads You'll be spending plenty of time kneeling on the floor; do yourself a favor and get a pair of comfortable knee pads. They'll make the job much easier.

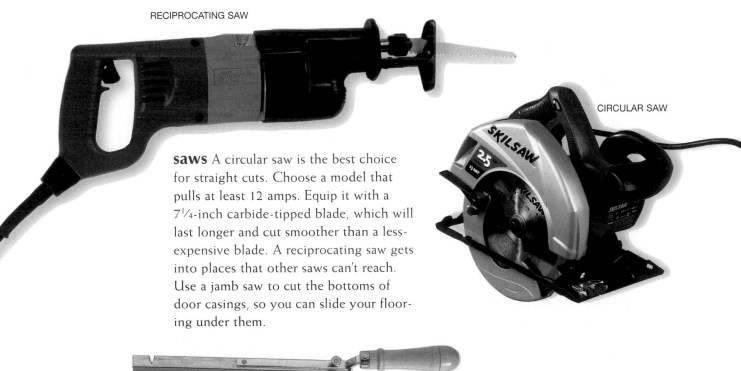

RECIPROCATING SAW

CIRCULAR SAW

saws A circular saw is the best choice for straight cuts. Choose a model that pulls at least 12 amps. Equip it with a 7¼-inch carbide-tipped blade, which will last longer and cut smoother than a less-expensive blade. A reciprocating saw gets into places that other saws can't reach. Use a jamb saw to cut the bottoms of door casings, so you can slide your flooring under them.

JAMB SAW

demolition tools A flat pry bar is indispensable for dismantling and prying up old flooring. A floor scraper quickly pries up ceramic or resilient flooring, and allows you to work standing up. Finish the job of scraping with a straight scraper or taping blade.

PRY BAR

DRYWALL SQUARE

drywall square Designed for use with drywall, this large tool makes quick work of measuring and marking cement backerboard or plywood.

STRAIGHT SCRAPER

knives A utility knife (see page 64) is an all-purpose tool. It will also cut cement backerboard but the going will be tough; a backerboard knife is faster and easier to use.

FLOOR SCRAPER

BACKERBOARD KNIFE

drill A ³⁄₈-inch variable-speed, reversible drill is powerful enough to drive screws for anchoring backerboard. If you choose a cordless drill, get one that pulls at least 14 volts. Buy a magnetic sleeve and several #2 Phillips screwdriver bits. This w. enable you to drive screws more quickly than yo. can pound nails.

CORDLESS DRILL

layout tools

A successful tile installation starts with layout lines that are straight and square. Accurate measuring and marking are essential to getting the job done right.

CARPENTER'S LEVEL

JURY STICK

level A carpenter's level, also called a spirit level, tells you if a line is plumb or level. To check a level for accuracy, place it on a flat surface and note the position of the bubble. Flip it upside down; if the bubble is in precisely the same place, the level is accurate.

jury stick Also called a layout stick, a jury stick eases the task of laying out a complicated tile floor or wall. You can make one on the job site, using a straight board and a pencil; follow the directions on page 121.

CHALK LINE

chalk line and straightedge
A taut string makes a perfectly straight line;
with a chalk line, you can snap a mark on
a floor or wall. Use a straightedge to mark
a line or to check how tiles line up. Tile
setters use aluminum straightedges, but
a metal carpenter's level or the
factory edge of a sheet of
plywood also work
fine.

STRAIGHTEDGE

SQUARE

square and tape measure
Use a framing square, also known as a
carpenter's square, to see whether two lines are
perpendicular. A 25-foot tape measure is the best
tool for measuring. The hook should slide back
and forth smoothly. Retracted, it accurately
measures "wall-to-wall"; extended, it hooks
on a board end for an equally
accurate measurement.

TAPE
MEASURE

tools for cutting tile

For most ceramic floor tiles, you can make straight cuts
using a snap cutter, but you will need either a nibbling
tool or a wet saw (see page 62) to make a cutout. For
stone tile, use a wet saw. To cut round holes, use a drill
with a masonry bit, or a carbide-tipped hole saw.

snap cutter Most tiles can be quickly
cut along a straight line using this inexpensive tool. Check that your snap
cutter is large enough for the tiles you
need to cut. It should have an adjustable
guide, to ease the job of cutting several
tiles the same size. Better models have
replaceable blades, also called scoring
wheels. A handheld snap cutter eases the
task of cutting mosaic tiles.

SNAP
CUTTER

CARBIDE-TIPPED
HOLE SAW

nibbling tool This cutting
device, also called
biters or tile nip-
pers, can take a bite
out of almost any tile, though the
going will be slow. If you have
only a few such cuts to make,
this tool may save you the trou-
ble of renting a wet saw. A nibbling tool is
also useful when you need to shave less
than half an inch from a tile.

NIBBLING
TOOL

grinder and saws Equipped with a
masonry blade, a grinder will cut quickly
through any type of ceramic or stone tile.
You can achieve similar results using a circular saw equipped with a diamond blade
or a masonry blade. For curved cuts, use a
hacksaw with a rod saw blade. Holes for
pipes and fittings are neatly made with a
carbide-tipped hole saw.

MASONRY
BLADE

GRINDER

HACKSAW WITH A ROD SAW BLADE

wet saw Also called a tub saw, a wet tile-cutting saw produces precise, clean cuts. With it, you can even cut ¼-inch-wide slivers out of most types of tile. The water sprays continuously onto the blade, preventing it from wearing out. Adjustable guides make it possible to produce cuts at 45 degrees or other angles. Unless your plans include several tiling projects, you'll probably want to rent rather than buy a wet saw.

LOWE'S QUICK TIP
Some wet saws cost little more than the price of a two-day rental. The diamond blade will be of lower quality than the one in a rental saw; it will wear out quickly if you cut very hard tile such as porcelain. Make sure its tray is large enough to handle your tiles. Test to see if you can make accurate cuts easily.

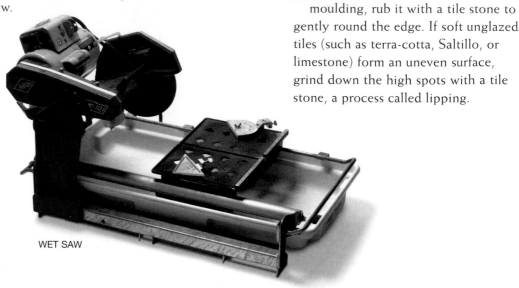

WET SAW

tile stone If a cut edge will not be covered by moulding, rub it with a tile stone to gently round the edge. If soft unglazed tiles (such as terra-cotta, Saltillo, or limestone) form an uneven surface, grind down the high spots with a tile stone, a process called lipping.

tools for **setting** tile

To set tile properly in thinset mortar, you must mix the mortar so it is free of lumps. It must then be spread to form a flat surface with consistent notch lines. You'll tap the tiles so they are level. Last, you'll spread grout and clean the surface.

MIXING PADDLES

mixing tools
Small amounts of thinset mortar can be mixed by hand using a margin trowel (see facing page). But for most jobs a mixing paddle is worth the cost because it saves a lot of work. For an average-sized job, a small paddle designed to be used with a ⅜-inch drill will do fine, as long as the drill is strong. For larger amounts, rent a ½-inch drill and a large mixing paddle.

mallet and beater board
To tap tiles into place, use a beater board. Buy one with a rubber face, or improvise by using a flat piece of wood about 5 by 10 inches in size. (Some people wrap the wood with carpeting, but this makes it less precise.) You can tap the block lightly with a hammer, but a rubber mallet is lighter and easier to control. To bed large tiles, especially if they are irregularly shaped, tap them directly with a rubber mallet.

laminated grout float Purchase a grout float with a face that is laminated with hard rubber. After using the float to press grout into the joints, the hard rubber surface acts as a squeegee, so you can wipe tiles virtually clean of excess grout.

notched trowels Choose trowels with thick, comfortable handles made of wood or rubber. Check that the blades, and the teeth, are straight. Follow the mortar manufacturer's directions to choose a notched trowel with teeth that are properly sized for your material. The thicker the tile, the deeper the notches must be.

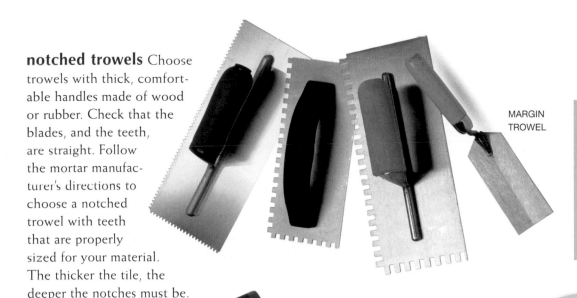

MARGIN TROWEL

LOWE'S QUICK TIP

A margin trowel is a handy all-purpose tool. Use it to mix mortar and grout; spread mortar in tight places; back-butter tiles; and scrape away dried mortar.

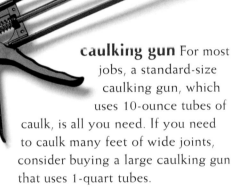

caulking gun For most jobs, a standard-size caulking gun, which uses 10-ounce tubes of caulk, is all you need. If you need to caulk many feet of wide joints, consider buying a large caulking gun that uses 1-quart tubes.

wiping tools Have a bucket of clean water and a large sponge on hand to wipe the tiled surface after grouting. A wet towel can be used for the initial wiping. To clean away grout or mortar that has hardened, use a scrubbing tool with a fiberglass mesh pad; anything harsher might scratch the tiles.

tools for **resilient flooring**

Flooring that is flexible, such as vinyl tiles or sheets, linoleum, carpet tile, and wood parquet, is easier to prepare for, cut, and install than ceramic tile. Only a modest collection of tools is needed.

JIGSAW

underlayment stapler Plywood underlayment, typically ¼ inch thick, can be fastened by driving nails or screws. However, an underlayment stapler is much faster, and the resulting indentations are easier to fill when you smooth the floor. You will probably want to rent rather than buy either a pneumatic or a hand-driven stapler.

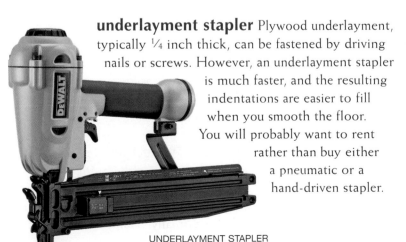

UNDERLAYMENT STAPLER

saws Cut underlayment and wood parquet with a circular saw (see page 59) or any other power saw. For cutouts or curves, use a jigsaw, also called a saber saw.

utility knife Slice through vinyl, carpet, and linoleum with a utility knife. Buy a professional-quality knife, with a large, comfortable handle and a mechanism that keeps the blade firmly in place while you cut. A standard knife blade works fine for all cutting needs, though you may find a hooked blade easier to use when cutting sheet goods.

vinyl tile cutter Rent this tool (see page 156) if you have plenty of commercial vinyl tiles to cut. With it, you can easily and quickly cut a series of tiles to the same width.

tools for **strip flooring**

Installing a strip floor—especially a hardwood floor with narrow strips—calls for plenty of repetitive cutting and fastening. Set up the work area with easy-to-use power tools to ease the task. Use a power miter saw (see facing page) to cut the boards.

small-notched trowel Spread adhesive (organic mastic) using a trowel with notches of the size recommended by the manufacturer (see page 63). Vinyl adhesive typically calls for notches that are $5/32$ by $1/16$ inches; for wood parquet, you likely will need a trowel with $1/8$-inch pointed notches.

FLOORING ROLLER

flooring roller Use a roller to squeeze out bubbles and waves from sheet flooring. A large, heavy roller is used while standing up. A less bulky hand roller (shown) does the job just as well, but you must work on your knees.

hammer and nail sets You will sometimes need to face-nail a board that cannot be reached with a stapler. Drill pilot holes, drive nails with a hammer, and sink the nail heads below the surface using a nail set (see facing page).

flooring fasteners You will probably rent rather than buy these tools. A flooring stapler (left) has a base that fits over the tongue side of a tongue-and-groove strip. Powered by a compressor, the stapler drives a long staple at a 45-degree angle through the back of the tongue to fasten the strip securely and invisibly. A hand-operated nailer must be whacked very hard; a pneumatic-assisted version (right), which requires a compressor, is easier to use and drives staples more reliably.

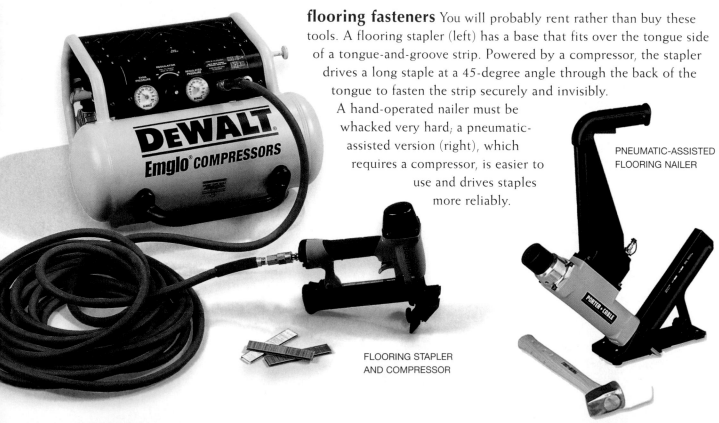

PNEUMATIC-ASSISTED FLOORING NAILER

FLOORING STAPLER AND COMPRESSOR

EDGING SANDER

floor sanders To sand and refinish an existing floor, or to sand and finish a new hardwood floor, rent two types of sanders. A drum sander does most of the work. If possible, get a model that runs on 220-volt current; it will work more efficiently than a model that uses standard 120-volt current. For the places where the drum sander cannot reach, use an edging sander.

DRUM SANDER

tools for **baseboard**

For a professional appearance, wood base moulding needs to be cut crisply and to the precise length. With the right tools, this is not difficult. Measure for cuts using a tape measure (see page 61).

POWER MITER SAW

power miter saw You can achieve precise cuts using a hand miter saw and miter box, but a power miter saw greatly lessens the struggle.

coping saw This tool is indispensable for creating tight inside corners, and is not as difficult to use as you may think.

COPING SAW

nailing tools You certainly can fasten mouldings using a hammer and nail set, but you will need to work quite carefully to avoid dinging the wood. A pneumatic nailer sets the nail heads perfectly with no damage to the moulding, and allows you to hold the board with one hand while you drive the fastener with the other.

NAIL SETS

HAMMER

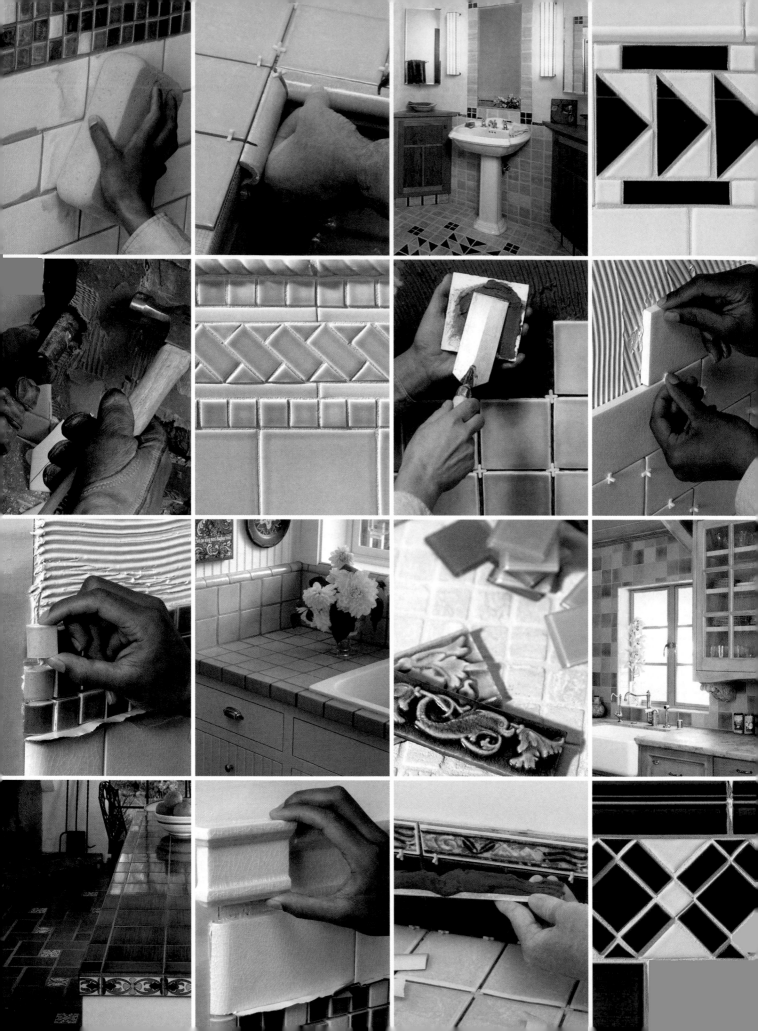

wall and counter tiles

TILING A WALL OR A COUNTER IS IN MANY WAYS EASIER than tiling a floor. The tiles are lighter and easier to cut, and you can work from a sitting or standing position. On the other hand, a wall or counter is closer to eye level than a floor is, so imperfections are more apparent. Tiles must be installed in straight rows with consistent grout lines, and they must form a consistently even surface.

In this chapter we give fail-safe instructions that enable a homeowner to achieve professional results. For instance, rather than simply snapping guide lines and installing tiles against them, we recommend using a temporary guide board called a batten, which makes it easy to get off to a straight start. We show how to install backerboard, which any handy person can do, rather than a thick mortar bed, which is a challenging type of installation best left to the pros. Where appropriate, we recommend setting wall tiles in organic mastic, which allows you to correct mistakes easily.

The most common wall tiles are soft ceramic with a shiny glaze, fairly small (4 by 4 inches is popular), and factory-perfect in size so they have consistent joint lines. However, almost any ceramic or stone tile can be installed on a wall; nowadays it's not unusual to see irregularly shaped, porous stone tiles, for instance. Countertop tiles, however, must be stronger. Most people prefer tiles with a hard glaze that is easy to wipe clean. Browse pages 14–29 for ideas, and consult with a Lowe's tiling specialist to be sure of the right tiles for your situation.

Lowe's installation services can arrange for professional installation of every type of tiling shown in this chapter. Once you request professional services, a Lowe's-approved contractor comes to your home, takes measurements, and presents an all-inclusive bid for the work and materials. There is a modest charge for this bid; the charge will be deducted from the installation cost should you decide to hire the contractor. The bid is binding: the contractor will not add extra costs unless you agree. Lowe's guarantees that the work will be done to your satisfaction and in a timely manner.

preparing a wall for tiling

WALL TILES DON'T GET WALKED ON, BUT THEY DO GET BUMPED, AND THEY CAN crack if the substrate is weak. New wall tiles strengthen a wall only slightly, so don't count on the tiles to tie together a wall with cracks or to firm up a wall that feels flexible when you press on it.

testing and patching

A standard new-home wall, composed of a single layer of ½-inch drywall attached to studs that are spaced 16 inches apart, is just strong enough for most tiling projects. An older plaster wall in good condition is actually stronger.

Test a wall by pressing it with the heel of your hand at various points. If drywall has come loose, drive drywall nails or screws through the drywall and into the studs behind it. For a plaster wall in which plaster has come loose from the underlying lath, you have a more difficult problem. Either remove the plaster (a messy job) and install drywall, or "skin over" the entire surface with a layer of drywall, attached with screws driven into

LOWE'S QUICK TIP

If the wall to be tiled will be exposed to only occasional moisture, you can install greenboard (see pages 70–71). If it will get wet regularly, install cement backerboard (see page 81).

DRYWALL PATCH

DRYWALL SCREW

studs. However, this latter solution thickens the wall, so you may have to modify the wall mouldings.

To patch a small hole in drywall, purchase a drywall patching kit. For a hole or damaged area larger than 6 inches square, use a drywall saw to cut out a rectangular area around the damage. Cut two 1 by 4 nailers a couple of inches longer than the width of the opening. Position the nailers behind the opening (left) and attach them with screws. Cut a piece of drywall to fit, and attach it with screws to the nailers. Apply fiberglass mesh drywall tape and joint compound to the edge of the repair, let it dry, and sand smooth.

To patch a hole or weak spot in a plaster wall, chip out all the loose plaster. Cut a piece of drywall that is of the same thickness as the plaster so that it fits approximately in the opening, and attach it to the lath with screws (above). You may need to buy ⅜-inch drywall. Fill the gaps with joint compound, let it dry, and sand smooth.

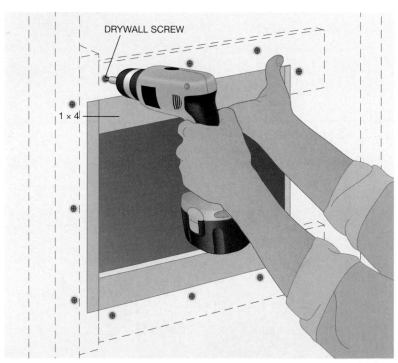

DRYWALL SCREW

1 × 4

removing obstacles

Whenever possible, avoid cutting tiles to fit around an obstruction. You will achieve more professional-looking results—and the job will proceed much more smoothly in the long run—if you remove the obstruction and replace it after the tiles have been installed. Detach and remove towel racks, soap dishes, toilet paper dispensers, cabinets, and mouldings that are in the way.

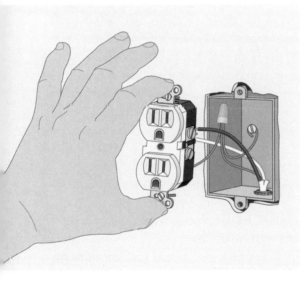

If you will be tiling around an electrical switch or receptacle, shut off power to the circuit by switching off the circuit breaker or unscrewing the fuse. Use an electrical tester to make sure that the power is off. Remove the cover plate and the screws that hold the switch or receptacle in place, then gently pull it outward. Make sure any wire splices are covered with wire nuts or tape, and wrap electrical tape around exposed screw terminals. Once you are certain the switch or receptacle is safe, you can restore power. Do not use a receptacle while it is pulled out. To reinstall after tiling, see page 78.

If you will be installing tiles directly onto the existing wall surface, scrape away any loose paint. Then rough up the entire surface with a hand sander to make sure the adhesive will bond firmly.

check for **plumb** and smoothness

Hold or tape a carpenter's level against a straight board, and hold the board up against the wall near a corner. If a wall is out of plumb, it will not be parallel to a vertical grout line on an adjacent wall. In addition, test various points along the walls to see if there are any waves. A wave will be most visible if it is near a corner. See page 71 for ways to correct waves or an out-of-plumb wall.

tiling over **existing** ceramic tile

Even if existing wall tile is firmly attached, there are two problems to overcome before you can tile over it. First, the glazed surface may be too slick for adhesive to adhere. The glazes on wall tiles are usually soft, however, and can be roughed up with a belt sander (below). Consult with a Lowe's tiling expert to make sure that the mastic you use will stick firmly to the roughed-up tiles. Second, the extra layer of tiles will stick out from the wall, meaning that you'll have to find a special way to finish the edges. Radius bullnose may be the solution (see the illustration on page 80).

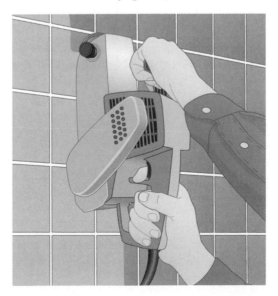

LOWE'S QUICK TIP

If you attach the tiles to the wall using organic mastic, the tiles will closely follow the contours of the underlying wall. If you use thinset mortar, you will be able to significantly straighten the wall while you apply the mortar. However, thinset is a bit tricky to use on a wall; see pages 84–86.

preparing other types of wall surface

A substrate for wall tiles obviously doesn't need to be strong enough to walk on, but it must be firm so it will not flex, as well as stable so it will not expand and contract during changes of temperature or humidity. It must also have a porous surface that the adhesive can grip; organic mastic or thin-set adhesive is likely to come loose from a surface that is glossy or oily.

Adhesive does not stick to the underlying wall material, but to the surface. For instance, if paint or wallpaper is starting to peel, the tile adhesive will peel off as well, dislodging the tiles.

wallpaper By design, wallpaper paste is weak; it's just strong enough to hold the paper. Strip all the wallpaper (there may be several layers) before tiling. Remove wallpaper even if it has been painted over.

wood paneling All types of wood paneling—from cheap sheets with a wood-grain veneer to solid tongue-and-groove planks—expand and contract with changes in the weather. Do not tile over wood of any sort. Instead, remove the paneling and patch the underlying wall.

concrete A basement wall made of concrete may be a suitable surface for tiling. Use a grinder to level any bumps. Scrub the wall with a concrete cleaner to be sure all oils are removed, then brush on liquid concrete bonding agent. Basement walls often develop cracks after a decade or two; to protect tiles, install an isolation membrane (see page 117).

brick or block Tile adhesive will have no trouble gripping the rough surface of brick or concrete block. However, masonry walls are usually uneven, making it difficult to install a smooth tile surface. Straighten out a masonry wall by applying a skim coat of brick mortar mixed with some extra Portland cement. If a powdery white substance (called efflorescence) appears on a brick wall, or if bricks are crumbling, the wall is getting damp fairly often and tiles will not stick; consult with a mason before tiling.

installing greenboard

Moisture-resistant drywall, commonly known as greenboard or blueboard, is available in ½-inch-thick 4-foot-by-8-foot sheets. The long edges are tapered to accommodate the thickness of the drywall tape and joint compound used to seal the joint. The short edges are not tapered; wherever two nontapered edges meet in a butt joint, the thickness of the tape and joint compound will result in a slight outward bump in the wall surface. Plan your installation to include as few butt joints as possible.

cut, snap, and cut again Measure for the cut, and subtract ¼ inch. (Because the cut will be ragged, the piece will be slightly longer than you measured for.) A drywall square (below) makes quick work of scoring square lines across the width of a sheet. Hold the square firmly against the cut line, and use a utility knife to score a line. Bend the sheet back until it snaps, then cut through the back side.

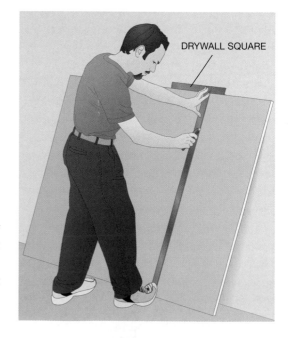

DRYWALL SQUARE

cut holes with a drywall saw If

you need to cut a hole for a pipe, measure and mark the center of the hole, then mark the circle. Plan a hole large enough that the greenboard will be at least ¼ inch away from the pipe at all points. Score the circle with a utility knife. Cut the hole with a drywall saw (right); keep the saw to the inside of the scoring as you cut.

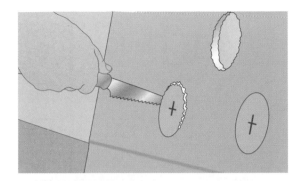

attach the greenboard Use the dry-

wall square to draw lines indicating the centers of studs. Hold the sheet in place up against the studs (a helper will make this easier), and drive screws or drywall nails into the studs. Each fastener head must dimple the surface inward, but not so far that it breaks the paper, or it will lose holding power.

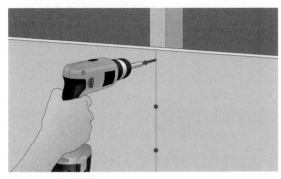

tape the joints Cut and apply mesh

tape. Using a 6-inch taping blade, smoothly cover the tape with joint compound. With an 8-inch taping blade apply one or two additional coats of joint compound, feathering the edges for a smooth transition between the joint and board. Sand between the coats.

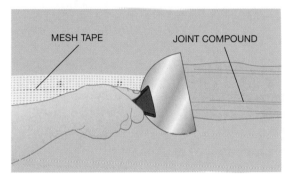

MESH TAPE   JOINT COMPOUND

STRAIGHTENING A WALL

If a wall has serious waves near the corners or is more than ½ inch out of plumb, take steps to straighten things out. Otherwise, you'll have to cut each corner individually and end up with grout lines that aren't parallel to the corners.

Adjusting with compound

To correct concavities in an existing wall, or to bring a wall into plumb, you'll need joint compound, a 12-inch-wide taping knife (above right), and plenty of patience. Apply joint compound and spread it with the taping knife so it looks fairly straight. Check your work with a straightedge, a level, or both, and adjust as necessary. After the compound dries, sand it

smooth and check again. It may take several applications to make the wall smooth and plumb.

Shimming

If a wall is out of plumb or wavy, use a level to draw a plumb line next to it on the adjacent wall. Every 8 inches or so along the out-of-plumb stud (or wall, if you are skinning over it), nail a shim that is thick enough to come up to the plumb line. (Cut shims with a utility knife.) Hold a level against the shims to double-check for plumb. On the adjacent wall, draw arrows pointing to the thickest parts of the shim (right). When you install greenboard or backerboard, drive fasteners at those points.

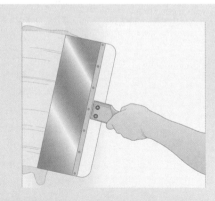

laying out for wall tile

ONCE YOU HAVE PREPARED THE WALLS AND MADE SURE THEY ARE PLUMB AND flat (see pages 70–71), it's time to plan exactly where the tiles will go. The main goal when laying out wall tiles is to avoid a row of very narrow cut tiles. Narrow tiles look awkward and emphasize any imperfections in adjoining walls. A secondary goal is symmetry: whenever possible, center the tiles on the wall so that the cut tiles at either side are the same size.

An obstruction such as a window can make the layout much more complicated, because you also need to avoid having narrow tiles around its sides.

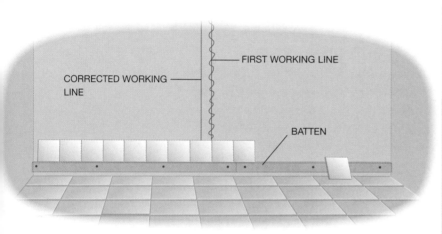

CORRECTED WORKING LINE

FIRST WORKING LINE

BATTEN

The neat symmetry of the tiling in this bathroom is the result of careful layout. By anticipating the location of each tile you not only avoid narrow tiles that emphasize imperfections in the wall, but you'll make your job go faster and easier.

install a **batten**

Decide how high the second horizontal row of tiles will be above the floor. If the floor beneath is fairly level and the bottom of the tiles will be covered with a base moulding, position the second row above the floor by the height of one tile plus an inch or so. If there will be no base moulding, and the bottom row of tiles must meet the floor precisely, plan to cut all the bottom-row tiles to about three-fourths height.

Use a level to draw a horizontal working line for the second row, and also draw a plumb vertical line in the exact center of the room. Attach a batten—a very straight board—with its top edge against the horizontal line. A long strip of plywood with one factory edge makes an ideal batten.

Position tiles in a dry run on top of the batten, starting at the centerline and running to one adjacent wall. If the tiles are not self-spacing, add spacers between them. If this layout leads to a narrow cut tile at the end, mark a corrected vertical line, moving it by the width of half a tile in either direction.

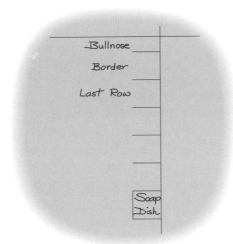

Bullnose
Border
Last Row

Soap
Dish

mark for borders and for accessories

If the tiles will not reach to the ceiling, decide where to position the top of the installation. Make a jury stick (see page 121) and hold it vertically to mark for the courses of field tiles (the tiles that cover the bulk of the wall surface), the border pieces (if any), and the rounded-edge bull-nose pieces at the top.

Soap dishes, toilet paper holders, towel racks, and other accessories are mounted to the wall after or while the tiles are set (see page 82). Choose accessories that fit into the space of one tile. To make sure that you remember to leave space for each accessory, mark its location on the wall.

handling obstacles

Small obstacles such as electrical receptacles or switches are not usually considered in the layout; an occasional narrow cut tile is not a problem. However, if an obstacle is large and at eye level, it may be the focal point of the wall. In that case, it's important to avoid narrow cut tiles around it, and preferable to make the cut tiles on either side the same size.

Use a jury stick to check whether there will be a narrow vertical row of tiles along either edge of the obstacle (below). If so, you may have to make a choice between placing narrow tiles there or putting them at the wall edges. Also use the stick to determine whether there will be a narrow horizontal row of tiles just below or above the obstacle. If so, you may choose to raise or lower the batten.

If a room has more than one highly visible obstruction, you'll probably have to make some compromises. If any of the obstructions is seriously out of plumb or level, try to place wide cut tiles there.

LOWE'S QUICK TIP
The moulding piece below a window sill, called the apron, can be removed and replaced after the tiles have been set. You can also remove it permanently and tile all the way up to the window sill. No other window mouldings can be treated this way.

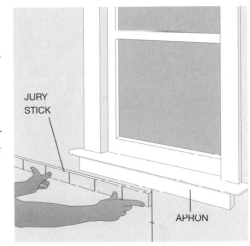

JURY STICK

APRON

USING BORDERS

The most popular way to enliven a wall of tiles is to run a decorative border along the top, and sometimes along the sides as well. Both need edge trim or bullnose pieces (see page 76) to make the transition to the wall surface. Often it makes sense to choose affordable tile for the bulk of the field and splurge on a border to dress up the installation. A border need not be installed at the top or around the perimeter. A border set in the middle of a field of tiles can also provide an eye-catching accent.

Three tile borders are shown here. Lowe's offers a selection of borders. Even more can be special-ordered. While such ready-made options are often a good place to start, you should feel free to make up your own design. To be safe, buy all the tiles from the same manufacturer so they will fit together.

Carefully think through the entire layout. It helps to make a detailed drawing, using graph paper. One simple but effective border uses a row of thin tiles and a finish cap, with a row of field tiles sandwiched between. To add more interest, use strips of mosaics, tiles tilted to look like diamonds, or triangular tiles.

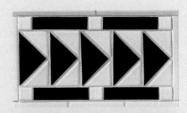

tiling a wall

IF THE WALL SUBSTRATE IS WELL PREPARED, INSTALLING THE TILES WILL BE A straightforward job. Double-check to see that the surface is flat and firm, and that adjoining walls are plumb.

Organic mastic comes ready-mixed, is easy to apply, and allows tiles to be adjusted up to 30 minutes after installation. Thinset mortar is more difficult to work with, but it is more resistant to water. Use mastic for walls that will stay relatively dry, and consider thinset for a wall that will often get wet, such as a tub enclosure (see pages 80–87).

LOWE'S QUICK TIP

If brick-shaped tiles are installed one on top of two, as shown in Step 2, draw two vertical working lines near the center of the wall, representing the leading edges of alternating courses.

1 Using a trowel with notches recommended by the mastic manufacturer, scoop mastic out of the tub and spread it on the wall. Do not cover the working lines. As much as possible, apply the mastic with long, sweeping strokes. Hold the trowel at the same angle all the time, to ensure a setting bed of consistent depth. The trowel teeth should lightly scrape the wall surface.

2 Press each tile into the adhesive. Avoid sliding a tile more than half an inch. Add spacers as you go. Every 15 minutes or so, check the entire installation to make sure no tiles have strayed out of alignment. Using a cloth dampened with water or mineral spirits (depending on the type of mastic used), wipe away any mastic that squeezes onto the surface of a tile.

3 Tap the tile surface with a mallet to make sure the tiles are embedded in the mastic and to form a smooth wall surface. If a tile's surface is raised noticeably above the surface of its neighbor, try tapping it tighter against the wall using a rubber mallet. If this doesn't do the trick, you may have to remove some tiles, reapply mastic, and start again.

self-spacing tiles

Some tiles, such as those shown at right, have two nubs on each edge, so that when the tiles are butted together, a perfect grout line is created between them without the need for spacers. Installing these self-spacing tiles is quick and easy. If a cut tile of this type is slightly larger than it should be, don't force it in. Cut a new tile, or reduce the size of the cut tile by rubbing the edge with a tile stone.

irregular tiles

If the tiles are precisely made, simply set spacers in each corner along each edge. However, if the tiles are not consistent in shape or size (stone or hand-made Saltillo tiles are examples), you will have to improvise. Depending on how irregular they are, you may choose to use standard spacers and turn some of them sideways, as shown on the facing page. With some tiles, you can adjust spacing by pushing the spacers in or pulling them outward. Other options include scraps of cardboard or wedge-shaped plastic tile spacers. Whichever method you use, check every other row or so to see that the tiles form a reasonably straight horizontal line.

cutting wall tiles

Most ceramic wall tiles are softer than floor tiles and can be easily cut with a snap cutter or rod saw. If a ceramic tile is too hard for a rod saw, use tile nippers, a wet saw, or both together (see pages 126–127). Stone tiles must always be cut with a wet saw (see page 127).

To make a cutout with a rod saw, hold the tile firmly, with the area to be cut overhanging the work surface (right). Saw with steady, moderate pressure. When turning a corner, take care not to twist the saw—you may crack the tile.

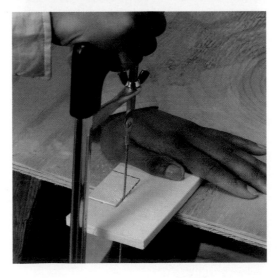

LOWE'S QUICK TIP
Do not attempt to straighten out a wall by more than 1/4 inch or so using organic mastic. If it is applied thicker, it may never fully harden.

trim tiles

To finish off the unglazed edges of field tiles, add bullnose pieces (also called caps), which have one finished edge. At an outside corner, use a corner piece or a "down-angle" tile, which has two finished edges. (For more information on trim tiles, see pages 94–95 and 134.)

Bullnose tiles are supposed to have the same dimensions as the field tiles, but don't be surprised to find they are slightly smaller. Leave a bit more space between them to maintain straight grout lines. If you have square tiles, you can compensate for this variation by positioning the bullnose tiles so their grout lines do not line up with those of the field tiles.

1 Spread the mastic right up to the edge line of the area to be tiled, but no farther. All the tile should be embedded in mastic, but any excess mastic must be cleaned away.

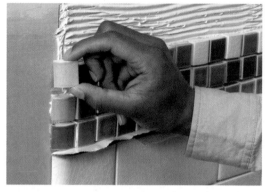

2 Set the bullnose pieces as you did the field tiles, then press or tap with a beater block. In this installation there are both small mosaic bullnose tiles and larger field-tile bullnoses.

3 Wherever two edges will be exposed, install a decorative corner tile (shown) or a down-angle tile, which has two rounded edges.

4 Using a rag dampened with water (or mineral spirits if the manufacturer's instructions require it), thoroughly wipe away all excess mastic.

accessories

Soap dishes, towel racks, toothbrush holders, and toilet paper dispensers often get pulled or bumped. Some installers therefore adhere them to the substrate with a strong adhesive, such as thinset mortar or silicone adhesive. Others deliberately use a weak adhesive such as organic mastic so

the accessory will come out in one piece rather than breaking if someone leans or pulls too hard on it.

Some accessories attach not to the substrate but directly to the tiled wall. Following manufacturer's instructions, drill small pilot holes in the tiles using a masonry bit, tap in plastic anchors, and drive the mounting screws.

grouting and finishing

Wait for the adhesive to completely harden before grouting. Usually allowing 12 hours is enough, but if the room is humid or if you spread organic mastic thickly, it could take a day or two. If you can move a tile to the side using your hand, you need to wait longer.

Use unsanded grout for joints less than $\frac{1}{8}$ inch wide, and sanded grout for wider joints. Unless the grout is fortified with powdered latex, mix it with liquid latex even if the directions say you can mix it with water only.

Prepare as much grout as you can use in 20 minutes or so. In a clean bucket, mix the liquid with the powder (a margin trowel works well as a mixing tool) until the grout is free of lumps and about as thick as toothpaste. Wait 10 minutes, then stir again.

1 Scoop grout out of the bucket with a laminated grout float, and smear it onto the wall. Working in sections about 4 feet square, push grout into the spaces between the tiles. Hold the float nearly flat and sweep it diagonally across the tile surface so that it does not dig in. At all points, press the grout in by moving the float systematically in at least two directions.

2 Tilt the float up and use it like a squeegee to wipe away most of the grout from the face of the tiles. Be careful to scrape diagonally so that the edge of the float cannot dig into the grout lines.

3 Dampen a sponge and wipe the tiles gently. Rinse the sponge every few minutes with clean water. If you see a gap in a grout line, push more grout into the gap using your finger, and wipe away the excess. Wipe the surface two or three times.

4 Run the sponge gently along the vertical lines, then along the horizontal lines, to achieve grout lines of consistent width and depth. If you're having trouble making consistent lines, try tooling the joint by running the rounded handle of a tool or toothbrush along each line. Allow the grout to dry, then buff the surface of the tiles with a dry, lint-free cloth.

LOWE'S QUICK TIP
Avoid using ready-mixed grout, which comes in buckets. It is easier to use but is not as durable. In addition, if the grout cavity is wider than $\frac{1}{8}$ inch, ready-mixed grout will shrink, leaving unsightly cracks.

caulking

If your grout is not white, a tile supplier may sell a caulk that matches it. Pure silicone caulk is the easiest to keep clean; silicone-reinforced latex caulk will dull if wiped often. "Tub and tile" caulk performs almost as well as silicone.

Making clean caulk lines is a skill that you can learn quickly. Practice on scrap pieces until you feel you can control the flow of caulk and make a line of consistent thickness. For another method of caulking, see page 87.

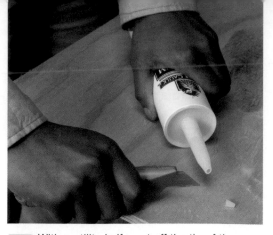

1 With a utility knife, cut off the tip of the caulking tube nozzle. The closer to the tip you cut, the thinner the bead of caulk. Some people like to cut at a steep angle, while others cut the tip almost straight across. With some caulking tubes, you also need to poke a long nail or a wire down through the nozzle to break a seal. Load the tube into a caulking gun.

2 Squeeze the caulking gun trigger until caulk flows; push down on the release button to stop it. Place the nozzle tip on the joint you are caulking, squeeze the trigger, and move the nozzle along the joint as you continue to squeeze.

3 If you manage to squeeze out a line of caulk that is straight and smooth, you can just leave it. For a more finished look, dampen a rag or sponge with water or mineral spirits and run it along the caulk line to smooth the joint.

REPLACING ELECTRICAL DEVICES

When the tiling is done, you'll need to replace any electrical devices removed earlier. At your main electrical panel, shut off power to the circuit supplying the switch or receptacle. If the electrical box for the switch or receptacle is recessed more than ¼ inch, insert a box extender as shown. Attach the device to the box, running the screws through the extender tabs. The ears of the device should rest on the tiles. Replace the cover plate, and restore power at the main panel.

BOX EXTENDER   EAR

INSTALLING STONE TILE ON WALLS

Some types of natural stone stain easily, and some are translucent. Use white thinset when installing light-colored marble or other stone; gray thinset or brown organic mastic can subtly muddy the stone's color. If you choose a grout that is not similar to the color of the stone, check with the tile supplier to make sure the grout will not stain the stone.

Wall tiles (right) made of polished marble, granite, or other stone are usually large— 12 inches square. They are butted up against each other with very thin grout lines. Unless the tiles are installed perfectly flat, any variation between them will be obvious.

Installation techniques are not much different than for other types of wall tile, except that you have to be very precise. Carefully examine the substrate. Check walls to see that they are flat and smooth; correct even the most minor imperfections. When you spread the mortar, hold the trowel at the same angle at all times so the setting bed is a consistent depth. Constantly check and recheck that the surfaces of adjacent tiles are on the same plane. Don't be surprised if you have to remove a tile and reset it in order to achieve a smooth wall.

For a uniform appearance, any exposed tile edges should be finished ahead of time to make them as shiny as the tile surface. The best way is to have them professionally buffed; a tile dealer may know a place where you can arrange for this to be done. If you'd like to try a do-it-yourself method, you can sand the edges with very fine sandpaper, then brush on two or more coats of clear lacquer.

Rough stone wall tiles (left) offer a less demanding alternative. The earthy look of large, rough tiles made of limestone, marble, or slate is an increasingly popular option— especially for bathrooms. In most respects, the installation of such tiles is much easier than with smooth tiles. A slightly uneven surface is generally considered acceptable— even desirable. The edges do not have to be polished. The only potential concern is the weight of the tiles. If a tile is not firmly embedded in thinset of the correct consistency, it could fall out during installation. There's no need to brace tiles temporarily; just make sure they are well set.

LOWE'S QUICK TIP

Natural stone varies from tile to tile in color and pattern. Examine tiles from all the boxes, laying them out based on color and thickness. You may choose to "shuffle" the tiles so that there will be an even distribution of tiles with certain characteristics.

tiling a tub surround

A TUB SURROUND IS ONE OF THE MOST COMMON TILING PROJECTS. IN MOST cases, the tile extends about 4 feet above the tub. On the sides, you can either stop the tile at the edge of the tub (see page 86) or extend the tile surface past the tub so a vertical row of trim tiles reaches the floor. Tiling a shower stall is nearly identical, except that you'll run the tile to within a few inches of the ceiling. (Running the tile to the ceiling is usually avoided because ceilings are seldom perfectly level.) While similar to tiling a wall, tiling a tub or shower is more complicated due to working around the faucet or shower control and the installation of such amenities as soap dishes, niches, and seats.

gathering the pieces

Purchase bullnose tiles for the outside edges along the top and the sides of the installation. You'll probably need two outside corner pieces or "down-angle" tiles, which have bullnose edges on two sides. One common border, shown on page 85, combines outside trim pieces and thin liner pieces, with a row of field tiles sandwiched in between. The thin trim pieces may turn a corner and run vertically down the sides, or can run horizontally only, meeting the vertical outside trim.

preparing the substrate

Use cement backerboard as a substrate. Many tub surrounds are tiled using greenboard for the substrate. These installations can last a long time, but only if the grout and caulk are kept in perfect condition,

LOWE'S QUICK TIP

Thinset mortar stays strong when it gets wet; organic mastic weakens in time if it is left damp. However, thinset is somewhat difficult to use for wall tiling, because it must be kept at just the right consistency— not too wet and not too dry—as you set the tiles. If you don't feel confident using thinset (see page 84), switch to organic mastic, and afterward take special care to maintain the caulk and grout lines.

with no holes. However, even a small gap in the grout or caulk will let in water. Greenboard (or worse yet, standard drywall) will then crumble and fall apart.

removing plumbing Faucet handles attach in different ways. In most cases, you first need to pry off a decorative cover in

the center of the handle with a small screwdriver. Loosen and remove the screw that's underneath and pull off the handle. If there is an escutcheon (flange) behind the handle, it may simply lift off, or you may have to loosen a small setscrew first. To remove a stuck handle, tap it gently from side to side, or spray the screw and behind the handle with penetrating oil spray.

To remove a spout without damaging it, stick a wooden dowel (or a wooden hammer handle) into the opening, and

AVOIDING DEMOLITION

If you use radius bullnose for the edge, you need not remove the existing substrate. Install cement backerboard onto the surface of the wall. Unlike conventional bullnose edging (see page 76), a radius bullnose piece has a lip that wraps around the backerboard at the edges. "Down-angle" radius bullnose pieces are used on outside corners.

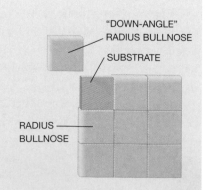

"DOWN-ANGLE" RADIUS BULLNOSE

SUBSTRATE

RADIUS BULLNOSE

lever it counterclockwise. If the spout is shaped so that this will not work, wrap the faucet with tape or a rag, and use slip-joint pliers or a pipe wrench (facing page). Use the same technique to remove a shower arm.

removing tiles and substrate To protect a tub, cut pieces of rosin paper to fit inside it. Anchor the paper with wide masking tape so the paper won't rip as you work. Place a dropcloth in the tub and position a piece of plywood on top of the tub to catch falling debris. Clean the area often so tile shards do not rip the paper.

Some tiles can be easily removed with a prybar and a hammer (right). However,

if the tiles are set in a thick mortar bed, you will need to whack away for hours using a hammer and a cold chisel.

Once the tiles are off, mark the wall to show the outline of the new tiled surface, and remove the substrate to within an inch or two of the line. (If you go past the line, you will need to patch the wall—a fairly time-consuming process.) For a plaster wall, either remove the wood lath along with the plaster, or remove only the plaster. Repair any rot in the studs you have just exposed.

installing **backerboard**

Remove all nails or screws from the studs. Measure to find out how thick the backerboard must be to match the surrounding wall surface. To cut backerboard, see page 110. The side-wall backerboard must be flush with the abutting wall surface.

1 Place strips of ¼-inch plywood on the tub rim as spacers. This creates a gap between the tub and the backerboard that you will later fill with caulk. Without this caulk barrier, moisture will wick up into the backerboard. Starting with the back wall, cut pieces of backerboard to fit, allowing an ⅛-inch gap between pieces. Drive a few backerboard screws through the backerboard and into the studs. Make sure that the heads of the screws are sunk just below the surface of the board.

2 Measure and mark the backerboard for the center of each pipe. With a carbide-tipped hole saw, cut each hole about ½ inch wider than the pipe. Or, drill a hole in the center using a masonry bit, score the outline, and punch the hole out with a hammer. For a wall that is more than ¼ inch out of plumb, remove the backerboard and install shims (see page 71). Replace the backerboard and drive screws every 6 inches into the studs. Press fiberglass mesh tape along each joint. Mix a little thinset mortar (see page 84); trowel a thin coat over the mesh tape. Feather the edges and smooth any bumps.

tub amenities

It's not difficult to add customized features to a tub surround, as long as you plan ahead. Some features can be added as you tile, while others require that you build in the needed supports or spacing when you install the framing and backerboard.

integrated soap dish Some soap dishes are attached directly to the substrate, while others are set into an opening cut in the wall. If possible, purchase a soap dish that is the same size as the tiles. That way, you can simply leave one tile out, and install the dish in the resulting opening. Otherwise, you will need to cut tiles to create an opening of the correct size. As you tile, hold the soap dish in place to make sure it will fit.

Install the soap dish after the tiles have set, either before or after grouting. Butter the back of the soap dish with thinset, organic mastic, or silicone adhesive. Push the dish into position, and wipe away any adhesive that oozes out. Apply masking tape to hold the dish in place while the adhesive sets.

shower seat A triangular shower seat can be supported between two rows of tiles; it does not need to be recessed into the substrate. The row of tiles directly below the seat must be cut ahead of time to accommodate the thickness of the seat. Experiment to find the precise height for these tiles, so that after the seat is installed, the row of tiles directly above it will end up at the correct height. Note that the tiles on either side must be notch-cut. Apply silicone adhesive to the back edges of the seat, and slip the seat into place against the backerboard. Allow the silicone to set for several hours before you install the rest of the tiles.

shampoo niche For the base of the niche, purchase a shelf made of solid material. Some types can be cut with a circular saw; others require a wet saw. Before you install the backerboard, cut two 2-by-4 crosspieces to fit between the studs that are at each side of the planned niche, and use 3-inch screws to install one crosspiece above and one below. Bear in mind that after the backerboard and tiles are installed, the finished opening will be about 1½ inches smaller in either direction than the framed opening. Cover the sides and back of the opening with backerboard.

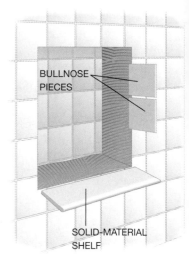

BULLNOSE PIECES

SOLID-MATERIAL SHELF

When you tile the wall, cut and install tiles that go to the edges of the opening. Cut the shelf to overhang the wall by an inch or so. Spread mortar on the bottom of the opening so the mortar is thicker at the back than at the front to give the shelf a slight downward tilt for drainage. Tile the niche. Cut and install bullnose tiles along the inside edges of the opening to create finished corners. The pieces just above the shelf will need to be cut at a slight angle because of the tilt in the shelf. Fill in remaining spaces with field tiles.

laying out the job

In general, lay out the walls for tiling as described on pages 72–73, but adapt the process for a tub surround as described below. If you will be tiling around a window, see page 87. Plan for amenities like a soap dish or shower seat now as well (facing page).

For a bathtub that is perfectly level in both directions, you can install full-sized tiles running horizontally at the bottom. If the tub is slightly out of level, install a bottom row of half- or three-quarter-sized tiles; this will allow you to cut some a bit larger than others. On each wall, install a batten—a perfectly straight board—so that it is level and can support the second horizontal row of tiles (right). Secure the battens with screws driven into the studs.

do a dry run You may want to do a vertical dry run of tiles to find out where the top of the installation will be. Or, use a jury stick (see pages 61 and 121). Next, do a horizontal dry run. Set as many full tiles as possible on the battens, with spacers if you will be using them. Adjust them as needed. On the back wall, it's important that the vertical rows of cut tiles at either end be the same size.

On the side walls, determine where you want the installation to end, then use the dry run (or jury stick) to check the size of the cut tiles at the inside corners. You may need to adjust the layout so that the cut tiles will be at least half-sized.

draw the lines Once the dry-run tiles are where you want them, draw layout lines. Mark the back wall, placing a grout line near the center of the wall. On each side wall, mark where the bullnose pieces will end. Remove the tiles, and use a level to draw plumb lines vertically from those three marks. Use a framing square to make sure that the lines are square with the batten.

MAPPING ACCENT TILES

If your installation will include decorative or different-colored tiles, map their locations after you have done your dry runs. This is easily done on a piece of graph paper.

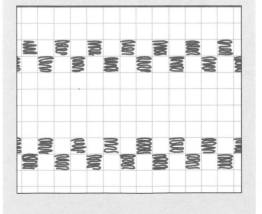

LOWE'S QUICK TIP

If the back wall has a window, it is liable to rot, especially if it is wood. Consider replacing it with glass block; it should have at least one louvered section to provide ventilation. A salesperson at Lowe's can guide you in its installation.

mix and apply **thinset**

In a 2-gallon bucket, combine thinset powder with latex additive (see page 129) to make enough thinset to last for 20 minutes or so. Hand-mix it with a margin trowel, or use a small mixer on an electric drill, until all the lumps are gone and the mortar is about the thickness of mayonnaise.

When it is properly mixed, the thinset should be almost thick enough to stick to a trowel held sideways, but not quite. Let the mixture set for 10 minutes, then stir again; it will be a bit thicker. The ideal mortar is just stiff enough to hold the shape of trowel lines on the wall, but wet enough so that you are sure tiles will stick.

Using a $\frac{1}{4}$-inch-by-$\frac{1}{4}$-inch square-notched trowel, spread thinset over about 10 square feet of the wall. Do not cover up the layout line.

installing the tiles

Check that the batten is level and the layout lines are plumb. Tiles set in organic mastic can be adjusted up to 30 minutes after setting them, but tiles set in thinset mortar should not be moved after 5 minutes. Check alignment every few minutes.

applying spacers To install irregularly shaped tiles, check every other horizontal row of tiles for level, and closely follow the plumb layout line in the center of the wall. Use scraps of cardboard as spacers, folding them double if needed.

If you are installing regularly shaped tiles that are not self-spacing, place a plastic spacer at every corner, as shown at right. Self-spacing tiles (see page 75) simply butt against each other. With either type of tile, once you have installed 10 tiles or so, there is no way to change the alignment.

Don't worry if the tiles go slightly awry from the layout line; it's more important that the tile corners align with each other.

On the back wall, you have a margin for error; the cut tiles can be as much as $\frac{1}{4}$ inch short. Any such gaps will be covered by the thickness of the side wall tiles.

tile the side walls On the side wall that has no plumbing, install the first two rows of full-sized field tiles, then measure and cut pieces to fit at the corner. Cut them precisely: there should be no more than a $\frac{1}{16}$-inch gap at the corner, but you should not have to force a tile into position.

If a tile is slightly too wide, use a tile stone to shave off a little, or discard the piece and cut a new tile. Keep the tile-cutting guide in position so you can easily cut tiles for the next rows.

You may need to adjust the cutting guide slightly as you move up the wall; few walls are absolutely plumb. Finish with the border and trim tiles as you did on the back wall.

On the side wall that has the plumbing, install as many full-sized tiles as is possible. Temporarily prop any unsupported tiles in place so they will stay in horizontal alignment. Then measure for the tiles that must be cut to go around the pipes (see Step 4).

tiling around pipes In most cases, you will need to cut a notch in a tile to go around a pipe, as shown. If a pipe falls in the middle of a tile, measure to the center of the pipe, and bore a hole using a drill equipped with a carbide-tipped hole saw (see page 61).

If you lack a carbide-tipped hole saw and need to cut a hole, drill a series of closely spaced $\frac{1}{4}$-inch holes around the entire perimeter of the hole, and gently tap out the center with a hammer.

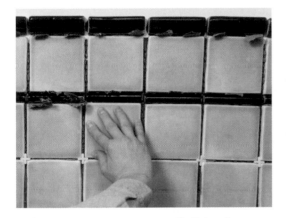

1 Cut tiles with a snap cutter or a wet saw (pages 126–127). Before you start to install tiles on the back wall, cut a few tiles to fit at the edges. Leave the saw's cutting guide in position so you can cut more.

2 Once the thinset or mastic is applied, work along the batten, pressing tiles firmly into the mortar. Add cut tiles on either side as you go. To be sure the tiles will stick, use a straight trowel to butter each piece with a thin coat of mortar.

3 Finish the back wall. Install all the tiles above the batten for the back wall, including the cut pieces at the corners, the border (if any), and the bullnose tiles at the top. Then move on to the side walls.

4 Install the full-sized tiles closest to a pipe, then hold a tile in place and mark it for a cut. Use a square to mark both sides of the notch.

5 Most wall tiles can be cut using a rod saw (see page 61). A wet saw (shown), grinder, or nibbling tool (see page 126) also works. Make the cut about ¼ inch larger than it needs to be.

6 Test that no part of the tile ends up closer than ⅛ inch to the pipe. If the mortar has begun to harden while you were cutting the tile, scrape the mortar away and back-butter the tile.

tiling down to the tub

The bottom row of tiles should be ⅛ inch above the tub, to prevent cracking as the area expands and contracts due to changes in temperature. To install the bottom row, first remove the batten, and scrape away any dried thinset. Cut tiles to fit, allowing for the ⅛-inch gap above the tub edge. If possible, spread thinset on the wall; otherwise, back-butter the tiles and press them into place (below).

Cutting the tile located near the outer edge of the tub also requires special care. The bullnose tile at each outer corner of the tub could be cut straight like the others, but you'll achieve a neater appearance if you curve-cut it to follow the curve of the tub (below). Cutting this piece is tricky; prepare a cardboard template with a utility knife. Trace the outline onto a bullnose tile, and cut it carefully with a rod saw (see page 61).

LOWE'S QUICK TIP

On the side walls, you may choose to extend the tiles past the tub by the width of a tile or two and run the outermost tiles along the tub and down to the floor. In that case, remove the baseboard trim, install the tiles, and cut and install the baseboard to meet the tiles.

finishing

Wait overnight, then remove any spacers. Wherever the mortar is less than ¼ inch below the surface of the tile, scrape it out with a grout saw, a small screwdriver, or a utility knife to keep the mortar from showing through the grout. Clean all mortar off the surface of the tiles using a damp cloth or a scrubbing tool.

grouting Purchase sanded grout for tiles spaced apart by ⅛ inch or more, unsanded grout for narrower grout lines. If the grout powder does not contain latex, mix it with liquid latex rather than water.

Follow the manufacturer's instructions for mixing the grout. You may need to mix an entire box or bag at once in order to ensure uniformity of color. Add liquid in small amounts at a time and mix by hand in a bucket, using a margin trowel (see page 63) or a putty knife, until the grout is just liquid enough to pour. Wait 10 minutes, and stir again. If it is too stiff, add a little more liquid.

Scoop the grout out of the bucket with a laminated grout float, and push the grout into the lines between the tiles with the float held nearly flat. Move the float in at least two different directions at every point, to ensure that the grout is fully pushed in. Once you have grouted an area about 10 feet square, tilt the float up at a steep angle so you can use it as a squeegee. Scrape away most of the excess grout, keeping the float angled so it cannot dig into the grout lines.

After you have grouted a wall, lightly clean the surface with a large, damp sponge. Turn the sponge over when it gets caked with grout, and rinse it often in clean water. Once all the walls have been grouted, rub the surface lightly with the sponge.

Examine the grout lines closely: you want them to be uniform in depth and width. You may need to tightly wad up a sponge or use the handle of a toothbrush or a tool to smooth (known in the trade as "striking") each individual joint. If you find any gaps, push in a little grout with your finger and rub with the sponge again.

Sponge the surface one last time, then allow the grout to dry for a day. After the grout is dry, buff the tile surface with a clean, dry cloth until it shines.

caulking Before caulking, remove the protective covering from the tub and clean the tile and the tub where the caulk will go. Dry thoroughly. Purchase a "tub and tile" caulk that matches your grout.

The caulk line where the tile meets the tub is critical, both for appearance and for protection of the substrate. You can squirt a line of caulk and tool it with your finger (see page 78), but for a more professional result, use the tape method (right). Begin by applying a piece of masking tape along

both sides of the joint. Caulk the joint, and smooth the caulk with your finger. The caulk will go onto both pieces of tape. Then pull away the pieces of tape to reveal a neatly caulked line.

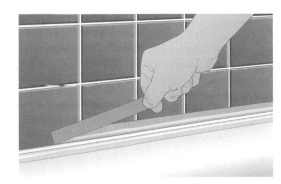

TILING A WINDOW RECESS

Windows located above bathtubs are liable to rot. The solution: remove all window trim, cover the exposed areas with backerboard, and tile over it. If the window itself is rotting, install a vinyl replacement window or glass block. Lay out the wall tiles so as to avoid narrow slivers around the window—both the horizontal rows under and perhaps above the window, and the vertical rows on either side.

First, install all the wall tiles except the cut tiles around the window recess. Cut and install the partial wall tiles and the recess tiles at the same time so you can make adjustments if necessary.

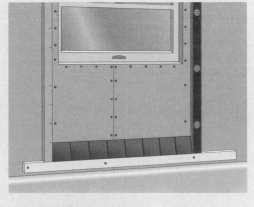

The cut edges of the wall tiles should come right up to the sides of the recess. When you do a dry run, the bullnose tiles should rest just against the cut edges of the wall tiles. The thickness of the mortar will produce a 1/8-inch grout spacing.

When tiling the recess, install bullnose tiles on the sides first. Their front edges should just cover the unfinished edges of the wall tiles. Next, install the recess tiles at the top. You may want to use organic mastic for these tiles, because thinset does not have as much hanging power before it sets.

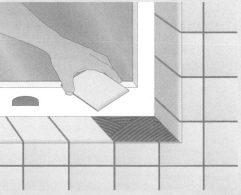

When applying mortar for the sill tiles, mound it up toward the back so the tiles will be tilted slightly downward, allowing water to run off easily. Grout the tiles and carefully caulk the inside corner where the tiles meet the window.

countertop & sink
design options

TILED COUNTERTOPS HAVE BECOME INCREASINGLY POPULAR AS HOMEOWNERS discover that they are easy to keep clean, and require only a small amount of additional maintenance. With the use of epoxy grout, even grout sealer is unnecessary.

countertop options

Tiling a countertop allows you to choose among a dazzling array of colors and styles. Make a scale drawing of your installation, and go over it in detail with a tile specialist at Lowe's to make sure you get all the parts you need. For the front edge of the counter, you will need trim pieces such as V-caps, rounded edges, or simple bullnose pieces. Make sure you have special pieces for any outside and perhaps the inside corners of the front edge, as well as for the backsplash (page 95). You may also choose among special trim pieces for a

more richly textured look. If you'd like additional options to choose from, ask your Lowe's salesperson for a catalog from which you can special-order.

sink options

If you're going to the trouble of putting in a new countertop, it probably makes sense to invest in a new sink as well. The plywood and backerboard making up a countertop substrate must be cut slightly differently for different types of sinks. Choose your sink and read the installation instructions before you install the substrate. And make sure that the opening in the base cabinet is large enough for the sink. For a kitchen installation, you will need a special sink base that has no drawers. You will probably need to install the sink near the center of the sink base so that it will not bump into either side of the cabinet.

Stainless-steel sinks come in a variety of price ranges; the more expensive models have a shinier surface that is easier to clean than that of cheaper models. If you buy one, make sure that yours has sound-deadening insulation. Enameled steel and acrylic sinks are inexpensive, but not durable; spend a little more for

Because it is tough, waterproof, and wonderfully decorative, tile is an ideal material for backsplashes and countertops (this page). It can even be used to cover an entire wall (facing page) for a surface that is both colorful and practical.

an enameled cast-iron sink, which will stay attractive for decades.

A "self-rimming" sink is the easiest to install. Cut the opening and test to see that the hole is the correct size, then tile the countertop and place the sink in the hole (see Step 2 on page 91). Self-rimming sinks are easy to install, but crumbs tend to collect along and under the rim; this is particularly true of stainless-steel self-rimming sinks.

For an alternative that is easier to clean, install a "flush-mounted" sink. Cut the hole

in the plywood, install the sink, then lay backerboard up to the rim of the sink. Bullnose tiles can then be installed on top of the backerboard and overlapping the rim of the sink.

Or choose an "underhung" sink. This is a difficult installation because of the number of cut tiles, but the result is attractive and easy to clean. Screw the sink to the underside of the plywood. Install narrow tile pieces along the vertical surface above the sink, and top off the edge where it meets the countertop with bullnose tiles.

LOWE'S QUICK TIP

Plan the backsplash at the same time you plan the countertop. You may choose to tile just 4 inches, or you may wish to do the entire wall between the counter and the wall cabinets.

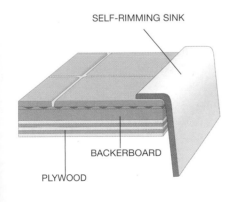

SELF-RIMMING SINK

BACKERBOARD

PLYWOOD

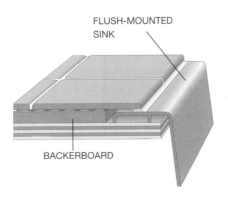

FLUSH-MOUNTED SINK

BACKERBOARD

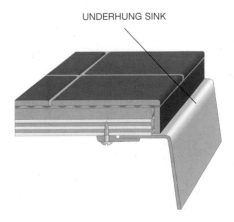

UNDERHUNG SINK

preparing a countertop

If you are installing new base cabinets, use shims on the floor and against the wall to make the cabinets level in both directions. Attach the cabinets with screws driven into the wall studs. In the case of an existing countertop and cabinets, you may be able to tile over the old countertop (see box on facing page). If the existing countertop is tiled, it may be possible to pry off the tiles and scrape away the adhesive.

Shut off the water to the faucet and disconnect the supply lines. (If you do not have stop valves under the sink to do this you'll have to turn off the main supply valve for the entire house.) Disconnect the drain as well, and remove the garbage disposer if there is one.

If the sink is cast-iron, slice through the caulking all around the underside of its lip, and pull the sink up. If the sink is stainless-steel, it is probably clamped to the countertop with a series of clips underneath. Crawl underneath with a flashlight and screwdriver. Loosen the screws, and slide or turn the clips so they no longer hold. Then pull the sink out.

Professionally installed countertops often have few fasteners—perhaps a screw driven up through the frame of the base cabinet every 4 feet or so. Use a flashlight to locate all the screws, and remove them. If construction adhesive or caulk has been applied to the underside of the countertop, slice through it with a utility knife. Pry the top gently with a flat prybar. If the top doesn't lift up easily, check again for fasteners; don't force it, or you may damage a base cabinet.

In preparation for installing the substrate, purchase sheets of plywood that are free of warping; store them stacked flat until you use them.

Before you begin work, protect the base cabinets from damage by covering them with plastic sheeting or construction paper. Also spread a dropcloth on the floor.

building a new substrate

Countertop tiles should rest on a surface—a substrate—that is solid and that can withstand moisture. The front edge must be thick enough to accommodate the edging you have chosen, and the substrate needs to be level in both directions.

In most cases, a layer of ¾-inch plywood topped with ½-inch or ¼-inch concrete backerboard will do the job. A standard kitchen countertop is 25 inches deep; a backsplash is commonly 4 to 6 inches high. You can modify these dimensions in order to minimize cutting of tiles.

1 Cut the plywood pieces so that they overhang the cabinets by about an inch. To ensure that the front and side edges are straight and square, install with the factory edges (rather than the edges you have cut) facing out. Attach the plywood by driving 1⅝-inch deck screws (which resist rusting) through the plywood into the cabinet base every 6 inches or so. Check the surface to make sure it is level; if necessary, remove screws and install shims. Cut a hole for the sink following the manufacturer's instructions. Lower the sink into the hole to make sure it fits.

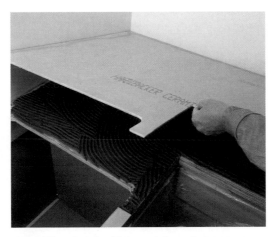

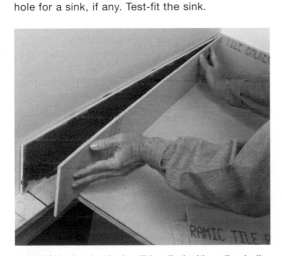

2 See page 110 for instructions on how to cut backerboard. Size and arrange the pieces so that any seams in the backerboard are offset at least 3 inches from any plywood seams. Lay out the pieces in a dry run. Make sure all the edges line up precisely with the plywood, including the hole for a sink, if any. Test-fit the sink.

3 Mix a batch of latex-reinforced or epoxy thinset mortar. Spread thinset over the plywood using a ¼-inch square-notched trowel. Lift up and install one piece of backerboard at a time. Lay the backerboard in the thinset, and drive 1¼-inch backerboard screws in a grid, spaced about 6 inches apart.

4 If the backsplash will be tiled with radius bullnose or quarter-round trim at the top, cut pieces of backerboard to accommodate the thickness and width of the backsplash. Butter the back of the strips with thinset, and press them into place.

5 Apply fiberglass mesh tape to the backerboard joints. Also wrap the front edges of the backerboard and plywood with the tape. Do not apply tape where the backsplash meets the countertop. Firmly press the tape in place.

TILING A LAMINATE COUNTERTOP

A "post-form" laminated countertop has a curved backsplash and a front lip. If it is in sound condition, it is possible to tile over it, if you use V-cap to cover the front edge and radius bullnose for the backsplash. Rough up the laminated surface with a hand sander or belt sander, then set the tiles in latex-fortified thinset mortar or epoxy thinset.

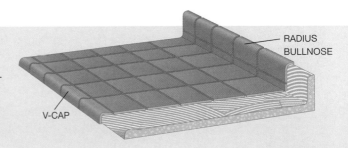

RADIUS BULLNOSE

V-CAP

laying out for the tiles

Expect to spend a good deal of time figuring the layout for your countertop tiles; a countertop may turn a corner and may have an obstacle such as a sink or cooktop, making the layout complicated.

Countertop tiles tend to be harder than wall tiles, which means that you may need to cut them with a wet saw. Even if you can cut the field tiles using a snap cutter, you may need to use a wet saw to cut any V-caps or other thick trim pieces.

using battens To ensure that the first row of tiles is laid in a straight line, consider using a batten. For V-cap trim, rip-cut a strip of plywood and attach it temporarily with the factory edge (which is perfectly straight) along the layout line (below, top). For bullnose tiles, use a strip of wood that is the same thickness as the edging tile, plus ⅛ inch for the thickness of the mortar. Attach it to the face of the countertop, and install bullnose tiles that rest on the batten and come flush to its front edge (left, center). For a wood edge trim, the field tiles should end exactly at the edge of the substrate. Attach a 1-by-2 board to the face of the substrate, and butt the tiles against it (left, bottom).

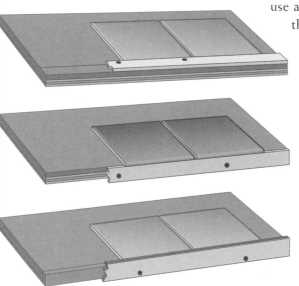

layout lines If you will be installing V-caps or other trim tiles along the front edge, you can make a simple layout line by holding a pencil against the trim piece as you drag it along the edge of the substrate. Install field tiles up to this line. Because of the thickness of the mortar used to set

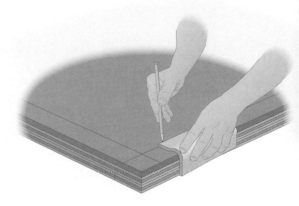

them, V-caps will actually be installed ⅛ inch or so in front of this line; this allows for a grout line between the field tiles and the V-caps.

laying tiles in a dry run

Before you prepare the mortar, position the tiles on the substrate with plastic spacers for the grout lines. Make adjustments as needed. Aim for a symmetrical look, with no narrow slivers of cut tiles.

For a countertop that turns a corner, start the layout at the inside corner. If you plan to install a flush-mounted or underhung sink (page 89), you may want to start the layout at the sink, so you can have tiles of the same size on both sides of the sink. If that layout approach ends up with a very narrow sliver, slightly

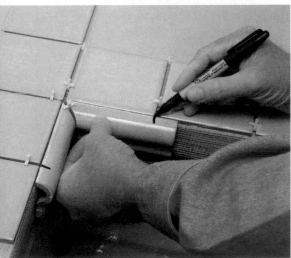

widening the grout lines may solve the problem. Alternatively, shift all the tiles over a bit. Once you have planned the layout, mark and cut tiles as needed (see pages 126–127).

cuts for the **corners**

Tiling a countertop may well call for some complicated cuts. It may take you a few attempts before you get these right, so have extra tiles on hand. If a tile must be cut at an angle as well as to length, make the angled cut first, hold the tile in place, and then mark for the length cut. Be sure to use spacers while marking (left).

To cut a pair of trim pieces for an inside corner, visualize how the cut should look; roughly draw it on the tile. Position the tile on the tray of the cutter so the tile is oriented the same way as it will be installed. Cut both pieces longer than they need to be so you can try again if necessary without wasting the tile. Test the pieces for fit as shown at left, using spacers, and cut to length.

Make sure you understand how all the pieces will go together. Remember to take into account the thickness of the mortar: field tiles will be about ⅛ inch higher than they were in the dry run; edging and backsplash tiles will come forward about ⅛ inch.

Install a flush-mounted or underhung sink before setting the tile (see page 89).

LOWE'S QUICK TIP

When measuring for cutting the tiles, take into account the width of the grout lines on either side.

INSTALLING TILES "ON POINT"

The decorative look of tiles set "on point," so they have diagonal grout lines, requires painstaking work but is not difficult as long as you have a reliable wet saw. Choose tiles with thick glazing so that you can round off the cut edges with a tile stone.

Practice cutting with a wet saw until you are sure you can make precise 45-degree cuts; you may need to slightly adjust the saw's sliding tray. Cut a number of tiles in half diagonally, at 45 degrees, and place them in a dry run along the layout line. Use as many full-sized tiles as possible, and make adjustments as needed to avoid small triangles.

setting the tiles

Leave the dry run in place. To be sure that you can follow the layout, remove only a few square feet of the dry run tiles at a time. Set all of them in mortar, and then do the same for the next few square feet of tiles in your dry run. In most cases, you should install the field tiles first, then the edging and the backsplash.

1 Mix as much latex-fortified or epoxy thinset mortar (see page 129) as you can use in a half hour or so. If it starts to harden, throw it out and mix a new batch. Spread it onto the backerboard using a ¼-inch square-notched trowel. To ensure a flat surface, hold the trowel at the same angle the entire time. Scrape away any globs of mortar.

2 Starting at the layout lines or at the batten, press both the full-sized and cut tiles into the mortar. Position plastic spacers to keep all the grout lines the same width. Use a straightedge to make sure the lines are straight, and tap the tiles into the mortar using a beater block (see page 130).

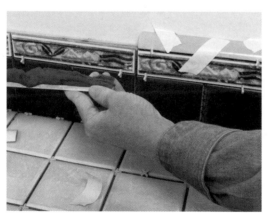

3 Back-butter the backsplash tiles, or comb mortar onto the backerboard strip with the trowel. Use spacers to hold the bottom back-splash pieces the width of a grout line above the field tiles. If there is a small quarter-round piece at the top (as shown), fill in the space above the backerboard strip with plenty of mortar, so the quarter-round can nest in it. If necessary, use strips of masking tape to hold the pieces together.

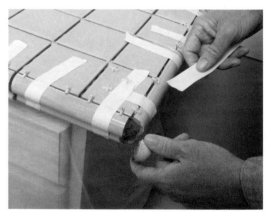

4 Either back-butter the edging tiles with mortar or apply mortar to the edge. Some types of edging, such as V-cap, can be simply set in the mortar because they rest on the horizontal surface of the substrate. However, if the edging attaches primarily to the vertical substrate edge, keep the grout line consistent by using spacers and add masking tape to hold the tiles until the mortar sets. Every few minutes, check to make sure that the edging pieces haven't begun to slide down; you may need to reapply the tape.

finishing the job

After the mortar has hardened overnight, remove any tape and plastic spacers. Use a laminated grout float to push grout into the gaps between the tiles and then squeegee away the excess. Wipe the surface and smooth the joints with a sponge, and buff the surface with a dry cloth (see page 133). Take special care to achieve consistent-looking grout lines, since they will be subject to scrutiny whenever people are working in the kitchen.

Use a grout saw or a utility knife to cut away the grout along the bottom of the backsplash, and apply a bead of caulk to this joint (see pages 87 and 116 for two caulking methods).

Install a self-rimming sink according to the manufacturer's instructions.

To put in a cast-iron sink, place a bead of silicone caulk all around the hole, and set the sink in it. Wipe away any excess caulk that oozes out.

To install a stainless-steel sink, apply a rope of plumber's putty to the underside of the sink, and press the sink into place. Clamp the sink to the underside of the countertop using the clips provided by the manufacturer.

LOWE'S QUICK TIP

Save time as well as hassles by hooking most of the plumbing—the faucet, drain, and garbage disposer—onto the sink before setting the sink in the hole.

TILING A BACKSPLASH WALL

The word "backsplash" can refer to a strip of tile or wood about 4 inches wide attached to the wall at the rear of the countertop. Or, it may refer to tiling on the wall behind the countertop—usually, the vertical space between the countertop and the wall cabinets, or between the range and the range hood. This space is often about 18 inches high.

Backsplash tiles are installed much like any wall tiles (see pages 74–79). The substrate does not have to be waterproof or especially strong; you can simply tile over any wall surface that is in sound condition. Any type of ceramic or stone tile can be used, as long as it is easily washable. Organic mastic is strong enough.

If backsplash tiles butt into a wall cabinet, simply run the field tiles to about ⅛ inch below the cabinet. Wherever the top edge of the tiles will be exposed, use bullnose trim pieces. Where backsplash tiles meet the countertop below or a cabinet above, fill the joint with caulk rather than grout to prevent cracking.

You'll probably need to cut tiles to fit around several electrical outlets or switches; see pages 69 and 78.

preparing for flooring

DON'T BE SURPRISED IF YOU SPEND MORE TIME PREPARING for your project than you do actually applying the flooring. Correct preparation of the floor substrate is critical. For instance, if vinyl tiles or sheet flooring are installed over a surface that has even minor imperfections, the finished floor will have unsightly pits or bumps. Ceramic tile installed over a floor that is not rock-solid will likely develop cracks in a year or so. If you choose to install directly on top of existing flooring, you must be sure that the adhesive will stick firmly to the surface. This chapter will show you how to install and prepare the right substrate for the flooring you have chosen.

Fortunately, new products and tools make substrate prepa ration easier. Ceramic tiles once had to be installed in a thick mortar bed—a difficult job that was best left to the pros. Now, cement backerboard makes it possible for do-it-yourselfers to create a firm bed. Underlayment for resilient flooring is easy to install if you use sheets that have a grid of X marks and equip yourself with a pneumatic underlayment stapler.

As you plan the job, consider the height of the new floor in relation to any abutting floor surfaces. Most people find it uncomfortable if the floor steps up more than $1/2$ inch (which usually takes place at a doorway). To minimize a step up, you may need to tear out, rather than install on top of, the existing flooring and underlayment.

Lowe's installation services can arrange for professional installation of every type of flooring discussed in this chapter. Once you request professional services, a Lowe's-approved contractor comes to your home, takes measurements, and presents an all-inclusive bid for the work and materials. There is a modest charge for this bid; the charge will be deducted from the installation cost should you decide to hire the contractor. The bid is binding: the contractor will not add extra costs unless you agree. Lowe's guarantees that the work will be done to your satisfaction and in a timely manner.

inspecting a floor

THE TYPE OF SUBSTRATE YOU NEED DEPENDS ON THE TYPE OF FLOORING YOU will install. Carpeting, wood parquet, wood strip, and laminate flooring have the easiest requirements: the substrate can be somewhat springy, and it does not need to be perfectly smooth. For vinyl tiles, sheet flooring, and cork, the floor can be a little springy but must be very smooth. For ceramic and stone tiles, the floor does not have to be very smooth, but it does need to be extremely firm.

know your floor

Even very strong ceramic or stone tiles can crack if they are installed on a floor that is not solid. Many wood floors are already strong enough to support tile, and most can be made so by installing a layer of cement backerboard (see pages 110–111). However, you may want to skip installing backerboard if it will raise the finished surface more than ¾ inch above an adjacent floor. A minority of floors have structural problems that backerboard cannot solve; in that case, either install resilient flooring or repair the floor before proceeding.

A floor that is strong enough for ceramic or stone tile will feel firm when a large adult jumps on it. If you feel any give, examine the structure. Find out how thick your subfloor is and how far apart the joists are. (If you need to remove existing flooring, do so before making any tests; see pages 106–108.)

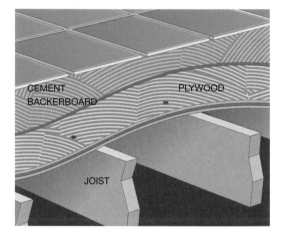

CEMENT BACKERBOARD · PLYWOOD · JOIST

To measure the thickness of the subfloor, look for a hole in the floor—perhaps one drilled for a pipe—or drill a 1-inch hole in an inconspicuous spot and stick a tape measure in the hole.

It's easy to find out how far apart your joists are spaced if the area below is an unfinished basement. If it's not, use a high-end stud finder that can detect joists even under wood flooring. Alternatively, drive a series of locator nails until you have found at least two joists. (Be sure to pull the nails up afterward.)

The following specifications satisfy normal residential requirements.

If joists are spaced 16 inches apart, you should have a layer of plywood at least ¾ inch thick topped with backerboard (above), or a total of 1⅛ inches of substrate.

If joists are spaced 24 inches apart, use a layer of plywood at least 1 inch thick (that is, two ½-inch sheets) topped with backerboard, or 1½ inches of substrate.

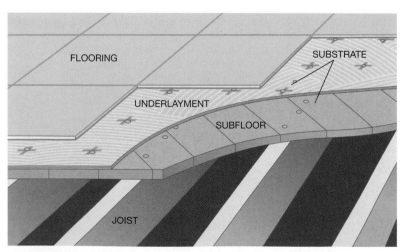

FLOORING · SUBSTRATE · UNDERLAYMENT · SUBFLOOR · JOIST

If you have an older home with angled 1-by plank subflooring (facing page, bottom), its strength depends on the type and condition of the planks. In very old homes, these may be rock-solid maple. If plank subflooring is firmly attached to joists, it is usually as strong as ¾-inch plywood.

If you want to install ceramic or stone tile over a floor that does not meet these requirements, or that feels springy when you jump on it, see pages 100–101 for tips on strengthening it.

silencing **squeaks**

Most floor squeaks can be solved simply by driving additional nails or screws. If you plan to remove the existing flooring, do so before fixing the squeak (see pages 106–108). Stand over the source of the squeak and examine the floor closely as you shift your weight and step around; you will likely see an area that moves up and down. Use a stud finder or drill a series of test holes to find the closest joist, and drive a series of 2½-inch screws (use only wood or deck screws) or 8d nails into the joist. If driving fasteners causes the floor to dip noticeably, the joist below has probably sagged; if so, drive shims as shown on page

101. If a squeak emanates from a place between joists, try fastening the top piece of plywood to the underlying piece (or planks) by driving a grid of 1⅝-inch screws.

patching a floor

If an area of the subfloor is rotted or weak, adjust the depth of a circular saw blade so that it cuts just through the subflooring without damaging underlying joists. Cut out a portion of the damaged area, determine where the joists are, and then widen the cut beyond the bad area so that it spans from joist to joist and forms a rectangle.

Cut two 2-by-6 nailers a little longer than the opening, and screw each to an outside joist. The top of each nailer should be the same height as the top of the joist it is attached to. Cut and install 2-by-6 blocking pieces to span between the joists, and attach them with angle-driven screws.

Install a plywood patch that has exactly the same thickness as the surrounding subfloor. (For instance, if the floor's thickness is ⅞ inch, use one piece of ⅝-inch plywood and one piece of ¼-inch plywood.) Anchor the plywood patch with screws driven into joists or nailers every 6 inches or so.

2 × 6 BLOCKING   2 × 6 NAILERS

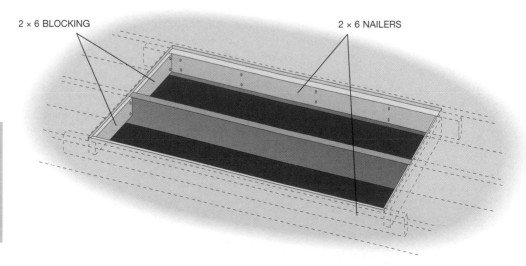

firming a floor

OFTEN, A FLOOR FLEXES NOT BECAUSE IT'S TOO THIN, BUT BECAUSE THE SUBFLOOR is inadequately attached. The solution may be to drive screws through the subfloor and into the joists. Use a stud finder to find the joists, and drive the screws using a drill equipped with a screwdriver bit. If you miss a joist, or if a screw does not grab securely, back the screw out. Adding cement backerboard in the course of remodeling will firm up the floor quite a bit.

adding a **sister joist**

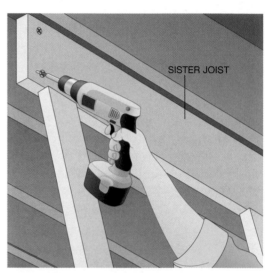

SISTER JOIST

If a joist has sagged, driving additional screws may have the unfortunate result of pulling the floor boards down, and will do nothing to strengthen a weak joist. When the problem involves multiple joists, call in a carpenter for advice. To shore up one or two joists, install a "sister" onto each (right). Cut the sister out of 2-by lumber, making it as long as possible. Press it up against the bottom of the floor and hold it temporarily in place by wedging a 2-by-4 support under it. Drive pairs of 3-inch wood screws every 8 inches or so to secure the sister to the joist.

installing **blocking**

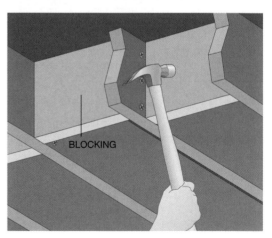

BLOCKING

To strengthen an entire floor, install blocking. From 2-by stock that is the same width as the joists, cut pieces to fit tightly between the joists. Tap the blocking into place between the joists so that pieces are offset from each other

LOWE'S QUICK TIP

To fix a serious problem such as a cracked joist, make "sisters" out of structural materials made for the job. Order either strips of reinforcing metal or "glue-lam" pieces, essentially extra-long and extra-thick strips of plywood.

ARE THE JOISTS STRONG ENOUGH?

If a floor seems generally weak even though the subflooring is thick enough, the joists may be undersized. Local building codes vary, but in general, if joists are spaced 16 inches apart, they should follow these guidelines. If your joists are too small for their spans, install sister joists onto each of them, or consult with a carpenter.

JOIST SIZE	MAXIMUM SPAN
2-by-6	8'6"
2-by-8	11'
2-by-10	14'
2-by-12	17'

by 1½ inches as shown (facing page, bottom) to simplify nailing. Drive 3-inch screws or 16d nails to anchor the blocking to the joists.

adding metal **bridging**

Steel bridging (right) will not add as much strength as blocking, but it will reinforce to some extent, cut down on squeaks, and is easier to install. Purchase bridging pieces that are made to fit the spaces between your joists—usually, 14½ inches. Wedge each piece tightly into position and drive a nail or screw through each hole. Where the spacing is smaller, install a piece of blocking instead.

installing **shims**

If a joist sags or if you see a space between the subfloor and the joist, purchase a packet of wooden shims. Drive them into the gap by tapping with medium pressure—hitting them too hard will cause the floor to rise. Drive shims every 2 inches or so. After you have driven a group of shims, go back and tap them all to make sure they are snug. From above, drive a series of fasteners into the joist.

firming from on top

Adding another layer of subflooring that is ½ inch or thicker will substantially strengthen a floor. Ideally, you should use plywood for lower layers and use either cement backerboard (if you are installing ceramic or stone tile) or ¼-inch underlayment (for vinyl tiles or sheet flooring)

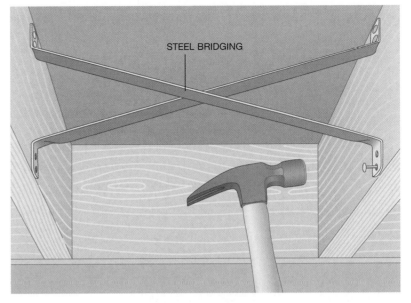

STEEL BRIDGING

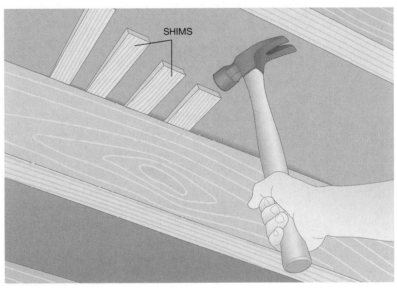

SHIMS

for the top layer. The structure will gain strength if you drive plenty of fasteners—long screws every 6 inches into joists, and shorter screws (just long enough to penetrate all the way through the subfloor) in a grid every 8 inches between the joists. Setting backerboard in a bed of mortar, or setting plywood in flooring adhesive, will also add firmness.

LOWE'S QUICK TIP

If the floor above a basement is sagging, have a carpenter install a beam with adjustable posts under the joists. The posts can be raised gradually over a period of months to bring the floor level.

removing fixtures
and other obstacles

IT'S VERY DIFFICULT TO INSTALL FLOOR TILES AROUND OBSTACLES, ESPECIALLY fixtures such as toilets and sinks. If at all possible, clear the floor entirely. In most cases, cutting tiles to fit around an obstruction is more time-consuming than removing the obstruction, tiling, and replacing the obstruction. And the resulting job will look neater.

   If hot and cold water supply lines (known as "riser tubes") protrude from the floor, consider calling in a plumber to move them to a wall. Even an old, heavy radiator can probably be removed. To remove a steam radiator—that is, one with only one pipe leading into it—shut off the heat, loosen the nut, and pick up the radiator. If you've got a hot-water radiator (one with two pipes leading into it), be sure to drain the heating system before removing the radiator; consult with a heating specialist to learn how.

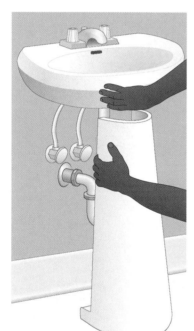

removing **sinks**

You may not have to remove the entire sink—only the portion that rests on the floor. Many pedestal and wall-hung sinks rely on a wall bracket for support. However, if you have a vanity, the sink and cabinet must be removed.

pedestal and wall-mounted

sinks Check to see whether the pedestal is anchored to the floor with bolts; if so, remove the bolts. Gently lift up the sink and slide the pedestal out. If the pedestal does not come out easily, you may need to remove the sink. If a wall-mounted sink has legs reaching to the floor, you can probably remove them with little difficulty. You may need to twist the bottom portion of the legs to shorten them before removing them.

vanities To take out a vanity cabinet, you must first remove the sink. Close the shutoff valves, and check that the hot and cold water are off. Disconnect the riser tubes from the shutoff valves. With a large wrench, loosen the nut that connects the tailpiece (the straight drain piece con-

nected to the sink) to the drain trap below. If the sink is attached to the cabinet with adhesive, slice through the adhesive using a knife. Lift the sink out. Remove any screws or nails holding the cabinet in place, and remove it as well.

LOWE'S QUICK TIP

Once the pedestal or legs have been removed from a sink, take care not to lean on or bump the sink as you work. If it will be difficult for you to resist grabbing onto the sink as you tile, remove it first.

removing a toilet

Turn off the water supply at the toilet's shutoff valve. (If there is no shutoff valve, consult with a plumber; you may need to turn off water to the whole house.) Flush the toilet, and use a large sponge to remove as much water as possible from the bowl and the tank. With a large pair of pliers or a crescent wrench, unscrew and disconnect the riser tube, either at the toilet tank or at the valve.

Unless the toilet is particularly heavy, there is no need to disconnect the tank from the bowl. Most toilets are held in place by only two nuts, screwed onto bolts that anchor the bowl to the floor. (Some older models may have bolts holding the tank to the wall.) Pry the decorative covers off the nuts, and use pliers or a crescent wrench to unscrew each nut. If the nuts are too rusty to unscrew, cut through the bolts with a hacksaw.

Grasp the toilet bowl, and gently rock it back and forth until it comes loose from the wax ring underneath. Pick the toilet straight up, and carry it out. Some water may spill onto the floor. Scrape the wax ring off the floor. Stuff a rag into the pipe to seal off sewer gas. When reinstalling the toilet, you'll need a new wax ring.

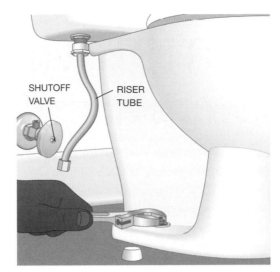

SHUTOFF VALVE   RISER TUBE

LOWE'S QUICK TIP

On a very old toilet, the tank (the upper portion) may be attached to the wall with screws. You must lift the tank lid to get at the screws.

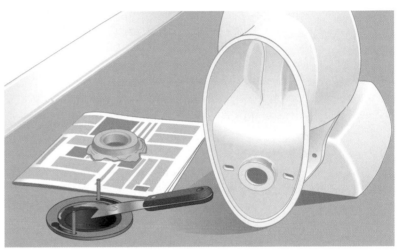

FLANGE EXTENDER

If new tiling raises the floor more than ½ inch above the toilet flange, a wax ring may not be thick enough to reseal the toilet to the flange. You can install two wax rings or use a toilet flange extender.

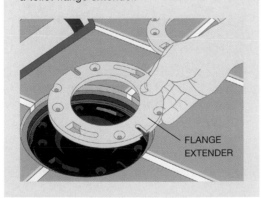

FLANGE EXTENDER

remove kitchen cabinets?

During a kitchen remodel, always install the flooring before you install the base cabinets. However, if the cabinets are already installed, removing them can be difficult—you first must remove the countertop and the sink with its appliances. You may be better off leaving the cabinets in place and tiling up to them; install base shoe or other moulding to cover the joint between the flooring and the cabinet.

If you will be adding a good deal of height to the floor—either by installing backerboard plus tiles or by installing strip flooring—be aware that the countertop will feel like it has been lowered by nearly an inch. This will be noticeable to a person working at the counter; another good reason to consider removing the cabinets before installing the flooring.

removing mouldings

MANY A HOMEOWNER HAS TRIED TO SAVE TIME BY LEAVING MOULDINGS IN PLACE and cutting tiles to fit. Don't make this mistake. Systematically remove or cut all mouldings. Plan your layout so that all tile edges will be covered once the mouldings are back in place. The only exception is wood baseboard with no separate "shoe" piece. If you have this type of moulding, you may choose to leave the baseboard alone, and install new shoe sections after tiling. If any of the existing moulding looks worn, remove it and replace it after tiling.

vinyl cove base Pry cove base off the wall using a stiff putty knife. To avoid damaging the wall above the moulding, insert the knife at the top of the base and push down. If the moulding is stuck tight, use a heat gun to soften the adhesive as you pry (right). Scrape any protruding globs of adhesive off the wall. Install new cove base after tiling (see page 135).

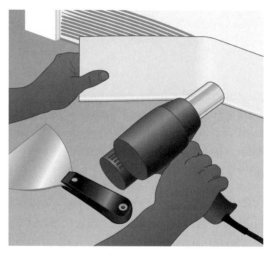

LOWE'S QUICK TIP

Old mouldings that look fine now may seem shabby when positioned against new tiles or other flooring. If your mouldings are dented or otherwise marred, achieve a total finished appearance by replacing them—or at least painting them.

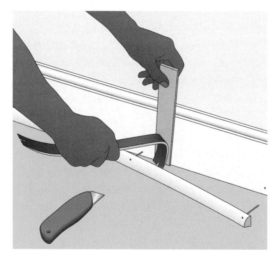

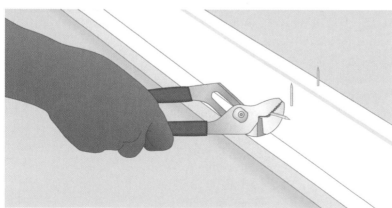

wood base shoe and baseboard If a room has wood baseboard with a smaller bottom shoe piece, you only need to remove the shoe. Using a utility knife, slice through the paint along the top of the shoe. Pry the shoe off using a flat pry bar and a scrap of wood to protect the baseboard (left). If the shoe is in good shape, write numbers on the back of the pieces so you can easily replace them later.

If there is only a baseboard, no shoe, you can leave the baseboard in place and tile to within a half-inch of the moulding, then cover the gap by adding base shoe.

If you plan to reuse mouldings, pull the nails through the back side (left), to prevent marring the surface. Firmly grab a nail with a large pair of slip-joint pliers and roll it backwards to pull the nail through.

cutting door mouldings If you will be installing backerboard or plywood underlayment, wait on this step until the material has been installed. Set a tile on the floor, and use it as a guide to cut the door casing with a hand saw. This will allow you to slide a tile under the moulding, which will save making complicated cuts in the flooring. If you will be tiling the floor on both sides of the door, also cut the bottom of the doorjamb and the stop, using the same technique.

CHOOSING AN UNDERLAYMENT

If a floor is solid and/or smooth, it may be possible to tile directly over it. If the existing surface is not up to the task, or if the area will get wet, install materials designed specifically for your type of flooring.

Some pros install tile the old-fashioned way, by pouring a thick slab of mortar and setting the tiles directly in it—a time-consuming operation that requires skill. Today, homeowners can achieve the same moisture tolerance and strength by attaching sheets of cement backerboard before setting the tiles.

Cement backerboard comes in two varieties, both made primarily of Portland cement, which retains its strength even when soaked with water. Mesh-reinforced cement backerboard is basically a slab of cement held together by embedded fiberglass mesh that wraps around both sides. Fibrous cement backerboard has fibers running throughout its body, and is smoother and a bit easier to cut. Both types are available in thicknesses ranging from ¼ inch to ⅝ inch, and in sheets of various sizes.

Attach either type of cement backerboard using special backerboard screws, which are strong and can be easily driven flush with the surface of the board. Standard drywall screws are much more difficult to drive flush, and are prone to break. Seal joints in the backerboard with fiberglass mesh tape and thinset mortar. Cement backerboard stays strong when it gets wet, but it does not repel water. If a floor is often subject to standing water, the water could seep through the grout, then through the backerboard and into the plywood below. To protect the wood below the backerboard, install a waterproofing membrane (see page 117).

Plywood is the best underlayment for nonceramic flooring such as vinyl tile, cork, wood parquet, and laminate tiles. It is inexpensive, is easy to cut and install, and can form a very smooth surface—an important consideration when applying thin resilient tiles that show every imperfection in the subfloor. Plywood designed for underlayment has a series of cross-shaped marks to guide you when you drive screws or nails in a grid pattern.

Ceramic or stone floor tile can also be installed on plywood, as long as the floor structure is firm and the tiles will not get very wet. However, plywood is more flexible than cement backerboard and it swells when moistened; for ceramic or stone tile, cement backerboard is the better choice.

removing flooring

IF THE FLOOR HAS EXISTING CERAMIC OR VINYL FLOORING, YOU CAN CHOOSE among three options: rough up the flooring and install new tiles directly on top; remove the old flooring before tiling; or, in the case of vinyl flooring, install backerboard directly on top, and then install tiles. Whichever option you choose, make sure the floor is strong enough (see pages 98–101).

ceramic tile You can install new ceramic or stone tile directly on top of firmly attached ceramic or stone tile. If the old tile is glazed, rough up the surface using a belt sander, a tiling stone, or a grinder to ensure that the thinset will adhere (see box below).

When the existing surface has deep-set grout lines, you can probably set large tiles on top with no problem, but small ones may be uneven. Experiment first by laying the new tiles down without adhesive; if they form an uneven surface, fill the grout lines with thinset. Allow the thinset to dry before starting the tiling job.

Removing ceramic tile can be very difficult, especially if the tiles are set in an old mortar bed. Start by chipping with a cold chisel and hammer (below left). Once the bulk of the tiles have been removed, use a floor scraper (facing page, right) to clean up the remaining mortar.

vinyl tile Try removing vinyl tiles with a floor scraper, a straight paint scraper, or a drywall taping blade. If the going is rough, soften one or two tiles at a time using a heat gun (below). Scrape up the adhesive as you remove the tiles.

LOWE'S QUICK TIP

If you need to remove the underlayment as well as the flooring, remove both at the same time (see page 108).

ADDING TILE ON TOP OF OLD FLOORING

If a single layer of vinyl tile or noncushioned resilient flooring is firmly attached, you can install ceramic or stone tile directly on top. For vinyl with a shiny surface, rough up the vinyl with a sanding block first. Where there is more than one layer of resilient flooring, or where the flooring is cushioned, remove the flooring.

sheet flooring Using a utility knife, make long cuts, about 8 inches apart, through the flooring. Use a scraper to pry the edges, and pull up a series of strips. Where the paper backing does not come up, use a pump sprayer to wet it with a weak solution of soap and water. Allow the liquid to soak in for a few minutes, then use a floor scraper or paint scraper to get up the rest. It may take several applications of liquid before the backing becomes soft enough to remove.

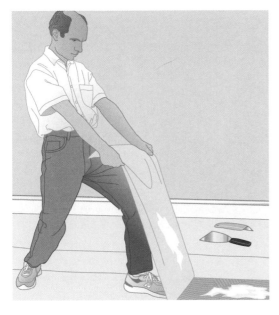 

carpeting Most carpets are held in place by barbed strips nailed along the base of the walls. To remove, grab a corner with a pair of lineman's pliers and pull. Use a utility knife to cut the carpet into manageable strips and roll up each for discarding.

Remove the padding and pry up any staples from the floor using a small screwdriver, utility knife, or lineman's pliers. Use a flat prybar to remove the tackless strips. Carefully gather them together (they've got lots of sharp tack points) and discard.

 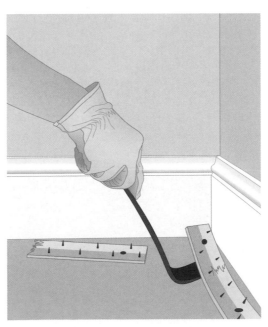

removing **underlayment**

Removing underlayment and flooring in one step can be quicker and easier than removing flooring alone, especially if they are firmly adhered. Be sure to wear gloves and protective clothing, because there will be plenty of sharp nails to deal with.

Determine how large you want the pieces to be, so you can fit them into your garbage container. Snap a grid of chalk lines on the floor. Equip a circular saw with a carbide blade that can cut through nails without dulling. Set the blade to cut through just the flooring and the under-layment, and no further. Cut along the chalk lines (right). Where the circular saw cannot reach, finish the cuts using a hammer and chisel, or a reciprocating saw.

Pry up the cut pieces with a pry bar (below left), then complete the job using a crowbar or wrecking bar. Carry the pieces out and discard. Use pliers to remove any pieces of nails that remain in the subfloor.

If the underlayment was installed using screws rather than nails, removal will be

a more painstaking task. First try prying up pieces; this may work if the screws are not too long. If the screws are too strong to pull up, remove the flooring (see pages 106–107). You may need to scrape each screw head with a putty knife or screw-driver to expose the screw head. Remove the screws using a drill equipped with a screwdriver bit (below right). If a bit becomes stripped, replace it.

LOWE'S QUICK TIP

To remove underlay-ment along with ceramic or stone tile, remove rows of tiles to expose strips of underlayment. Scrape away the mortar, which can quickly dull a circu-lar saw blade. Cut through the under-layment and pick it up as you would a vinyl floor; the tiles will likely dislodge as you do this.

creating a level surface

IF A SUBFLOOR HAS AREAS THAT ARE OUT OF LEVEL, IF IT HAS DIPS THAT NEED to be filled, or if you need to smooth a slightly bumpy surface, there is likely a leveling compound that can repair the problem. Consult with a flooring expert at Lowe's to find the product that best suits your needs. Choose a leveling compound that will stick to the material you will apply it over, and that can be installed at the thickness you need.

embossing leveler

Some resilient flooring, such as vinyl tiles and sheet flooring, will telegraph even the slightest of imperfections in the material they are adhered to. If you are installing these products over embossed vinyl tile or sheet flooring, or over ceramic tile, first apply embossing leveler. Paint the area with latex bonding agent to assure that the embossing leveler will bond adequately to the substrate. Mix the leveler with water or a latex additive, as directed by the manufacturer. Try to make a solution that is pourable but still fairly thick. Pour it onto the floor, and spread it by scraping lightly with a flat trowel. Use long, sweeping strokes. Work quickly because the leveler will set up in 15 minutes or less. Allow the leveler to dry, then scrape it lightly with

the trowel to assure bonding with the tile adhesive. Don't press too hard when you scrape, or you may dig up chunks of dried leveler. You may need to use a sanding block in spots.

leveling compound

Thinset can be laid thickly to correct a dip up to ³/₈ inch in depth (page 130), but for large areas use leveling compound. Bear in mind that it will not add to a floor's strength. If you install it on a floor that is springy, it may crack. Some leveling compounds are considered patching compounds. Others describe themselves as "self-leveling," meaning that they will achieve a smooth surface with little or no troweling.

1 If the area to be filled is bordered by other flooring, as shown, attach a board temporarily to act as a dam. (If you're filling an isolated dip, you won't need a dam.) To assure that the leveling compound will adhere to the underlayment, many leveling compounds require a bonding agent. The type shown is of two parts, mixed together and rolled onto the underlayment.

2 Mix the leveling compound with water or latex additive, as directed by the manufacturer, until you achieve a pourable solution that is free of lumps. Pour the leveler onto the floor and spread it with a straight-edged trowel. Don't overwork the surface. Just spread the compound so it is generally at the right thickness, then allow it to settle to a uniform smoothness.

3 Use a drywall taping blade or a flat trowel to feather the edges. If you will be installing thin vinyl tiles or sheets, sand the compound edges with a drywall hand sander before applying the adhesive.

laying cement backerboard

WHEN IT IS SANDWICHED BETWEEN MORTAR BOTH BELOW AND ABOVE, CEMENT backerboard forms a firm and rigid surface for floor tiles. (See pages 98–101 to make sure the floor will be strong enough for ceramic or stone tile.) Purchase either mesh-reinforced or fibrous cement backerboard, and special backerboard screws. With a chalk line, mark the floor to indicate the location of joists. Plan to install the sheets so none of the backerboard joints will be directly above joints in the subfloor. Also, stagger the joints in the backerboard so that there is no place where four corners meet. There should be a 1/8-inch gap between backerboard sheets, and a 1/4-inch gap between the sheets and the wall or baseboard.

1 Sweep the floor free of all debris, and lay down the sheet of backerboard to be cut. Measure for the cut, and subtract 1/4 inch, since the cut end will be rough. Mark both the top and the bottom of the cut, and hold a straightedge between the two marks. Or, make only one mark, and hold a drywall square, as shown. Using a cement-board knife, score a line. It may take two or three passes to cut through mesh-reinforced backerboard.

2 Turn the sheet upside down, or hold it on edge. Hold the board firmly on one side of the scored line and pull or push on the other side until it snaps. Score along the resulting crease on the back of the sheet until you have cut entirely through. Pick the sheet up on its side, and snap it back again to free the cut piece. If the cut edge is very rough, smooth it a bit with a tile stone.

3 Sweep the floor free of all debris. Mix thinset mortar (see page 129). Spread it on the floor using a ¼-inch square-notched trowel. Lay the sheet in the mortar carefully, so that you don't have to slide it more than an inch or so. Drive screws through the sheet into the joists every 6 inches, or as recommended by the manufacturer. Wherever the edge of a sheet is more than 2 inches away from a joist, drive screws along the edge every 4 inches.

4 Press fiberglass mesh tape over all joints. Using the flat edge of a trowel, spread a thin layer of thinset mortar over the tape. Feather it out on either side, and smooth away any high spots. After the thinset is dry, you're ready to begin tiling.

CUTTING HOLES

If you have a number of small holes to cut, purchase a carbide-tipped hole saw of the right size. To cut an occasional large hole, measure to the center of the hole, then use a compass to draw its perimeter. Use a masonry bit to drill a series of closely spaced holes along the perimeter. Tap the interior of the hole with a hammer. If the waste does not pop out easily, use a knife to cut through the fiberglass mesh (right).

You can also use a reciprocating saw, a hacksaw, or a jigsaw that is equipped with a masonry cutting blade to cut a notch or a cutout in a piece of backerboard.

installing plywood underlayment

PLYWOOD UNDERLAYMENT THAT IS 4 FEET SQUARE AND HAS A GRID OF X MARKS makes an ideal underlayment material for all floorings other than ceramic or stone tile. It is ¼ inch thick; if you need a thicker underlayment, use 4-by-8 sheets of AC or BC plywood. Make sure the plywood surface is free of knots and other imperfections.

fastening options

You can install the plywood using underlayment nails or screws, but an underlayment stapler drives the fasteners quicker, and the staples are easier to cover with patching compound. Rent a pneumatic stapler or a hand-powered stapler that you must pound firmly with a mallet.

keeping it smooth

As you work, keep in mind that any uneven seams, protruding fasteners, or other imperfections will eventually show up in your final flooring if you don't adequately deal with them now. This will likely be the most demanding and time-consuming step in your flooring project.

1 The underlayment is thin, and will follow the contours of the subfloor. If the floor is spongy or wavy, see pages 98–101 for ways to solve those problems. Go over the subfloor with a straight trowel, to make sure no fastener heads are sticking up. Drive screws where needed to secure the seams of the subfloor materials.

2 Starting at a corner of the room, lay several full-sized sheets on the floor. Use scrap pieces of plywood to keep the sheets about ¼ inch away from the walls, to allow for expansion. See that the joints are offset from the subflooring joints below by at least 3 inches at all points. Measure to see how you will need to cut subsequent pieces; you may choose to reorient the sheets to minimize cutting.

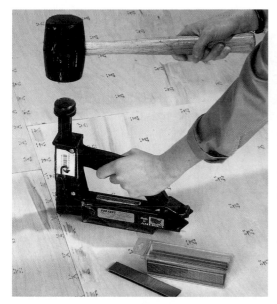

3 Starting at one end of a sheet and moving across it, drive underlayment staples (shown), underlayment nails, or deck screws into each of the X marks on the sheet. Make sure that all of the fastener heads are slightly below the surface of the plywood. To test, scrape the surface with a flat trowel or drywall blade. Where sheets butt together, see that they are at exactly the same height. If they are not, drive extra fasteners to force down the raised sheet.

4 After several full-sized sheets are installed, measure and mark the remaining sheets for cutting. Position any cut edges against the walls; a cut edge should never be in the middle of the room. Use a drywall square to mark the cut lines. Where a sheet needs to be cut at an angle, mark either end of the cutting line and snap a chalk line. Place two 2-by-4 boards across a pair of sawhorses or on a work table, and rest the sheet on top of the 2 by 4s. Adjust the blade of a circular saw to cut about ¼ inch deeper than the thickness of the sheet of plywood.

5 Mix up a small quantity of acrylic- or latex-reinforced flooring patch to the consistency of toothpaste. Use a flat trowel (shown) or a drywall taping blade to cover all the seams and the fastener heads.

6 Once the patch has dried, sand the entire floor smooth using a drywall-type hand sander. Keep sanding until the floor feels smooth when you run either your hand or a flat trowel over it.

preparing a concrete slab

EVEN STABLE CONCRETE FLOORS CAN DEVELOP CRACKS THAT CAN TELEGRAPH themselves up through a tiled floor. To ensure that a ceramic or stone tile floor will be free of cracks, first determine that the slab is stable. Then make any needed minor repairs, as shown on these pages, and apply an isolation membrane, as shown on pages 116–117.

is it strong enough?

If a concrete floor is still in good condition even after years of use, it is probably strong enough to support tiles. A slab should be at least 3 inches thick, with reinforcing metal to minimize cracking, and it should rest on a bed of well-tamped gravel.

Small cracks are usually only a cosmetic problem. For example, if the surface of the concrete has a weblike network of tiny cracks (called crazing), or if there are a number of small pits (called popouts), you don't have to worry that the strength of the floor is compromised. You can confidently install tiles on top.

However, if there is a crack wider than 1/4 inch, or if one side of the crack is higher than the other, the damage goes deep; call in a concrete professional for evaluation.

patching a crack

A trowel-applied membrane (see page 117) will stabilize cracks less than 1/4 inch wide. For a wider crack, chisel out loose particles from inside the crack and fill it with patching concrete as shown below. Purchase patching cement that is vinyl or latex reinforced. Just add water to the dry mix, and the product hardens in 15 minutes or so.

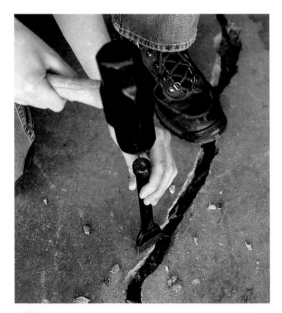

1 Use a hammer and cold chisel to "key" the crack—cut it away at an angle, so that the crack is wider at the bottom than at the top. Clean all loose material out of the crack using a wire brush.

2 Paint the crack with latex concrete-bonding agent. Mix a small batch of the patching compound and use a trowel to stuff the patch into the concrete. Scrape the surface, so that the patch is at the same height as the slab. Apply an isolation membrane over the crack before tiling.

patching a **damaged area**

If a part of your concrete floor is cracked or flaking, you may be able to patch it. Apply a patching compound and allow it to set, then apply an isolation membrane before laying tiles on top.

1 Draw a geometric shape around the damaged area. Using a grinder or a circular saw equipped with a masonry blade, cut the lines about ½ inch deep. Chisel out the area inside the cut lines. Using a wire brush, clean away all loose matter. Dampen the area and clean with a scrub brush. Allow to dry, then brush again. Paint the damaged area with latex bonding agent.

2 Mix a batch of vinyl concrete patch so that it is just liquid enough to pour. Trowel the patch into the cut-out area, filling it to match the surrounding area.

3 Use a flat trowel or a concrete float to smooth the surface level with the surrounding concrete. If the area is wider than 2 feet, use a straight board to level the patch.

leveling high and low spots

Drag a long, straight board across the floor, and look for high or low spots. With a pencil or crayon, mark all the high spots, as well as any depressions deeper than ½ inch. Fill depressions using leveling compound, as described on page 109.

Some high spots can be chipped away using a hammer and chisel. In larger areas, use a grinder equipped with a masonry blade (right). Don't worry if you grind a little too low; the dips can be filled in when you trowel on the thinset.

expansion joints and membranes

BUILDING MATERIALS SUCH AS WOOD SUBSTRATES, CONCRETE SLABS, GROUT, and even tiles expand and contract slightly with changes of temperature. In most cases, this movement is not a problem, especially if you use latex-reinforced or polymer-modified thinsets and grouts that have a bit of flexibility. However, if you are tiling directly over a concrete slab, or if you have different substrate materials that abut under the tiles, or if you are installing a section of tiles that is longer than 30 feet, take steps to ensure that the movement will not cause the tiles or the grout to crack.

expansion joints

Ceramic and stone tiles expand and contract so slightly that there is rarely an impact on residential floors in small rooms. However, if tiling adjoining rooms will result in more than 30 linear feet of tile, fill the grout line at the doorway with caulk instead of grout to create an expansion joint (right). Use silicone caulk that matches the color of the grout; allow it to dry completely before grouting. The caulked line will be flexible, so that tiles can move without cracking.

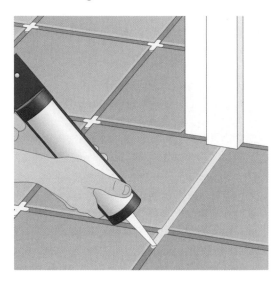

If you are installing tile on a very large floor, you'll need to buy contractor-style expansion joints instead, and install them at regular intervals.

A wall moves differently than the floor below it. If floor tile abuts wall tile (or a base made of tiles), caulk the joint rather than grouting it (below).

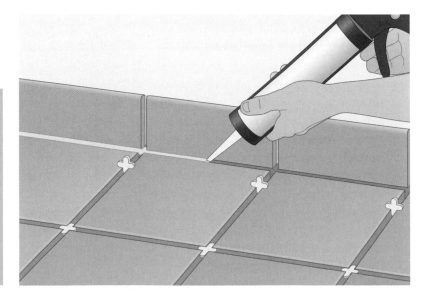

membranes

In most cases, ceramic or stone tile can be installed directly on top of a backerboard or plywood underlayment. However, if the floor or a portion of the floor may tend to flex or shift, consider installing an isolation membrane. And if you think the floor will get wet for prolonged periods, it's a good idea to install a waterproofing membrane. Consult with a tile expert at Lowe's to choose the membrane product that will work best for your situation.

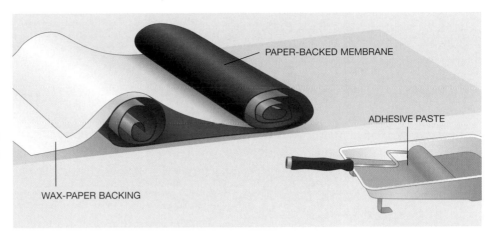

PAPER-BACKED MEMBRANE

ADHESIVE PASTE

WAX-PAPER BACKING

paper-backed membrane
Sweep and mop the floor to clear away even the smallest bits of debris. Roll the membrane out and use a utility knife and a straightedge to cut pieces to fit. Follow the manufacturer's directions regarding how much the side-by-side pieces should overlap. Once all the pieces have been cut, note the order and direction in which each piece will be laid, and set them to one side.

Follow the manufacturer's directions regarding how to spread the adhesive paste. Most recommend using a notched trowel or a thick-napped paint roller. Proceed systematically to avoid working yourself into a corner. Spread adhesive for one membrane sheet, install it, and then go on to the next sheet.

To install a membrane sheet, roll it onto the adhesive. Do not press on the sheet until it is positioned correctly. Work slowly and carefully to smooth out all wrinkles. To thoroughly embed the membrane in the adhesive, run your hand or a paint roller over the surface. Occasionally lift up a corner of the membrane to check that the adhesive is sticking uniformly. Once it has set, you can apply thinset and begin setting tiles.

sheet membrane
Begin by sweeping or vacuuming the floor clean. Roll the membrane onto the floor, cut the pieces to fit, and roll them back up again. Spread thinset mortar (probably the same material you will use to install the tiles) on the floor, using a notched trowel.

Roll the membrane onto the thinset, taking care to avoid any wrinkles. Repeatedly run a hand-held floor roller (see page 163) over the membrane to embed it firmly in the thinset. Once the thinset sets, you can apply thinset on top of the membrane and install the tiles.

see page 163

LOWE'S QUICK TIP

If a concrete floor abuts a wood one, the two surfaces will move separately. Within a concrete surface, an isolation joint (a gap filled with caulk or fibrous material) creates two separate slabs, which may also move separately. In either case, apply a 2-foot-wide isolation membrane over the joint.

RADIANT HEAT

Radiant heat gently and evenly warms a room. No matter which type of flooring you are installing—with the exception of thick pile carpeting—you can install radiant heat under it.

Electric radiant heat is the easiest to install. Since in most areas electricity is expensive, it's usually best to use it in small rooms. Mats that contain low-voltage cables can be stapled under the subfloor onto an exposed basement ceiling. If you are installing ceramic or stone tile, you can lay the mats on the substrate and apply the thinset over them. Carefully follow manufacturer's instructions; it is easy to damage the mat and its circuitry during installation.

Hot-water radiant heat consists of a long plastic tube that snakes around a room. If placed on top of the substrate, the tubing is typically set in plywood sheets that have been specially cut with grooves to accommodate the tubing. The tubing is connected to a boiler or to an existing hot-water system. Carpeting and strip flooring can be installed directly on top. Vinyl or sheet flooring requires an additional layer of underlayment. Cement backerboard should be laid before installing ceramic or stone tile over the tubing.

ceramic and stone floor tile

FLOORS COVERED WITH TILES MADE OF FIRE-HARDENED clay or natural stone are remarkably durable. In Rome, the Middle East, and elsewhere, floors that are thousands of years old remain intact and still look beautiful. These floors have endured not only because of the choice of materials, but because they were installed carefully. This chapter will show you how to install a tile floor that will look attractive and remain rock-solid for generations.

Most ceramic tile has a classic appearance and therefore is likely to outlast changing styles. Still, there are a wide variety of colors and shapes to choose from (see pages 14–29 for examples).

A tile installation must begin with a very firm substrate. Follow the instructions in the previous chapter to ensure that your substrate is firm and will not flex, or eventually grout or tiles will crack. At the same time, make sure that the finished floor will not be more than ½ inch higher than any abutting floor surfaces.

Plan the job carefully. Before you start setting tiles, you need to know where each tile will be placed. This chapter explains how to determine the best arrangement. It will also help you choose thresholds and baseboard and the optimal locations for them.

Though it may seem daunting, installing ceramic or stone tile requires no special skills. If you have some experience measuring and cutting lumber, you will have no trouble cutting tiles with the right tools. As you lay the tiles or grout the joints, pause from time to time to check that the installation is straight and even. If you catch a mistake within 15 minutes or so, you can correct it easily; if you wait longer, fixing it will be much more difficult.

Lowe's installation services can arrange for professional installation of every type of flooring shown in this chapter. Once you request professional services, a Lowe's-approved contractor comes to your home, takes measurements, and presents an all-inclusive bid for the work and materials. There is a modest charge for this bid; the charge will be deducted from the installation cost should you decide to hire the contractor. The bid is binding: the contractor will not add extra costs unless you agree. Lowe's guarantees that the work will be done to your satisfaction and in a timely manner.

laying out for a tile installation

ONCE YOU'RE ASSURED THE FLOOR IS STRONG ENOUGH AND SMOOTH ENOUGH for tiling, it's time to plan the layout. There are three basic considerations to think through.

■ Avoid ending up with narrow tile slivers along one or more walls. However, if you are sure that one edge of the floor will always be hidden (by furniture, for example), then you may opt to install slivers there in order to have full pieces along the opposite wall.

■ Try to center the tiles so that the cut tiles on opposite sides of the room are the same size—but only if you can do so without ending up with slivers. This is particularly important if the room is small.

■ If a room is out of square, adjust the layout to hide this imperfection as much as possible. When it is inevitable that one edge of the floor will have tiles that slowly increase in width, choose the least visible edge. Plan so that the tiles along this edge are as wide as possible; narrower tiles make the imperfection more obvious.

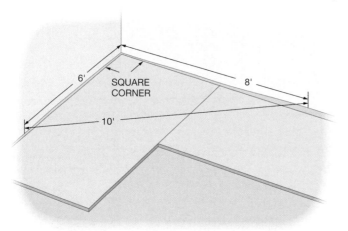

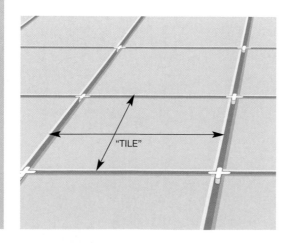

is the room **square?**

Lay full sheets of plywood or backerboard (which have exactly square corners) on the floor with the edges 1 inch away from both walls. Measure to see whether either wall goes out of square along its length. Also check for waves in the walls.

Alternatively, use the "3-4-5" method. Mark one wall precisely 3 feet from a corner, and the other wall 4 feet from the corner. If the distance between these two marks is exactly 5 feet, then the corner is square. If the room is large enough, use multiples of 3, 4, and 5, such as 6, 8, and 10 (as shown at left) or 9, 12, and 15.

dimensions of the tile

To plan a layout accurately, you need to take into account not just the size of the tile but also the width of the grout line. For layout purposes, the size of a "tile" means the tile plus one grout line in either direction.

making a dry run

It's easy to make a mistake when mathematically figuring a layout on paper. A dry run is more accurate. Lay complete rows of full-sized tiles, with spacers (see tip on facing page) in place, on the floor in at least two directions (below). This will tell you the exact size of the cut tiles along the edges. Chances are, you'll make an adjustment or two once you see the layout. You can use the dry run to mark the floor for working lines.

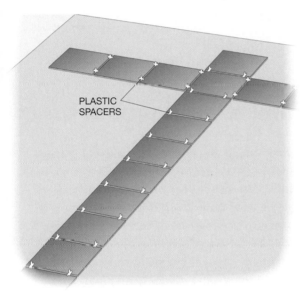

PLASTIC SPACERS

making a jury stick

If a room is large or the layout is complicated, a jury stick (also called a layout stick) can simplify the planning process. Find or cut a thin, straight board, such as a strip of plywood or a piece of moulding, about 8 feet long. Set the board on the floor next to some tiles laid with spacers in a dry run (right), positioning the board's end in the center of a grout line. Mark the board at the center of each grout line.

Use a jury stick as a kind of instant dry run. When laid on the floor, it quickly tells you how many tiles will fit in a given area, as well as how wide the cut pieces will be.

the working lines

Once you've settled on a layout, it's time to draw working lines as guides. First, decide where you want to start tiling. Plan so you will be able to avoid stepping on recently laid tiles. In some cases, it makes sense to start in the middle of the room; in other cases, it's best to start close to a wall. If a room has only one door, start at the far end of the room and work toward the door. Make sure you never have to reach across more than 2 feet of tiles to lay a cut tile. Using measurements, a dry run, or a jury stick, make pencil marks at either end of the first row of tiles.

Have a helper hold one end of a chalk line centered on one mark. Or tack a nail at the mark, and hook the chalk line to it. Center the chalk line over the other mark, pull the line taut, pick it straight up several inches, and let go. If the resulting line is not clear, rewind the line and snap it again. If it is still not clear, roll up the line to recoat it with chalk, and try again.

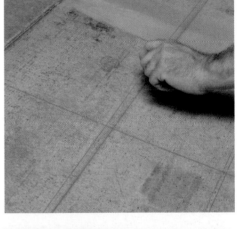

LOWE'S QUICK TIP

Marking measurements accurately is very important. Unfortunately, a simple pencil mark can be ambiguous — which end is correct? To clearly mark a working line, draw a V-shaped mark at each end, with the tip of the V representing the exact end of the line.

JURY STICK

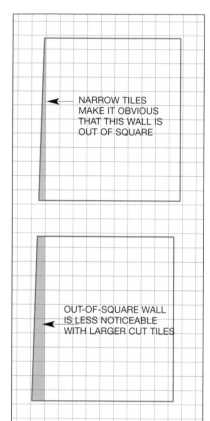

← NARROW TILES MAKE IT OBVIOUS THAT THIS WALL IS OUT OF SQUARE

← OUT-OF-SQUARE WALL IS LESS NOTICEABLE WITH LARGER CUT TILES

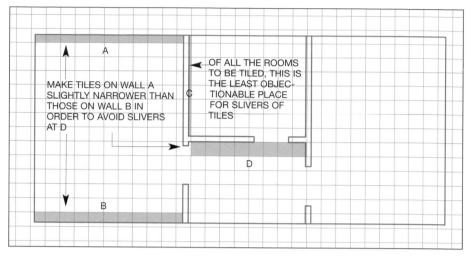

A

← MAKE TILES ON WALL A SLIGHTLY NARROWER THAN THOSE ON WALL B IN ORDER TO AVOID SLIVERS AT D

C

← OF ALL THE ROOMS TO BE TILED, THIS IS THE LEAST OBJEC-TIONABLE PLACE FOR SLIVERS OF TILES

D

B

make drawings
for complex installations

If a room has more than four corners or is more than 1 inch out of square, or if multiple adjacent rooms that share doorways are involved, make a drawing to help you visualize the job. Draw the area to be tiled on graph paper. Decide on a scale that is easy to use—one tile (including top and side grout lines) per graph square, or one tile per four squares. Draw the room accurately. Measure so that your drawing shows any out-of-square walls. Make several photocopies of this room drawing so you can experiment with different tile layouts.

If a layout is complicated—particularly if you are tiling adjacent rooms—you will probably need to make compromises. For instance, after you've made one drawing, you may decide to move all the tiles over an inch or two to avoid or hide slivers, or to minimize the visual impact of an out-of-square wall.

laying out for **diagonal** tiles

To mark for tiles that will be laid diagonally in a room, snap two perpendicular chalk lines that meet in the exact center of the room. Use a full sheet of plywood as a guide or the 3-4-5 method (see page 120) to make sure that the lines are exactly perpendicular. Then, measuring very precisely, along all four lines mark points that are equally distant from the center.

Now snap chalk lines (or draw lines with a straightedge as a guide) that connect the marks you have just made; this will result in a square that is tilted at a 45-degree angle to the room. Use the sides of this square as working lines for laying out the room.

Lay tiles in a dry run. You may need to shift the tiles over an inch or so in order to avoid small triangular tiles at the edges.

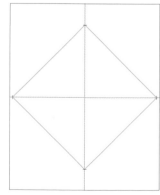

the **grid** system

If your tiles are slightly irregular in shape, it will not work to use plastic spacers. Instead, mark the floor with a grid of squares that hold nine tiles each (below). Lay three tiles next to each other, spaced as you would like them to be when the floor is finished. Measure the width of the three tiles, and add the width of one grout line; this is the length of each side of one layout square.

Measure the room and make a plan that will avoid thin slivers at any wall. Draw a series of V-shaped marks, spaced according to the size of the squares, along all four walls. Snap chalk lines in each direction. Check that the squares are the same size, and that the lines are perpendicular to each other.

When you lay the tiles, apply mortar in the inside of a square, taking care not to cover the lines. Set the tiles in the mortar (see pages 130–131). Align two sides of each square with the chalk lines; the other two sides should be one joint's width away from the lines. Stand back and examine the tiles. Make any needed adjustments before moving on to the next square.

starting with a **batten**

To ensure that your first line of tiles will be straight, tack down a long, straight board known as a batten. The factory edge of a ¾-inch sheet of plywood makes an ideal batten, because it is perfectly straight and thick enough that tiles cannot slide over it. Position the batten next to a working line, and drive several screws to hold it firmly to the floor. Butt the first row of tiles up to it. Once the mortar starts to harden, remove the batten. You may be able to use it again elsewhere.

LOWE'S QUICK TIP

Decide where you want to begin tiling. Work from one corner of the room toward the door so you do not tile yourself into a corner. You may choose to cut the perimeter tiles as you work. Or, install all the full-sized tiles, wait for the mortar to harden, and then cut and install perimeter tiles the next day. (This option will cut down on rental time for a wet saw, if you need one.)

marking tiles for cutting

MOST CUT TILES ARE COVERED BY MOULDING, A CABINET, OR AN APPLIANCE
and so do not need to be precise. Just make sure the tile edge will not show after the
moulding is installed, and leave a gap of at least ⅛ inch between the tile and the wall.
Depending on the threshold you choose (see pages 140–141 for options), the tiles that
will abut it may need to be cut very exactly.

straight cuts

While it's possible to use a tape measure to
measure for cutting tiles, most tilers find
that the tape quickly gets gummed up with
mortar. A quick and accurate method is
to first lay all the full-sized pieces you can,
then mark for straight cuts. Against the
wall, place a spacer (a piece of tile is
shown) that is ¼ inch or so thicker than
the grout line. Place the tile to be cut on
top of the adjacent whole tile, aligning the
two precisely. Set another tile on top of it,
and slide the top tile against the spacer.
Take care to keep it above any mortar as
you measure. Use the top tile to draw the
cut line (right).

TILE TO BE
CUT

marking for **inside** corners

At both walls, position spacers that are
about ¼ inch thicker than a grout line.
Place the tile to be cut directly on the tile
nearest the corner, and align it precisely.
Place another tile on top, slide it against
one of the spacers, and mark one side of
the cut. Then slide it over against the
other spacer and mark for the other side
of the cut (right). Erase or cross out the
portions of the lines that will not be cut.

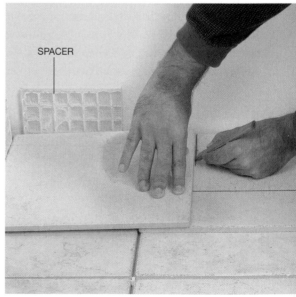

SPACER

outside corners

At an outside corner, often a tile needs to be cut in an L shape. If one side of the cut will abut a threshold or a doorjamb, that side will need to fit precisely.

1 Install or dry-lay all the full-sized tiles. Placed the tile to be cut directly on top of the tile nearest the corner, and align it precisely. Set spacers against both walls. Where the cut will be covered with moulding, the spacer should be about ¼ inch thicker than the grout line. Where the cut must meet a surface precisely, the spacer should be the exact thickness of a grout line.

2 Set a full-sized tile on top of the tile to be cut, and slide it against one of the spacers. Use its edge as a guide to mark the tile below. Where the top tile meets the front edge of the other spacer, make a small mark.

3 Slide the full-sized tile back and carefully transfer the mark onto the tile to be cut.

4 On the tile to be cut, use a square to draw a line from the small mark to the line. Erase or cross out the portions of the lines that will not be cut.

MAKING AN ACCURATE NOTCH

To mark for a pipe or other irregular-shaped notch, position a spacer that is about ¼ inch thicker than a grout line against the wall. Cut the tile to width, using the technique for a straight cut (see facing page). Slide a notch-measuring tool against the obstruction and the spacer. Place the tool on top of the tile to be cut, and slide it back ¼ inch so the notch will not touch the obstruction. Mark the tile for the notch.

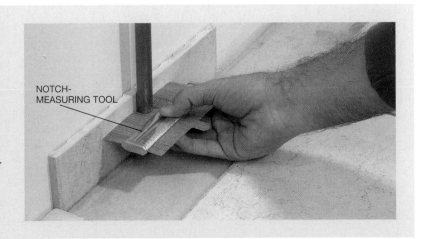

NOTCH-MEASURING TOOL

cutting ceramic and stone tiles

ALL THE CUTTING TECHNIQUES DESCRIBED ON THESE PAGES WORK FOR CERAMIC, quarry, and most porcelain tiles; stone, terra-cotta, cement-body, and some porcelain tiles should be cut with a wet saw only. Ask a tile specialist at Lowe's which tools are needed to cut the tiles that you are buying. For instructions on cutting wall tiles, which tend to be softer than floor tiles, see page 75. To mark tiles for cutting, see pages 124–125.

CUTTING
FENCE

snap cutter

Mark a cut line on the tile with a pencil or a felt-tipped marker. Position the tile firmly against the cutter's front guide so the cut will be square. Lift up the handle, and position the cutting wheel at the front or rear edge of the tile (depending on the type of cutter you are using). Press down with moderate pressure, and push or pull the wheel to score a line all the way across the tile. It's best to score a single, continuous line, but if you score an incomplete line, go over it again. Allow the cutter's wings to rest on either side of the scored line, and push down on the handle; the tile will snap in two. Brush away all debris from the base of the cutter before making the next cut.

nibbling tool

This tool, also called tile nippers, enables you to take small bites out of even very hard tiles. On many floor jobs, you can make the vast majority of cuts using a straight cutter, but you will need to make one or two cutouts or notches. Rather than renting a wet saw for a few cuts, a nibbling tool may be the answer.

To make a cut that runs in two directions (below), first score the lines using a snap cutter. Then start taking small bites out of the cutout area. The key is to nibble slowly, taking lots of tiny bites; if you take a big bite, you'll probably shatter most of the tile. Work your way slowly toward the corner of the cut. When you reach the scored lines, you can nibble more accurately.

It is usually not possible to cut off less than ½ inch from a tile using a snap cutter. To remove a slender slice from a tile, score the line with the snap cutter, then use a nibbling tool to break off the waste side of the cut, piece by piece.

It may seem unlikely that this simple tool can cut curves and notches in hard floor tiles, but all it takes is practice and patience. Nibbled cuts often will not be crisp and precise, but they are accurate enough for most purposes.

NIBBLING
TOOL

ANGLED CUTTING FENCE

wet saw

A tile-cutting wet saw makes the cleanest cuts in floor tiles. A rented saw typically has a pump that squirts water through a tube onto a rotating diamond blade. The pump must be submerged in water at all times; if the blade cuts even for a few seconds while it is dry, it will dull. You can also buy an inexpensive type of wet saw that partly submerges the blade in water, eliminating the need for a pump.

If the saw is properly equipped with a splash guard, you can use it indoors as long as you don't mind some scattered spray, but working outside is usually best. Set the saw on a worktable or a piece of plywood set atop two stable sawhorses. For a saw that has a pump, fill a 5-gallon bucket with water and position it on the ground nearby, set the pump in the water, and test to make sure there is a continuous stream directed at the blade while it is on. For other saws, just make sure the water supply is filled.

straight cuts To make a straight cut (above left), slide the tray all the way back toward you and position the tile, pressing it firmly against the guide. Turn on the saw, make sure the blade is getting wet, and slide the tile forward. Hold the tile firmly in place on the tray at all times. Push the tile slowly into the blade as you cut.

angle cuts For a 45-degree cut (above right), use a special angled cutting fence like the one shown. Protractor-type fences are available if you need to make cuts at angles other than 45 or 90 degrees.

notches To cut out a notch, first use a snap cutter to score the frontmost cut line. Hold the tile at a steep angle so that your saw blade will cut a little deeper on the back side of the tile. Make a series of cuts, about ¼ inch apart, all of which end at the cut line (below left). Finish the cut by using a nibbling tool to clean up the edge (below).

SNAP-CUT LINE

cutting **mosaics**

LOWE'S QUICK TIP

As long as the cuts do not need to be precise, you can cut mosaic tiles using a nibbling tool (see page 126).

To remove full tiles from a mosaic sheet, simply cut through the paper or plastic web backing using a utility knife. To cut individual tiles, first score them using a snap cutter. Or, using a square as a guide, score with the cutting wheel of a hand cutter (right). Center the hand cutter's wings over the scored lines and squeeze to complete the cut.

tiling around **pipes**

When cutting around plumbing or heating pipes, take care to keep the tile at least ¼ inch away from the pipe on every side. Otherwise, when the pipe heats up and expands, it could crack the tile. In most cases, you can use a pipe flange (also called an escutcheon) to cover the gap between the pipe and the tile.

To measure to the center of a pipe (middle left), place the tile to be cut directly on top of an adjacent tile, and slide it until it touches the pipe. Mark the spot where it touches.

A pipe that is attached to a faucet seldom can be easily disassembled in order to slip a tile over it. So if a hole falls in the middle of a tile, cut the tile along the center of the pipe, notch-cut each of the two resulting pieces, and lay them on either side of the pipe (middle right). The result will be slightly unfinished-looking, since you will have a visible cut line.

If you are able to slip the tile over the top of a pipe, bore a hole. If you have a number of holes to bore, or if the hole must be precise, use a carbide-tipped masonry hole saw (bottom left). Otherwise, draw a circle using a compass, and drill a series of holes along the circle using a ¼-inch masonry bit (bottom right); tap the center with a hammer to complete the cut.

mixing and applying mortar

ONCE THE MORTAR STARTS TO HARDEN—SOMETHING THAT CAN HAPPEN QUICKLY, depending on weather conditions—adjusting the position of a tile is all but impossible. Before you start laying tile, review pages 98–127 to make sure everything is ready. See that the floor is strong and the surface is smooth and level. Remove all obstacles and, to the extent required, the base moulding. Plan ahead for any thresholds (see pages 140–141). Set tiles in a dry run and draw the layout on the floor. If you plan to cut tiles as you go, get your cutting tools ready.

The instructions for this project apply to any ceramic tile, including porcelain pavers, quarry tile, cement-body tile, and terra-cotta tile. (Additional directions for installing stone tile and mosaics are provided on pages 142–143. If you are laying irregular tiles using the grid system, see page 123.)

LOWE'S QUICK TIP

Fill a 5-gallon bucket about two thirds full with water, and keep it nearby so that you can place the mixing paddle in it when you are not mixing. Every time you insert the paddle into the water, very quickly turn the drill on and off, to partially clean the paddle.

the order of work

If a room is small and uncomplicated, plan to set all the tiles in one day. For a larger job, you may choose to install only the full-sized tiles on the first day. Then you can install the cut tiles a day or two later, after the full-sized tiles have set solidly enough that you can walk on them. If you are renting a wet saw for the cuts, this ensures that you will not have to pay for an extra day of rental.

Plan the tiling sequence so that you will never need to step on a tile that you have just laid; doing so could move it out of alignment. If you expect to tile the room in one day, try to make sure that you will never have to lean over more than 2 feet of just-installed tiles in order to measure and place a cut tile. If doing so is unavoidable, have a large piece of plywood on hand that you can lay on top of the tiles.

mixing mortar

For most applications, use gray thinset mortar with a liquid or powdered latex additive. If the tile is at all translucent (as with glass tile or marble), use white thinset mortar. A small amount of mortar can be mixed by hand with a margin trowel or a 4-inch taping knife, but you'll save trouble and produce a more reliable mix with a mixing paddle and a rented ½-inch drill. Mix only as much thinset as you can use within 30 minutes or so (allot less time if the weather is dry and warm). The dry mix and the liquid should be at room temperature.

Pour a few inches of latex (or use water, if the dry mix has a latex or polymer additive in it) into the bucket, then add the powdered thinset. Set the paddle down into the bucket. Clasp the bucket firmly with your feet to keep it from spinning as you mix (right). Operate the drill in short bursts at first—liquid may spray out of the bucket if you hold the trigger too long. Keep mixing until all lumps are gone.

The thickness of the mortar is critical. It should be wet enough to slowly pour but also be thick enough to stick to a trowel when held upside down (right). Add liquid or powder as needed. Wait about 10 minutes, then mix the mortar briefly again.

laying floor tiles

FOR A PROFESSIONAL-LOOKING JOB, TILES SHOULD BE SET IN STRAIGHT LINES with grout lines of consistent width. In addition, the surface of the tiles should form a smooth plane. Check these alignment details every 10 minutes or so; adjusting tiles later than that can weaken the thinset bond. As you work, keep the job as clean as possible. Once mortar gets on your hands or pants, things get messy quickly.

LOWE'S QUICK TIP

If the floor is uneven, you can straighten it out by as much as ³⁄₈ inch using the thinset. To check that the mortar is level and even, gently set a level atop it; test in two directions. Wipe the level clean.

1 Pour some thinset mortar onto the floor, or scoop it out with a notched trowel. Use a trowel with notches sized for your type of tile (check the manufacturer's instructions). With the trowel held at a slight angle and with the notches facing up, spread the mortar over an area about 4 feet square, taking care not to cover any working lines.

2 Turn the trowel so the notches face down. For consistent mortar thickness, hold it at about a 45-degree angle and maintain the angle as you comb. Allow the teeth of the trowel to scrape the substrate gently, and use long, sweeping strokes wherever possible. Comb away any lumps of mortar. If the mortar starts to harden, don't try to salvage it by adding liquid; throw it out.

3 Set each tile as precisely in place as possible, so you don't have to slide it more than an inch or so. Align the first tile with two working lines, then set several additional tiles, inserting spacers at every corner. Don't press down on any tile.

4 Set a beater board—a straight piece of 2-by-6—over two or more tiles, and tap. This helps ensure that the underside of each tile is set firmly in the mortar. It also aligns the top surface of one tile with its neighbor. Periodically check to see that the tiles form a continuous, level plane.

5 Every 10 minutes or so, pick up a tile that you've just set, and look at the back. Mortar should adhere to at least 80 percent of the surface (as shown). If you find only partial adhesion, perhaps the mortar is too dry; scrape it off the floor and throw it out. Or perhaps the mortar was not combed to achieve a flat surface; re-comb it.

6 Remove any excess mortar as you go; it will be much harder after it dries. A carpenter's pencil works well for removing mortar between tiles. Or use spacers, as shown.

LOWE'S QUICK TIP

Some porous tiles, such as terra-cotta or quarry, may soak up so much moisture that the mortar does not adhere. If you find that the mortar is not grabbing, try soaking the tiles briefly in water, or wipe their undersides with a sponge, before installing them.

7 If tiles are irregular, or if a tile is to be set in a spot where the trowel won't fit, you will need to "back-butter" each tile. Apply enough mortar so the cut tile is as high as the adjacent one, but not so much that mortar oozes out of the grout line. You will also have to use back buttering if you choose to install cut tiles on a later day.

CHECKING AND ADJUSTING FOR STRAIGHT LINES

Make it a habit to stand up and examine the grout lines every 10 or 15 minutes. Stretch a string line next to a row of tiles, or butt a very straight board gently against the tiles; the factory edge of a piece of plywood works well.

Perform any minor adjustments as soon as possible. If you make a mistake, you can probably move five or six tiles, but no more. To adjust a tile slightly, place your hand on top, fingers splayed out. Press gently as you slide the tile. If you feel resistance followed by a sudden movement, the mortar has probably begun to set. Pick up the tile, scrape it and the floor clean of mortar, back-butter the tile, and place it again.

grouting

Once all the tiles have been set, allow the mortar to dry for at least 12 hours. In humid weather, or if any of the exposed mortar is not completely dry, wait another day. Don't walk on the tiles or apply grout unless the mortar is completely hardened.

Use a thin screwdriver to pry out all the spacers; take care not to nick the tile. Wherever mortar is less than ¼ inch below the surface of the tile, dig it out with the screwdriver or a grout saw.

Wipe away all mortar from the surface of the tile using a wet rag or a scrubber. Unless your grout lines are less than ⅛ inch wide, use a sanded grout. If the grout is fortified with a powdered latex or polymer, add water. If it does not contain powdered latex, add liquid latex, even if the directions say you can use water. Unfortified grout mixed with water is likely to crack.

LOWE'S QUICK TIP

If you are installing a type of tile that needs to be sealed, check with a Lowe's tiling expert to see whether it should be sealed before you apply the grout. If you apply grout over porous tiles that are unsealed, it may be difficult to wipe away all the grout, and you may need to clean the tiles with an acid solution (see page 210).

1 Pour a small amount of grout powder into a clean bucket. Slowly add liquid latex or water, mixing with a margin trowel as you go, until the grout is about the thickness of toothpaste and free of lumps. Wait 10 minutes, then mix again. If the grout is too thick, add a bit of liquid and remix.

2 Using a laminated grout float, scoop some grout onto the tile surface. Holding the float nearly flat, push the grout into the joints with sweeping back-and-forth strokes. At every point on the floor, be sure to push the grout with strokes running in two or more directions.

3 Tip the float up and use it like a squeegee to clear away most of the grout from the surface of the tiles. Move the float across the tiles diagonally, so the edge of the float does not dig into any grout lines. Aim to remove at least three quarters of the surface grout, but don't worry if you miss a few spots.

jointing and wiping

Once the grout has been firmly embedded and most of the excess has been wiped away, it's time to remove the rest of the excess grout and tool the grout lines to make them consistent—a process called jointing. This step is more than "just cleaning." A tile job that has been carelessly jointed will look unprofessional and may lead to cracks and voids in the grout.

Have a bucket of clean water on hand, so you can continually rinse the sponge. As soon as the water starts to get murky, change it.

As you work, take care not to step or kneel in the grout lines. Work systematically, one section at a time.

1 Dip a large sponge in clean water and then squeeze out some of the water, so it is wet but not dripping. Gently run the sponge across the tile surface to wipe grout from the tiles, but do not dig into the grout lines. Rinse the sponge often. Repeat this process at least once.

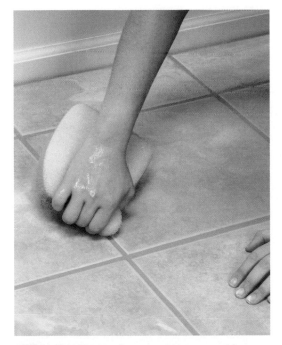

2 A tiled floor surface should have grout lines that are nearly level with the tiles—just slightly below the tile surface. Deeper lines will be hard to keep clean. Moisten a sponge with clean water and wring it out so it is just damp. Run it along each grout line, working first in one direction, then in the other. You may find it easier to work if you ball up a corner of the sponge, as shown.

3 Buff away the haze. Allow the grout to dry; it will become lighter in color. Using a dry, lint-free rag, buff the tiles until they shine. If any holes or gaps appear in the grout lines, fill them with grout.

tile base pieces and cove base

FOR A CRISP LOOK AND EASY MAINTENANCE, CONSIDER TILE BASE OR VINYL COVE base with a ceramic or stone tile floor. Of the the two, vinyl is the easiest to install, but tile looks more permanent. To install wood mouldings, see pages 178–183.

base tile

Install tile base pieces after the floor tiles have been set and the mortar has hardened. You may be able to use base tiles that have the profile of base cove (see facing page); this allows them to cover a larger gap between the flooring and the wall and makes them easier to clean. In addition to standard base tiles, purchase a corner piece—which has a bullnose edge—for each outside corner.

Set the tiles in a dry run. If the flooring is level, you can simply set the base tiles on top of it. If the floor is uneven, it may help to raise the base tiles ⅛ inch or so above the floor with spacers. Check that

the tops of the tiles form a level line. If they don't, adjust the tiles so this most visible part looks right. If possible, avoid having any base tile grout lines align with a grout line in the floor.

You can apply tile base pieces using thinset mortar, but if you use organic mastic (made for use with wall tiles) you'll find it easier to adjust the position of the tiles. Apply the adhesive using a narrow notched trowel, or back-butter the base tiles (see page 131). Once the adhesive has set, caulk the joint between the base and floor, and let the caulk dry. Then apply grout in the other joints.

LOWE'S QUICK TIP
You may be able to purchase base pieces that match the floor tile color. However, when a matching color is not available, install a tile base of a contrasting color.

1 Start at an outside corner, using a full outside corner piece, and work toward the wall. If you end up with a narrow sliver at the corner, it will probably look best if you cut two tiles—rather than one—at close to half their original size.

2 At an inside corner, you will need to make a cutout in one of the base tiles, as shown. A wet saw is easiest for this, but you can also use a hacksaw equipped with a rod blade if you work carefully.

vinyl base cove

Flexible vinyl base cove is easy to mop clean, and fairly quick to install. It comes in 4-foot-long strips, or in rolls with a self-adhesive backing. Be sure to purchase base cove that is wide enough to cover any paint lines or other imperfections on the wall.

This product is easy to cut and can be adhered in place quickly, but outside and inside corners can be tricky (see methods below). Purchase cove base adhesive in caulking tubes. Also get a cove base nozzle (Step 3), which attaches to a caulking tube and quickly produces a line of adhesive that is just the right width and thickness.

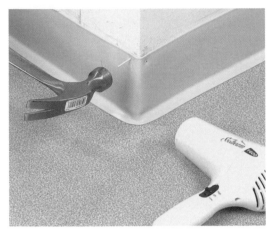

1 Start at an outside corner. If you simply bend the vinyl and press it into place, the bottom lip will nearly disappear and the top edges will detach from the wall. So use a heat gun or a blow dryer to soften the vinyl. Press the piece in place to see that it will lie flat against the wall and the floor at all points. You may need to drive a brad at each side of the corner, near the top.

2 If the heat gun is not doing the trick, it may help to very carefully cut through half the thickness of the vinyl at the corner. You can do this with a utility knife, but a rasping plane (shown) or a hand plane is easier to use and less likely to cut all the way through the base cove.

LOWE'S QUICK TIP

To make a straight cut in vinyl base cove, place the base on a scrap of wood, face down. Press an angle square on top, so the base is squeezed flat, and cut with a utility knife.

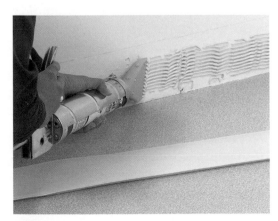

3 Apply the cove base adhesive using a caulk gun and a cove base nozzle, taking care to apply only behind the cove base. Press the cove in place, making sure it adheres to the wall at all points. Wipe off excess adhesive with a damp rag.

4 At an inside corner, make a cope joint similar to that for a wood baseboard (see page 181). Install a straight-cut piece on one wall. Cut the other piece to fit the profile of the straight-cut piece. Test the fit; you may need to modify it.

floating ceramic tiles

FLOATING TILES—TWO-TILE PANELS WITH TONGUE-AND-groove edges—allow you to skip several steps required with conventional flooring tile. First, no tedious floor preparation (including the installation of the backerboard) is required. In addition, you don't need to mix and apply thinset mortar or apply conventional grout. Even cutting is simplified—you use a circular saw equipped with a special blade.

As a result, floating ceramic tiles can be installed almost as quickly and easily as floating engineered or laminate flooring (see pages 194–197). This means that you can completely install a floor—including the grouting—in one day.

Installing floating ceramic tiles is a quick way to transform a floor. Not only do they install in less than half the time it would take with standard tile, they can be easily replaced when it comes time to redecorate.

quick and comfortable

AEROSOL GROUT

TILE-CUTTING JIGSAW BLADE

CIRCULAR-SAW BLADE

UNDER-LAYMENT

THRESHOLD/ TRIM

THRESHOLD/ TRIM TRACK

Because the floor is set on top of a cushion underlayment (see Step 2, facing page), the floor has a bit of give to it, making it more comfortable than conventional stone or tile floors. However, this flexibility comes at a slight cost: the grout used in this system must be flexible—it is actually much like caulk—so you cannot apply grout sealer to it. Thus it will be somewhat more likely to attract dirt, and a little harder to keep clean. However, special cleaners are available to maintain the floor in pristine condition.

This product is fairly pricey, but may be worth the cost because installation is so speedy. It will almost surely be less expensive than hiring a pro to install a standard ceramic tile floor.

getting started

The subsurface should be strong and free of squeaks, but it need not be rock-solid as for standard ceramic tile (see pages 98–101). It must be fairly even so the tile panels do not bend. Remove obstructions and mouldings, and undercut any door casings (see pages 102–108).

Each floating tile panel has two tiles and covers about 2 square feet. In addition to the tiles (get enough to match your square footage, plus 10 percent), purchase enough underlayment to cover your floor. It comes with the tape you will need to fasten it together.

You can cut the tiles using a standard wet saw, or you can purchase a set of tile-cutting blades—one for a circular saw and one for a jigsaw—that are made for cutting this product.

The grout comes in an aerosol can and is available in several colors. You can use any base moulding and threshold materials you choose, or buy threshold-base materials that match the flooring (see Steps 9 and 10, page 139).

1 To check that the floor is even enough, set a tile panel on edge at various locations on the floor. If there is a gap at the bottom wider than 1/8 inch, straighten the subfloor by driving more screws or by using leveling compound (see page 109). Alternatively, test with a 6-foot-long straightedge and repair any gaps that are greater than 3/16 inch.

2 Roll out the underlayment material, and cut it to fit so it is within 1/2 inch of the wall. Do not overlap the pieces of underlayment—butt them edge to edge. Use the tape provided to attach the pieces together.

3 If the layout of your room is such that furniture will hide an edge or two, you may be able to simply start in the most visible corner with a full panel. Before you do, set the panels in a dry run and use the procedures described on pages 120–123 to avoid ending up with narrow pieces. For every other row, you will need to start with a single tile. To cut a panel in half, simply turn it upside down and cut through the backerboard exactly over the grout line as shown.

4 Trimming the tiles is easy, but it does create dust, so you probably want to cut outside. Firmly position the tile and, using a square as a guide, cut through the tile side. Wear protective eye wear because tile chips will fly. Cut slowly, exerting only medium pressure.

PROJECT CONTINUES ➡

5 A jigsaw cuts more slowly and makes it difficult to produce a straight cut, but it creates far less dust, so you can use it for cutting indoors. Use a jigsaw to cut any notches (shown) or to make curved cuts.

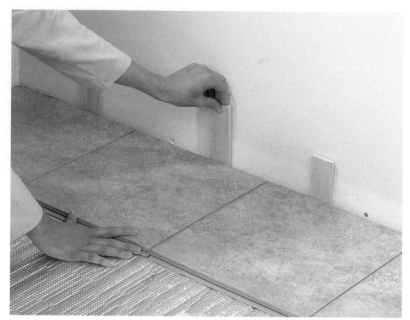

6 Set the first row against the most visible wall, with the tongue facing out. Use spacers to keep the tiles at least ¼ inch away from the wall, to allow for expansion. Use a string line or a straightedge to make sure this first row is perfectly straight. Support the two-tile panels with two spacers each, so they will not go out of alignment as you press against them.

7 For the second row, start with a single tile (that is, a half panel). Hold it with its front edge slightly raised and slip the groove into the tongue of the first row's panel, then lower it. Check that the joint is tight at all points, then install the next panel as shown. Continue adding rows of panels; every other row should start with a single tile.

8 Cut the panels for the last row so they fit snugly against spacers without having to be forced into place. Press down on the back of the panels to snap them into the tongues of the tiles in the previous row.

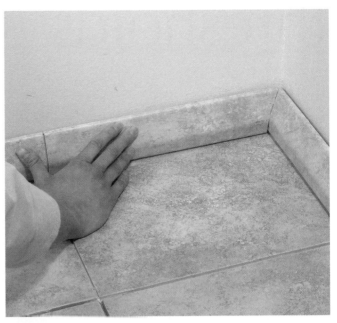

9 You can purchase transition strips to finish off the edges. (However, these strips work only if the abutting floor is a tile's thickness lower than the tiles. If the abutting floor is at a different level, see pages 140–141 for threshold options.) To install a transition strip, first cut the metal channel to fit, and attach it to the floor with screws. Then cut the transition strip and press it down until it snaps into the channel.

10 You can also use a transition strip as a base moulding. Attach the channel to the wall, and snap the pieces into place. You will need to cope-cut moulding pieces at an inside corner (see page 181).

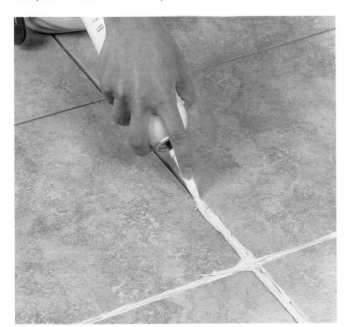

11 Once all the flooring is in place, apply the grout. Insert the tip of the aerosol applicator into a grout joint, press the nozzle, and pull back as the grout comes out. Fill the joints slightly higher than the surface of the tiles. Don't worry if you overfill; the material is easy to wipe away.

12 Using a large, damp (but not wet) sponge, level the grout. Press very lightly, and run the sponge in circles rather than in straight lines to avoid creating voids in the grout joint. Rinse your sponge often in cool water to keep it and the floor surface clean.

choosing and installing
thresholds

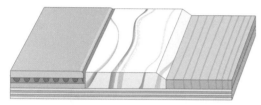

FLUSH WOOD

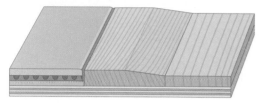

SOLID MATERIAL

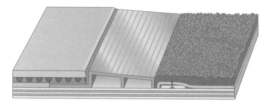

CARPET STRIP

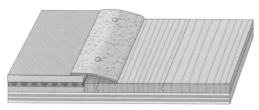

METAL STRIP

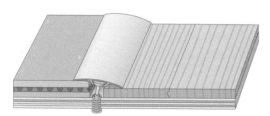

MULTI-FLOOR TRANSITION

THE PURPOSE OF A THRESHOLD IS TO PROVIDE A SMOOTH, attractive transition from one type of flooring to another. Where the tiled floor will be higher than an adjacent floor of wood, tile, or carpet, plan a graceful step-down. The flooring department at Lowe's has a good selection of options. For flush thresholds and the carpet strip, the tiles must be cut to fit precisely against the threshold. The other thresholds rest on top of the tiles, so the tiles do not have to be cut as precisely.

threshold options

- A flush-wood threshold is ideal for transitioning to a wood floor. If a standard hardwood threshold does not slope down far enough, use a belt sander to increase the angle.

- A flush-marble or solid-material threshold may have straight or beveled edges. The edges of both adjacent floorings must be cut exactly to butt up against the threshold.

- A carpet-strip threshold installs next to a strip that grabs the carpeting from underneath with a series of sharp points.

- An on-top metal or wood strip is the least expensive option and is easy to install. It fastens in place with screws or tacks. However, it tends to collect dust and debris.

- A multi-floor transition strip is easy to install, and can pivot to seal tightly against the flooring on both sides. It comes with special fasteners that fit into holes bored into the subfloor.

- Oak transition thresholds (shown below), available in a variety of shapes to accommodate various types of flooring, rest on the top of the tiles like an on-top metal strip. Each creates a tight seal and so collects less dust. Such thresholds can be used to make the transition from tile to vinyl, or tile to laminate, and between tile and carpet.

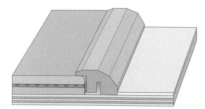

HARDWOOD TILE-TO-VINYL

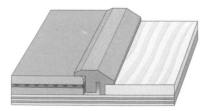

HARDWOOD TILE-TO-LAMINATE

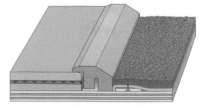

HARDWOOD TILE-TO-CARPET

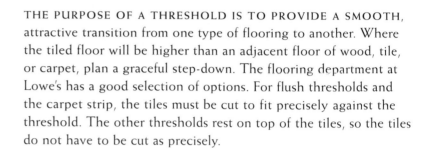

installing thresholds

Always wait for the tile grout to harden completely before installing any type of threshold. Thresholds in doorways usually should be positioned directly under the door when it is closed, so each room's flooring stops in the center of the doorway.

using a temporary guide If you installed a new threshold before tiling and tiled up to it, it would get scratched when the floor is tiled and grouted. Instead, temporarily attach a straight board, such as a strip of plywood, that is the same thickness as the threshold. Cut the door stop at the bottom so the guide (and later, the threshold) can slide under it. After tiling, remove the guide.

flush wood and solid-material thresholds Cut a wood threshold with a miter box; use a wet saw to cut a marble or solid-material threshold. To attach a wood threshold, slide it tightly into place, drill pilot holes, and drive nails or screws. To attach a marble or solid-material threshold, test that it fits, then remove it and lay a bed of mortar or silicone sealant. Set the threshold carefully in place. For both types of flush thresholds, caulk the joint between the threshold and the tile.

multi-floor transition strip Mark a straight line to indicate the center of the strip, about ½ inch away from the tiles. Drill four or five ¼-inch pilot holes along the line. Slide nylon fasteners onto the underside of the strip, and position them where the holes are. Use a rubber mallet to tap the strip down and drive the fasteners into the hole. The fasteners flex to accommodate varying floor levels.

installing stone tile

BOTH POLISHED AND ROUGH STONE TILE CAN USUALLY BE installed wherever ceramic tile is used. In general, employ the same techniques as those shown on pages 120–133. Take extra care that the substrate is firm, because stone tiles, though hard, are easy to crack. You'll probably have to make all the cuts with a wet saw rather than a snap cutter or nibbling tool.

Though they may not appear so, light-colored marble, travertine, and other natural stones are actually somewhat translucent. Gray thinset adhesive can show through enough to muddy their appearance. Use white thinset instead.

rough stone tile

LOWE'S QUICK TIP

Even when polished, many types of stone soak up stains readily. As a result, grout of a contrasting color may stain the stone as you apply it. Choose a grout of similar color, or consult with a tile expert at Lowe's before using a grout of a different color.

Tumbled marble and other porous stones usually are installed with wide grout lines; the finished floor is not expected to be perfectly smooth. As a result, installation is much less nerve-wracking than for polished stone. A wide choice of borders and decorative insets is available for use with porous stone.

If the tiles are irregular in shape, use the grid method to lay out and install them (see page 123). Some types look irregular but are actually precise squares; check to see whether you can use spacers when installing them.

It can be difficult to clean grout from porous stone. In most cases, you should seal the tiles before applying grout. When you apply the grout (below left), wipe the tiles with a clean, wet sponge early and often (below right), using clean, cool water.

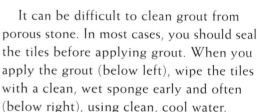

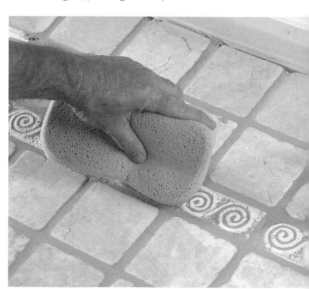

polished stone tile

Typically, formal-looking polished stone such as marble or granite is installed with thin grout lines. Use $1/16$-inch spacers and unsanded grout.

Because these tiles are placed so closely together, even the slightest discrepancy in height would be noticeable. Be sure to start with a substrate that is absolutely smooth and clean. Some natural stone tiles are slightly warped. Before applying mortar, lay a number of tiles next to each other to test for imperfections in size.

Also take extra care while combing the mortar to achieve a very even surface. When you set the tiles, check constantly for changes in level and use a beater board (right) to make corrections.

INSTALLING MOSAIC TILES

With small mosaic tiles, every square inch must nestle firmly in the mortar, or else one of the individual tiles may come loose. Doing this can be tricky since the paper or mesh backing that holds mosaics together interferes with the ability of the mortar to adhere. To make sure that all the tiles stick, a sheet of mosaics must be pressed firmly into the mortar. This causes mortar to ooze up through the many grout lines, making installation a messy operation.

To ensure firm adhesion, spend a little more for epoxy thinset. If you work carefully, however, standard thinset mortar, mixed with liquid latex, should do the job.

In either case, mix the mortar a little wetter than you would for regular tiles—it should be just firm enough for the ridges made by a notched trowel to hold their shape. The job will go slowly, so mix small amounts at a time. As you lay the sheets in mortar, check often to make sure all the tiles are sticking. Tap the tiles firmly into the mortar using a beater board. When mortar oozes up between the tiles, wipe it off with a damp—not wet—sponge; getting the remaining mortar wet could weaken it. Wiping the mortar away to a depth of at least $1/4$ inch is a tedious but necessary job.

If the individual tiles are large enough, you can cut mosaics using a snap cutter. However, a nibbling tool is usually easier. To make a precise cut in a small tile, first score the line with a snap cutter, then cut with a nibbling tool. (For instructions on cutting mosaic tile, see page 128.)

When you apply the grout, you won't be able to tool every line as you would with larger tiles. Keep wiping the surface lightly, over and over again, until the grout lines are consistent.

setting a patterned floor

THE TILE DEPARTMENT AT LOWE'S CARRIES MANY DECORATIVE TILES THAT CAN be arranged to make an eye-catching patterned floor. In addition to many colorful tiles that can be used for accents and combined into medallions, there are assembled mosaic sheets that can be used as borders. The pattern shown on these pages demonstrates how off-the-shelf elements can be combined into a design that incorporates several popular elements—a border that creates the impression of a throw rug, a center medallion, and some small decorative pieces set "on point."

planning the pattern

A patterned floor calls for meticulous planning to avoid unattractive slivers of tile. It also calls for planning ahead if you want to special-order borders or completed medallions. Draw several plans and do as many dry runs as it takes to know where each tile will be and that the look of the edge tiles is acceptable.

If a flooring pattern uses a set ensemble of tiles whose size cannot be adjusted, set it in a dry run in the center of the room to see what will happen along the walls. Consider moving the pattern an inch or two out of center to avoid slivers. Other patterns can be adjusted for size. Lay the floor out for an attractive overall fit of the surrounding tiles and then design the patterned section.

1 After installing a solid substrate (pages 98–111), use the techniques described on pages 120–123 to measure the room and plan the layout. This project includes angled tiles. On graph paper, make a drawing that shows all the tiles.

2 Lay tiles in a dry run that is large enough to confirm that you will not end up with slivers or a line of tiles that increases in size along its length. Check that the border forms a rectangle with square corners. Place the medallion in the center of the bordered area and see that the tiles around it can be cut to attractive sizes.

3 You may choose to install a piece of plywood (shown) or wood battens along the layout lines marking the inside of the border, or you can simply tile up to the layout lines. Often it works best to install a section of border and immediately follow up with a few field tiles as you work around the medallion area.

TEMPLATE

4 Place the medallion in the center of the bordered area and dry-lay the tiles around it. To mark for complicated cuts, use cardboard templates that are the same size as the tiles. Cut the templates, see that they fit, then use them to trace cut lines on the tiles.

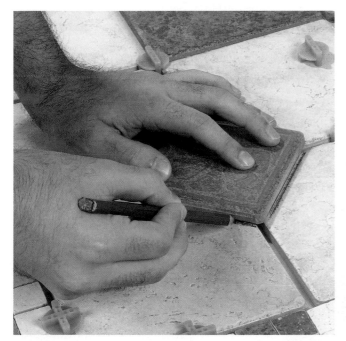

5 To make room for the accent diamonds, hold a diamond in place and mark a tile. Set the saw guide, cut four tiles, and test the fit. Adjust the guide as needed, and make all the remaining cuts at once—four tiles to surround each on-point tile you will install.

6 Set the rest of the tiles in thinset, using spacers or grid lines as needed. Allow the mortar to dry, then grout, tool, and wipe.

tiling a hearth and fireplace surround

A FIREPLACE HEARTH AND SURROUND IS A GREAT PLACE TO INDULGE IN EYE-catching color, beautiful patterns, or richly textured stone. Since they do not add up to much square footage, you can choose expensive tiles without breaking your budget.

The limited area to be tiled also offers some design challenges—there may be only a narrow space on the wall between the fireplace and the mantle, and wood moulding may encase a small hearth. If possible, avoid having some tiles that are cut noticeably smaller than others. You may be able to use a single row of large tiles (below). In general, use the tiling techniques shown on pages 126–133 for the hearth and those on pages 80–87 for setting wall tiles in thinset.

LOWE'S QUICK TIP
Install tiles for a fire-place project in latex-reinforced thin-set mortar; organic mastic weakens when it is exposed to heat.

fireplace possibilities

In older homes, the hearth rests on a thick slab of concrete, which is supported by massive framing (see diagram on facing page). Both the hearth and wall tiles are typically set in a thick mortar bed, making them very difficult to remove. If possible, find a way to tile on top of such existing tiles. In a newer home, the hearth tiles may be set on a sheet of backerboard, and the wall tiles may be set on drywall or on the brick of the fireplace. You should be able to remove these tiles.

Often, a wood mantle surrounds the wall tiles on three sides, with trim pieces (usually, quarter-round or cove moulding) covering the edges of the tiles. You may be able to remove the trim pieces, install the new tiles, and put back the original trim. If not, either butt the tiles against the mantle precisely, or install new trim pieces to cover the edges of the tiles.

You may find it possible to enlarge your hearth. If the tiles are flush with the height of the surrounding floor, you can lay concrete backerboard on top of the tile and extend the backerboard over the nearby flooring. Attach the backerboard to the tiles with epoxy thinset, and to the flooring with screws. Install tiles on top of the backerboard. For a hearth that is too small, but raised, you may be able to use concrete backerboard and wood framing to extend it.

getting **ready**

If the surfaces to be tiled are level and not glossy, they are ready for tiling. To tile over a rough surface like brick, check with a straightedge for high spots, and level them with a grinder. Then clean the surface with a mild solution of muriatic acid. For glazed tiles, go over the entire surface with a belt sander or a grinder to remove the glossy finish.

Mix a small batch of latex-reinforced thinset mortar. Use the flat side of a trowel to apply a thin "bond coat" of mortar to the surface. This fills in any grout lines and other irregularities.

Porous stone tiles must be sealed before they are installed, or the mortar will stain them permanently. Lay the stones out on a drop cloth and apply sealer with a brush or a rag to the top and sides of every tile.

LOWE'S QUICK TIP

If you are installing glazed tiles, you may want to use bullnose tiles around the inside edges of the firebox. Some installations also include a row or two of tiles inside the firebox, running vertically along the sides and sometimes along the underside of the top as well.

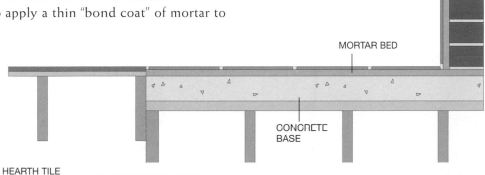

MORTAR BED

CONCRETE BASE

HEARTH TILE   CEMENT BACKERBOARD   TRIM

tiling **the hearth**

After the bond coat dries, apply thinset with a notched trowel and set the hearth tiles, using spacers to maintain consistent grout lines (see pages 130–131). Allow the mortar to set overnight. The hearth-tile edges can be finished with wood trim, or you may be able to use bullnose tile.

supporting **the wall tiles**

Construct a 2-by-4 wooden frame to serve as a temporary support for the first row of tiles above the firebox (right). Check that the tiles resting on it will be at exactly the correct height, and check that the support is level. Install the first tiles using the techniques shown on the following pages.

setting the wall tiles

As with the hearth tiles, use latex-reinforced thinset mortar for wall tiles placed around a fireplace. Use a large-notched trowel to apply the mortar, to ensure that the tiles are fully bedded. Make sure to purchase spacers so you can ensure consistent grout lines.

When installing large tiles like the ones shown here, spread only enough adhesive to accommodate two or three tiles at a time. Back-butter each tile with a thin coat of mortar to ensure a firm bond. Insert the spacers to maintain grout lines.

Press the tile firmly into place (below left). If necessary, use a beater block (see page 130) to embed the tile firmly and to bring its surface flush with the surrounding tiles. To make sure a tile is properly bedded, pull it out and examine the back; there should be pulled-up mortar on nearly the entire surface.

Place a level on top of a tile or row of tiles to make sure you are staying level (below). Adjust with the spacers if necessary. Wipe away any mortar from the surface of the tile before moving on to the next tile.

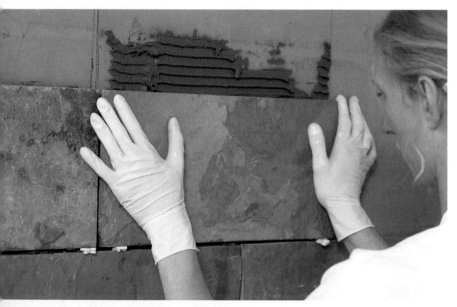

grinding bullnose edges

Wherever a tile edge is exposed, it should be finished with a bullnose edge. If bullnose pieces are not made for your tile, you can hire professionals to make factory-like smooth finished edges.

In the case of stone tiles, however, the edges do not have to be perfect, so you may choose to do it yourself using a grinder. Consult with a Lowe's tile specialist to choose the grinding disks that will work best with your tile.

Place the tile on a stable surface; you may want to clamp it in place to be sure it doesn't shift while you work. Equip the grinder with the roughest recommended disk. Turn the grinder on. Tilt the disk at a 45-degree angle to the tile. Using gentle pressure, set the blade on the far side of the tile and pull it toward you (left). It will take four passes or so to create a slightly rounded edge.

Switch to a slightly less coarse disk and repeat the process. Switch again to the smoothest disk, and repeat.

set the **bullnose** pieces

Cut the bullnose trim pieces to fit. Lay out a dry run, so you know that all the tiles are cut correctly and ready to install. Where a trim piece rests on top of another tile, spread a thick layer of thinset, taking care not to drip on the new tile. Gently set the trim piece in place, and use spacers to position it precisely. Wipe away any excess mortar. Place the adjacent trim tiles quickly, so you can make any adjustments in all the pieces before the mortar starts to set.

LOWE'S QUICK TIP

Once the mortar has set, apply a coat of sealer to stone-surface or porous tiles. Pay attention to the rate of absorption; some areas may be more porous than others and will need an extra coat. Let the sealer dry for the recommended amount of time, then grout the installation.

TILING UP TO A MANTLE

At Lowe's you will find a selection of mantles in various sizes and styles. In addition to the mantles on display, ask to see a catalog that shows more options, which you can special-order. Select a mantle that surrounds your fireplace symmetrically, so that the space above the firebox is the same width as the spaces on either side. You can adjust a mantle's height—but not its width—by cutting it.

On an existing mantle, there will probably be moulding. It can be removed and reused to cover the edges of your new tile. If there is no such moulding, you can purchase some and stain it to match the mantle. Alternatively, install tiles that tightly fit against the mantle.

If you are installing a new mantle, first place the mantle on the wall and mark its exact location. Tile the wall and perhaps partway into the firebox as well; install enough tile so that the mantle will cover the inside edges (top right). Following the manufacturer's directions, attach 1-by cleats to the wall, ¾ inch inside the marks (right). Set the mantle over the cleats; drive finish nails or finish-head screws to attach it to the cleats.

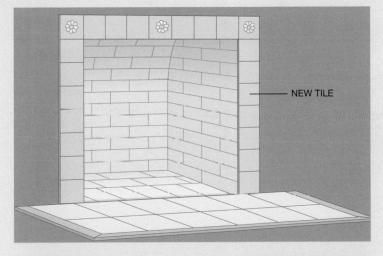

NEW TILE

CLEAT

MANTLE

vinyl flooring

VINYL FLOORING (ALONG WITH LINOLEUM AND RUBBER) IS resilient—it has a little give to it. Strip flooring, discussed in the next chapter, tends to be more resilient than ceramic and stone tile but not as much as these products.

Most resilient flooring products are sold as square tiles or as sheets, and are often the simplest to install. If your existing floor is level with the flooring of any adjacent rooms, adding ceramic or stone tile or hardwood flooring will likely raise it too high for a comfortable transition between rooms, especially if you need to install cement backerboard. Resilient flooring, however, typically adds ¼ inch or less to the floor. A homeowner with average do-it-yourself skills and a willing assistant can usually cover a room with resilient flooring or carpeting in a day.

Lowe's carries a wide selection of vinyl tiles in two general categories. Commercial tiles (often called "solid-vinyl," although they are actually about 80 percent vinyl) have color clear through and are ideal for heavy traffic areas. Surface-printed tiles (which are self-stick) offer the greatest variety of colors and textures. Peruse the possibilities on pages 30–33. You can also special-order even more options from an in-store catalog.

Because it is easy to cut and apply, you can custom-design vinyl or linoleum to create a one-of-a-kind floor. Mix different colors, for instance, or cut borders or accent inserts. Unlike ceramic and stone tile, the flooring in this chapter can be laid on a substrate that is less than firm. However, the underlayment must be extremely smooth.

installing tiles

IN MANY WAYS, INSTALLING COMMERCIAL AND SELF-STICK TILES, OR RUBBER tiles, is easier than installing ceramic or stone tile. The substrate does not have to be firm, because these tiles are flexible. Figuring the layout is easy, since most resilient tiles are 12 inches square, with no grout lines. No special cutting tools are needed; a utility knife does a fine job. An average-sized room is usually done in a day, and you can walk on the floor right away. Begin by removing all obstructions. Pry off the existing base shoe or base moulding, and replace it later, so all tile edges will be covered (see pages 104–105).

a smooth-enough surface

A resilient tile floor does have one stringent requirement: the underlayment must be completely smooth. Thin self-stick tiles with surface-printed embossed patterns will reflect every tiny imperfection in the sub-

strate. Even bumps $\frac{1}{16}$ inch high will be visible. Commercial tiles like those shown in the steps on pages 155–157 are thicker, but are only slightly more forgiving; the same is true of rubber tiles.

- If the existing flooring is a resilient product that is in good shape, glue down any loose pieces and carefully fill and sand any cavities. To install resilient tile over an embossed surface, first smooth the surface with embossing leveler (see page 109).

- If the existing floor surface is rough and would be difficult to smooth, cover it with plywood underlayment (see pages 112–113). Before installing resilient tiles on a concrete surface, use a grinder to take down any high spots and fill holes with floor patch. Clean an old concrete floor with a concrete cleaning product to make sure that the adhesive will bond.

After preparing the floor, run your hand over it to make sure there are no protrusions or indentations.

Many people prefer vinyl tile not only because of the variety of color and patterns available but because vinyl is comfortable to walk on and forgiving should you happen to drop a glass or a plate.

choosing tiles

Pages 30–33 show a selection of different types of resilient flooring tiles. Rubber and commercial vinyl tiles are installed in the same way; see page 154 for self-stick tiles. To get an idea of the final appearance, apply mastic and set a tile on the floor. Roll it or walk on it, and wait a couple of days for it to completely settle.

planning the layout

See pages 120–123 for instructions on laying out a floor. If you are installing 12-inch tiles, you will probably not need a dry run or a jury stick, since there is one tile for every foot.

However, for two or more colors of vinyl tile installed in a pattern, plan the layout using graph paper, or lay the tiles in a dry run on the floor to see how they look. All the tiles on a floor should be made by the same manufacturer to ensure that they will be precisely the same size. Check the lot numbers to be sure of color consistency.

the order of work

As you are deciding where to start installing the tiles, keep in mind that you cannot step on the adhesive after it has been applied with the trowel; you can, however, step on tiles as soon as they have been placed. Plan your order of work ahead of time. You can start in the middle of the floor by applying a small section of adhesive and tile and then work outward from there. A more straightforward approach is to trowel adhesive over the entire floor and then start laying tiles near the entry door, working inward.

The adhesive must be tacky but not hard when you apply the tiles. Assuming the room is at normal temperature and humidity, you will need to wait about an hour after applying the adhesive before you can install the tiles. However, if you are installing in a basement or other place with high humidity, it may take 12 hours or more for the adhesive to get tacky.

Once the adhesive is ready, all the tiles must be installed on the same day; otherwise, the adhesive will become too hard and the tiles will not stick.

INSTALLING LINOLEUM

True linoleum, which is composed of linseed oil, pine resin, powdered stone, wood fiber, and other natural ingredients, can be cut with a knife using a template, as for a vinyl floor. However, linoleum is laid in a latex adhesive made specifically for it. The adhesive must stand an hour or so before the linoleum can be laid.

Linoleum sheets are typically only 6½ feet wide, so most rooms will need at least one seam. Because factory edges are often imperfect, professional installers use a special edge trimmer to cut each piece before joining them together. Creating a tight seam involves the use of a seam scriber tool, as well as seam sealer. It takes some practice to make tight seams, so the job is best left to professionals.

Flooring professionals can also inlay patterns for you, including features such as borders, medallions, or other fanciful designs, using linoleum of other colors and patterns. In this way, you can have a one-of-a-kind custom floor.

LOWE'S QUICK TIP

If you are installing over an existing tile floor, offset the new tiles so that their edges are at least 2 inches away from the edges of the old tiles underneath.

spreading **adhesive**

Be meticulous about cleaning the floor surface: any construction debris will create bumps in the floor, and dust can keep mastic from sticking to the underlayment. First sweep, then vacuum, then wipe the entire floor with a damp rag, and allow it to dry.

Spreading adhesive for resilient tiles is not difficult, but you must work systematically. Tilt the bucket of adhesive and shake out a dollop onto the floor. Holding the trowel at about a 45-degree angle to the floor, spread the adhesive. Use long, sweeping strokes that overlap by an inch or so. Trowel away any excess adhesive immediately. Don't try to retrowel it a few minutes later, because the adhesive will have started to harden. Note that it's fine to cover the working lines with adhesive; they'll show through as the adhesive hardens.

LOWE'S QUICK TIP

Check the label on the adhesive to make sure your trowel has notches of the correct dimensions—usually, $5/32$ by $1/16$.

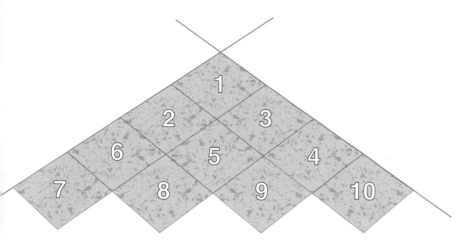

setting tiles

Lay tiles as shown at left. Whenever possible, set a tile so that it abuts two other tiles—not just one. As you set each tile, check that its corners align precisely with the corners of adjacent tiles. Have a rag and some adhesive remover or paint thinner on hand, and wipe up any excess adhesive immediately.

SELF-STICK TILES

The selling point for these tiles is that they have a sticky back, so they can simply be applied to a dry floor. However, many pros distrust the adhesive on the back of the tiles, and spread vinyl adhesive just as they would for nonstick tiles.

Lay these out as you would commercial tile. Peel off each tile's paper backing, and install the tiles along the working lines. Cut the edge tiles with the backing still in place; these tiles are typically so thin that they can be cut clean through with one pass of a utility knife—or they can even be cut with scissors.

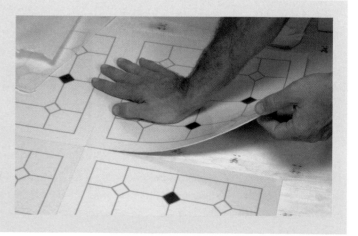

1 After half an hour or an hour, depending on the temperature and humidity, the adhesive will become translucent and tacky rather than wet. You now have 8 hours or so to lay the tiles. Gently place the first tile at the intersection of the working lines; don't push down on it. Examine the position of this first one very carefully to see that it follows the working lines in both directions.

2 Lay the next two tiles in place, and check to see that they follow the working lines and that the corners align perfectly. You should be able to adjust their position slightly; however, after three or four more tiles have been installed, adjustment will be virtually impossible. Continue laying tiles, following the order shown in the illustration on the facing page. Whenever you install a tile that butts against only one other tile, feel the corners to make sure that they line up precisely.

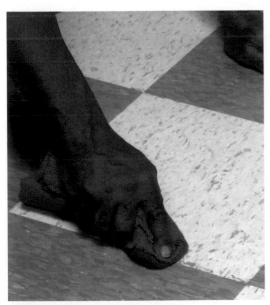

3 Occasionally, adhesive will squeeze up between two tiles. Immediately use a rag soaked with adhesive remover or paint thinner to wipe this away. Keep your hands and shoes clean of adhesive.

4 From time to time, stand up and walk all over the floor, pressing straight down with your foot to firmly embed each tile in the adhesive. Afterward, clean off any adhesive that squeezes out.

LOWE'S QUICK TIP

When cleaning excess adhesive from surface-printed tiles, be sure to use a solvent that will not dull the shiny surface; consult the manufacturer's instructions or check with a Lowe's tile expert to be sure.

PROJECT CONTINUES ➡

marking tiles for cutting

Once all the full-sized tiles in a section of the room have been installed, lay some plywood on the floor to use as a cutting surface, and start cutting and laying the perimeter tiles.

To measure for a straight cut, place a ¼-inch spacer against the wall. Turn the tile upside down, facing in the correct direction, and hold it over its future location, pressed against the spacer. Mark both sides for the cut. Make sure you keep the tile from touching the adhesive while you are measuring.

For instructions on marking tiles for inside and outside corners, see pages 124–125. (Keep in mind, of course, that with vinyl tiles you will not need to take grout lines into account.)

cutting tiles

If you have more than 50 tiles to cut, consider using a vinyl tile cutter (below), which reduces strain and mess and makes quick work of cutting a row of tiles all the same size. Most rental outlets carry this handy tool. Vinyl tile is only slightly more difficult to cut with a utility knife, however. As soon as a knife blade has become dull so that cutting is difficult, replace the blade.

Hold a straightedge between the two cut marks. (A full tile makes a convenient straightedge. Mark it with an X so you will not install it on the floor by mistake.)

With a utility knife, score a single line along the straightedge (below). Pick the tile up, grasp both sides firmly, and bend the tile until it snaps.

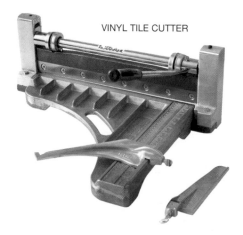

VINYL TILE CUTTER

MAKING A CUTOUT

When you need to make a cutout for an outside corner, first score a cut line in both directions, using a scrap of plywood as a work surface. Then repeatedly score the shorter of the lines until you have cut all the way through. Now you can bend the piece back and snap it off. Trim away any roughness with the utility knife.

fitting around a pipe

Because vinyl tile is relatively easy to cut, you'll find that fitting tiles around obstructions goes quickly. Should you make a mistake it is possible to shave off a bit more tile for a perfect fit—or even throw away the tile and start again.

Install field tiles before attempting to fit around an obstacle. Have a piece of scrap plywood handy to use as a cutting surface. Remember to firmly hold the tile being cut and keep your hand away from the direction of the cut.

1 If only a partial width of tile is needed, cut the tile to width (see facing page). Place the tile directly on top of the nearest installed tile, and slide it against the pipe. Mark the tile on each side of the pipe. Measure the distance the tile must travel toward the wall, as shown, and add ⅛ inch. This is the depth of the cut.

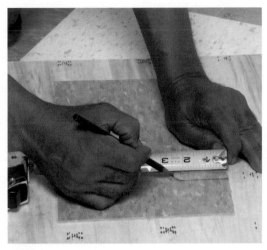

2 Keeping in mind that you want a gap of about ⅛ inch or so around the pipe, draw the outline of the front edge of the pipe. A tape measure can stand in as a handy straightedge for marking.

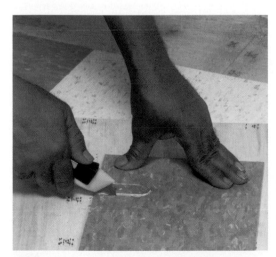

3 Carefully score along all the marked lines. Then slice repeatedly with a utility knife until you cut all the way through the tile. Remove and save the cutout piece. Check the tile for fit; you may need to enlarge the cut slightly.

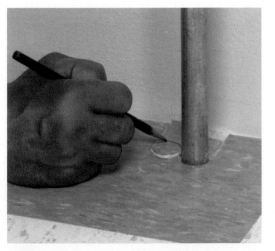

4 Install the tile. Hold the cutout in place, mark it, and cut it to fit behind the pipe. Install the cutout. Caulk around the pipe where it meets the tile. Install a pipe flange (escutcheon) to cover the caulk.

LOWE'S QUICK TIP

If you are installing surface-printed vinyl, which is very flexible, cut a single slit behind the pipe, then cut the hole for the pipe. Bend the tile to slip it around the pipe. After installation, caulk the joint between the vinyl and the pipe, apply seam sealer to the slit (page 163), and attach a pipe flange.

installing vinyl sheet flooring

SHEET VINYL IS MADE OF BASICALLY THE SAME MATERIAL AS HIGH-quality surface-printed vinyl tile. Better-quality products are ⅛ inch thick and have a strong surface coating, so they will not tear easily during or after installation. Installing vinyl sheet flooring is more difficult than installing vinyl tiles. If you make a mistake while cutting a tile, you can simply discard it and install another one. With sheet flooring, however, a mistake ruins the entire sheet.

For a successful installation, prepare an accurate template of the room. The steps on these pages will guide you through the process of using such a template. The flooring shown is laid in a continuous bed of troweled adhesive. A "loose-lay" vinyl sheet is adhered to the floor only around the perimeter of the room, using either a narrow strip of troweled adhesive or double-sided tape.

While vinyl sheet flooring is more difficult to install than vinyl tile, in most situations there are no seams to catch dirt or possibly come loose with time.

getting **ready**

Remove any obstructions, as well as the base shoe or the base moulding (see pages 104–105). Prepare the floor as you would for vinyl tile, either by installing underlayment or by patching the existing flooring (see pages 110–115). Sand the floor until it is completely smooth, and sweep and vacuum it.

Sheet vinyl is easy to cut. However, you should plan your layout to minimize the need for complicated cuts.

creating a **template**

Because you get only one chance to cut the vinyl sheet correctly, it is vital that you make an accurate template. (However, you do have some wiggle room because base moulding or thresholds will overlap the edge of the vinyl at almost every point around the perimeter of the room.) Some flooring sheets are rolled up together with a heavy paper sheet that can be used as a template. If your vinyl does not come with such a sheet, use rosin paper (also called construction paper or kraft paper).

1 Undercut door casings and other mouldings so you can slip the vinyl under, rather than having to trim it to fit around, the obstruction. A jamb saw (shown) makes the job easy.

2 Roll out a sheet of rosin paper lengthwise in the room. Try to avoid tearing the paper; if necessary you can mend tears with masking tape. Cut it a bit longer than needed.

3 As long as the wall is fairly straight, simply position the template about ¼ inch away from the wall. (Be sure the moulding is wide enough to cover the gap at all points.) If the wall is wavy, use a short straightedge to scribe a line that parallels the wall. Cut along the line, then slide the template so that it is ¼ inch away from the wall.

4 Once you have a piece of the template correctly positioned, cut a series of triangles out of the paper, about 2 inches wide and spaced about 16 inches apart. Press pieces of masking tape over the triangles to hold the template in place.

Roll out another sheet, overlapping the first by an inch or so. When it is correctly positioned, cut and tape triangles to hold it in place. Do not tape the seams yet.

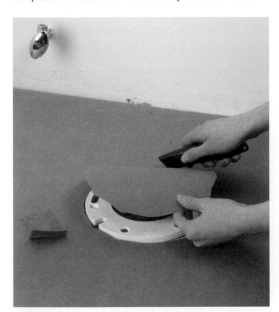

5 When you come to a raised obstruction (like this toilet flange), cut the hole a little small, then enlarge it to fit. If you make a mistake, simply cut a piece of rosin paper and tape it so it covers the gap. Be sure that any patching pieces are firmly adhered.

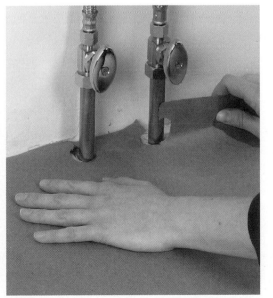

6 If you encounter a pipe or two, pull the paper back and make a slice long enough to extend from the front of the pipe back to the wall. Then cut a circle for the pipe and push the paper into place. The paper should be about ¼ inch away from the pipe.

LOWE'S QUICK TIP
The masking tape pieces that go over the triangles must be removed once the template is completed. As you apply each piece of tape, fold over the tip to create a little handle that you can easily grab when you pull the tape away (see Step 4). If the masking tape does not stick to the floor, the floor may be too dusty; roll up the template and wipe the floor with a damp rag.

PROJECT CONTINUES ➡

7 At a door opening, the vinyl will slip under the casing but must fit snugly against the jamb, where it will not be covered by moulding. Slip the template under the casing and use a patch piece to butt it against the jamb. The template should end at a point that will be under the door when it is shut.

8 Tape the succeeding sheets of rosin paper firmly together so the template becomes a single sheet that will not come apart when you roll it up. Examine the template carefully at all points to make sure that it fits all around the perimeter.

LOWE'S QUICK TIP

To be accurate, the template must lie flat on the floor at all points. If there is a bubble or a wave, slice through it with a utility knife, lay the two sides flat, and cover the slice with masking tape.

cutting and laying sheet vinyl

Once you are satisfied with the template, remove all the pieces of masking tape that cover the cut-out triangles. Carefully roll up the template, taking care not to rip it or pull apart the pieces.

You will need a work area that is large enough so that you can lay out the vinyl sheet. An adjoining room is best, but a deck, garage, or driveway are also options. Sweep the surface completely free of all debris; a small stone, for instance, could poke a hole through the vinyl if you step on it. Check the sheet as you roll it up to make sure no debris has stuck to it.

1 To get the vinyl to lie flat, roll it backwards, then unroll it. Lay the vinyl with the finished surface facing up, and smooth out any bubbles or waves. Place the template on the vinyl and adjust its position for the best appearance. You may want to avoid having a pattern line come very near a wall or you may want to center the pattern on the floor. Secure the template with pieces of masking tape every 12 inches or so around the perimeter and with tape over the cut-out triangles.

2 Trace the outline of the template onto the vinyl sheet. To be sure you are drawing a straight line, lay a framing square or a straight edge along the edge of the template. Remove the template from the vinyl sheet.

3 Before cutting, slip a piece of scrap wood or plywood under the vinyl. Use a utility knife equipped with either a hook blade or a standard blade. Where the vinyl will be covered with moulding, you can cut freehand, though you may find it easier to use a straightedge. Where the vinyl must be cut precisely, use a straightedge.

LOWE'S QUICK TIP
Some vinyl sheets may become permanently stained if you draw on them with a marker. Test on a scrap piece to make sure that you will be able to erase the line; you may need to use a pencil instead.

4 To cut a hole for a pipe, first use a speed square to cut a straight line from the edge of the sheet to the front of the pipe. Then cut the hole freehand. Plan to use a pipe flange (also called an escutcheon) to cover the gap between the vinyl and the pipe.

5 Assess the shape of the room and how you can most easily get the roll into the room to determine which end of the vinyl sheet should be rolled out first. Roll the sheet up so that the finish side is facing up. Work carefully, to avoid tearing the sheet. Inside corners are easily torn during the installation process. To strengthen an inside corner, apply a strip of duct tape at a 45-degree angle, as shown.

PROJECT CONTINUES ➡

6 Sweep the floor, vacuum, and then wipe with a damp cloth. Unroll the vinyl sheet, pushing the edges into the corners as you go. Run your hand along the surface to make sure there is no debris underneath. If you find a bump, reroll the sheet and remove it immediately. Make sure the vinyl lies flat at all points, with no bubbles or waves. Slip the vinyl under mouldings and around pipes. Pay special attention to any places—such as the doorjamb—where the vinyl must be positioned exactly.

7 If the gap between the vinyl and the wall is less than ¼ inch at any point, use a straightedge as a guide while you slice off a sliver with a utility knife.

8 You will roll up one half of the vinyl, apply adhesive, and roll it back onto the adhesive, then do the same for the other half. To keep the vinyl from shifting while you work, place two or more heavy objects on the part of the floor that will be rolled up second. Roll up half the floor, taking care not to tear the vinyl, or, if the shape of the room makes it necessary, fold it back on itself.

9 If the vinyl is folded back, take care not to step on the fold, which could crack it. Using the notched trowel recommended by the manufacturer, spread the recommended adhesive onto the floor. Aim for even coverage, with no blobs or gaps. If you purchased "loose-lay" flooring, apply the adhesive—either a strip of troweled adhesive or double-sided tape—only around the perimeter of the room.

10 Carefully unroll the vinyl onto the troweled adhesive, smoothing it with your hand as you go. Check that it is positioned correctly. Starting near the middle of the adhered section and moving outward, run a floor roller over the entire surface to remove any air bubbles. Once the first half of the floor is installed to your satisfaction, roll up the second half and repeat Steps 8 through 10 for the second half. If you have any seams to join—for instance, the slit behind a pipe—use seam sealer (see box below).

Once the floor is laid, clean away any adhesive on the surface using a solvent recommended by the flooring manufacturer. You may want to wait a day before installing the base moulding (see pages 178–183) so you won't have to deal with sticky adhesive getting on the mouldings.

If you find a captured air bubble after the floor has been laid and you cannot remove it by rolling, poke it with a needle and then roll it so that the air escapes via the pinhole. To seal the pinhole, apply a touch of seam sealer.

LOWE'S QUICK TIP

If the vinyl needs to move, you can probably make a correction of ¼ inch or less while you roll the floor. If it needs to move farther, pick the vinyl up off the adhesive and make adjustments.

JOINING TWO PIECES OF VINYL

If the floor is wider than a single sheet of vinyl, you'll need to create a waterproof seam between two sheets. Following the instructions on the previous pages, make two templates, one for each sheet, that overlap each other by 2 inches. Before cutting the two pieces of vinyl, spread them out with one overlapping the other, and see that the pattern matches. Set the templates on top, and cut the pieces.

Dry-lay the pieces on the floor. Once you are satisfied with the alignment of both pieces, use a straightedge to cut through both at once (top right). Hold

the blade of the knife in a straight vertical position as you cut, to ensure a tight seam. Remove the two thin scrap pieces that are produced.

Adhere the sheets to the floor. As a last step, focus on the seam line. Take care to keep everything perfectly clean as you work, and clean the seam completely using seam cleaner. Use a special applicator (right) to apply seam sealer to the joint. Avoid touching the seam for at least several hours; any dirt that gets into it before it dries completely will become a permanent part of the floor.

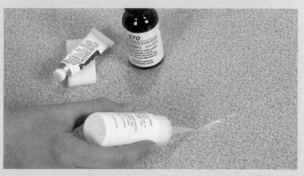

strip flooring

INSTALLING A STRIP FLOOR DOES NOT REQUIRE SPECIAL skills; if you are reasonably experienced at measuring and cutting wood, you should be able to install any of the floors shown in this chapter. Tools for fastening the flooring may be new to you but can be mastered with a few minutes' practice.

Subfloor requirements for strip floors are not stringent. The floor should be level, but it does not have to be completely firm because strip flooring is flexible. Solid wood flooring will add a good deal of strength to a floor; other types of strip flooring will add only a modest amount. Engineered and laminate flooring will raise a floor by about ½ inch; solid wood flooring will raise it ¾ inch.

A floor made from solid strips of wood must be sanded, stained, and finished after installation—a process that takes up to a week and fills the house first with dust and then with the odor of drying stain and finish. The other flooring projects in this chapter require no sanding and staining, and can be completed in a day—though you may want to apply a coat of polyurethane or floor wax for protection, adding another day.

At Lowe's you will find a wide array of wood and strip flooring (see pages 36–43). Engineered, parquet, and laminate floors are prefinished in a wide choice of hues. Solid wood flooring can be stained to most any color. For a distinctive look, combine two types of material or stain, or install an inlaid pattern (see pages 166–167).

Lowe's installation services can arrange for professional installation of every type of flooring shown in this chapter. Once you request professional services, a Lowe's-approved contractor comes to your home, takes measurements, and presents an all-inclusive bid for the work and materials. There is a modest charge for this bid; the charge will be deducted from the installation cost if you decide to hire the contractor. The bid is binding: the contractor will not add extra costs unless you agree. Lowe's guarantees that the work will be done to your satisfaction and in a timely manner.

floor designs

The alternating hues of birch flooring (above) lend an understated beauty to a contemporary kitchen. Contrasting wood tones can be used to make a spare but stunning border that mimics the look of an area rug (right).

A CLASSIC WOOD FLOOR FEATURES STRIPS RUNNING IN THE same direction, coated with the same finish. This arrangement showcases the wood grain's natural variations in color and pattern. If you'd like to spice things up, a few simple changes can make a big difference—for instance, using an unusual type of wood, mixing materials, inlaying a pattern, or choosing an unusual finish.

wood species

Natural wood flooring (either solid or engineered) is most commonly made of oak or maple—both of which are durable and reasonably priced. You do, however, have other options. At Lowe's, you can special-order many types of strip flooring that are not on display.

Pine flooring is often sold in 6-inch-wide strips. Many people love the casual look of its wide grain lines and occasional knots. It is a soft wood, easily scratched and dented, but in an informal setting that may not be a problem.

True walnut and cherry floors are extremely expensive and are usually used for accents. Brazilian hardwoods, sometimes labeled "cherry" or "walnut," are less pricey. Most have a beautiful, straight grain and are extremely stable and hard.

mixing materials

Natural wood grain harmonizes well with other natural materials, such as ceramic or stone tile. Various species and stains also mix and match nicely, so don't be shy about experimenting with materials or stains.

Create a custom look by alternating two types of engineered flooring. Or use

LOWE'S QUICK TIP

To create a stained pattern in a solid wood floor, apply a light stain to the entire floor. Then, mask a pattern and apply darker stain. Allow the stain to dry completely before applying a polyurethane finish. (See page 184 for a variation on this approach.)

two different species of solid hardwood strips for a more textured look.

Wood parquet tiles (see pages 168–171) are another option. They can be installed abutting engineered flooring, for added color and pattern variety.

patterns and borders

Ready-made wood borders and medallions can be special-ordered and installed by a do-it-yourselfer. However, for a more intri-cate or custom design, you probably want to hire a professional.

stains and paint

Judiciously applied, paint and solid-color stains can enliven a room yet still allow the wood's natural grain to shine through. The distinction between stain and paint is often blurred in such rooms; a lovely stain can be made by simply thinning a can of paint. (See page 185 for more on painting floors.)

installing parquet wood flooring

PARQUET TILES ARE MADE UP OF STRIPS JOINED INTO SQUARES. THE TILES FIT snugly together by means of tongues and grooves on their edges. See page 40 for tips on selecting parquet tiles. These tiles require a special adhesive, which may be either latex- or oil-based. For applying the adhesive, purchase a notched trowel of the size recommended by the adhesive manufacturer.

getting **ready**

The substrate for a parquet floor does not need to be completely firm, and it doesn't have to be very smooth. You can install parquet tiles directly over an old wood or vinyl tile floor, as long as the floor is free of major defects. Remove any obstacles, and remove or cut mouldings (see pages 102–105). Figuring the layout is easy, because the tiles are exactly 12 inches square, with no grout lines. See pages 120–123 for layout instructions. Parquet tiles are laid a small section at a time because the adhesive hardens quickly.

Sweep and vacuum the floor carefully; if the trowel picks up even a small crumb of debris, you will have to replace the affected tile. Parquet adhesive is particularly sticky and hard to clean, so try not to get it on your hands or knees. Clean up wayward adhesive immediately, using a rag soaked with soapy water (for latex-based adhesive) or paint thinner (for oil-based adhesive).

setting the tiles

Allow wood parquet tiles to sit in the room for at least a day so they can adjust to the ambient temperature and humidity. Start your installation near the center of the room, and set tiles in the order shown on page 154. Install the full tiles first.

1 Before you begin to spread the adhesive, assemble a group of 10 or so tiles on the floor and slide them together. Check that the edges and corners fit tightly. Occasionally two tiles will not fit because one has a slightly splintered tongue, or a groove that is clogged with debris. You may be able to correct the problem by cutting off the splinter with a knife or removing the debris with a screwdriver. If not, discard the tile. After test-fitting a group of tiles, stack them within easy reach so you can install them quickly.

2 Pour some adhesive onto the floor, or scoop it out with the notched trowel. Using long, sweeping strokes and working systematically, spread enough adhesive to cover about 8 square feet. Avoid covering any working lines and leave no blobs. Avoid re-combing after a few minutes because the adhesive starts to harden quickly.

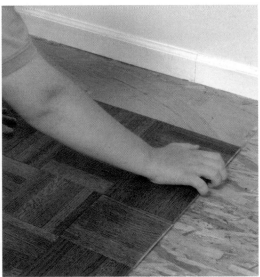

3 Set the first tile onto the adhesive at the intersection of the working lines. Push down gently, and twist it into perfect alignment. Disregard the tongues when aligning the tile with the working lines.

4 Set each successive tile next to its neighbor, and slide it into place. You'll be able to slide the tiles for a half hour or so. Sometimes they'll also move when you don't want them to. Every few minutes, check all the tiles and adjust them as necessary.

PROJECT CONTINUES ➡

PARTIAL TILE

5 As long as the adhesive is sticky to the touch, the tiles will adhere. Once the adhesive starts to skin over (so it feels tacky rather than gooey), adhesion will be impaired. Should this happen you'll have to scrape up the adhesive and start again. To ensure a firm bond, tap each tile with a rubber mallet. Check the alignment of the tiles and adjust if necessary. To test for firm adhesion, attempt to pry a tile up using a pry bar. If the tile refuses to come up after you've exerted moderate pressure, it is well stuck.

6 If the adhesive is starting to set up and some of the seams between tiles are not tight, insert the tongue or groove of a partial tile piece into the groove or tongue of the tile that needs to move. Tap the partial tile with a hammer.

INSTALLING TILES AT AN ANGLE

To lay out a pattern of parquet tiles set at a 45-degree angle, see page 122. To mark a tile for cutting, place the tile to be cut directly on top of a tile near to the wall, with its tongues facing in the right direction. Set ¼-inch spacers against the wall. Cut the tongues off of another tile, and use it for measuring purposes only. Set the measuring tile on top of the tile to be cut, slide it against the spacers, and mark for the cut.

MEASURING TILE

TILE TO BE CUT

CUT TILE GOES HERE

cutting **parquet** tiles

Do not apply adhesive to the floor where the cut tiles will go until a few minutes before you will install them. Because parquet tiles crack easily, it is wisest to cut them with a table saw, a radial-arm saw, or a power miter box. However, with care they can also be cut with a circular saw or a saber saw. Whichever tool you use, keep your fingers well away from the blade. It often helps to clamp the tile onto a worktable before cutting it.

marking To measure for a straight cut, place a ¼-inch spacer at the wall. Set the tile to be cut directly on top of the tile it will slide into. (Position the tile with its tongue and groove facing the correct way.) Place a full tile on top of the tile to be cut, slide it against the spacer, and mark for the cut. (To mark for cutouts and notches, see pages 124–125 and page 157.)

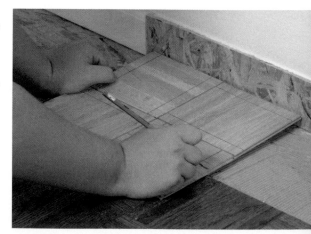

breaking apart If you need a half or a quarter tile, or a number of individual pieces, simply bend the parquet until the sections come apart (above). Sometimes, this is all the cutting you need to do.

straight cut If you cut the tile right-side up, a circular saw blade may produce unsightly splinters. Instead, transfer the cut line to the back of the tile. Hold the tile firmly in place with your hand against a supporting surface, or clamp it to a work table, and make the cut (above right).

cutouts and notches A cut that goes in two directions can be made with a circular saw, but it's easier with a saber saw (right). If you use a fine-cutting blade, you can cut the tile right side up. Apply tape to the bottom of the saw baseplate to protect the tile from scratches. Hold or clamp the tile firmly in place, and blow away the sawdust as you cut.

finishing the job

Use a recommended solvent to clean off all squeezed-out adhesive. Install base mouldings (see pages 178–183) and thresholds (see pages 140–141).

Most wood parquet tiles come with a fairly durable protective coating. In theory, if the tiles fit together tightly, the seams will be protected. However, tiles do not always align perfectly, and the protective finish will not last forever.

For a finish that will bead up water for years, add a coat of clear polyurethane once the parquet has been installed. Oil-based polyurethane is the strongest, but is illegal in some states for environmental reasons; latex-based polyurethane is nearly as strong. Prepare the surface by sanding it lightly, using a hand sander and 180-grit sandpaper. Completely remove all grit so that the floor is perfectly clean. Apply the polyurethane using a paintbrush or a special applicator. After the finish has dried, lightly sand it again.

installing a solid wood strip floor

STRIP FLOORS FIT TOGETHER BY MEANS OF A PROTRUDING tongue on one side of each strip that fits into a groove in the next board. Most solid flooring is 2¼ inches wide and ¾ inches thick. Nails—or flooring staples—are driven through the tongue into the subflooring. (See pages 36–37 to peruse the variety of options in solid hardwood flooring.) Once the floor is installed, it must be sanded smooth and finished (page 185).

A solid wood floor (unlike a laminate or engineered one) expands and contracts widthwise—not lengthwise—with changes in temperature and humidity. It is essential to have a ½-inch gap between the flooring and the wall to allow for this movement.

preparing for the job

The understated elegance of a solid-wood strip floor makes it a perennial favorite, its rich wood grain a subtle foil to carefully chosen furnishings. In the room above right, the dark wood tone contrasts with a light-colored table and chair.

The subfloor should be made of plywood or planks that are at least ⅝ inch thick and in sound condition so staples will grab firmly. It should be reasonably smooth and free of squeaks—new strip flooring may eliminate some squeaks, but you can't count on that. A single layer of ¾-inch plywood over joists that are 16 inches apart will be strong enough. See pages 98–109 and 112–113 for preparing a floor surface. Installing flooring is a major project, so plan carefully, taking the following into account.

- Flooring boards should be stored for a week or more in the room where they

A SENSE OF DIRECTION
When installing over existing planks or strip flooring (often used in older homes to make the subfloor), it is important that the new flooring run in a different direction. If it does not, the new floor will almost certainly develop unsightly waves. Run the new flooring in a different direction (perhaps at a 45-degree angle) or install underlayment on top of the old strip flooring (see pages 112–113).

will be installed, to adjust to the ambient temperature and humidity.

- You will need to cut boards one at a time, as you reach the end of each row. It will likely take two days to cut and nail all the boards.

- Once all the boards are installed, it will take a week or so to sand and seal the floor. This typically involves three passes with a sanding machine, an application of stain (if you choose), and two or three coats of finish (see page 185). This process will produce dust that can work its way into adjoining rooms, followed by unpleasant odors. You may choose to hire a professional to speed up this stage.

- Mouldings can be installed after sanding if they will be stained the same color as the floor. Otherwise, wait to install them until the floor is completely finished.

- Rent a pneumatic flooring stapler, and buy plenty of staples—you can return the boxes you do not need.

prepare the room

Remove obstructions and the base shoe or the base moulding. Undercut the door casings (right) so you can slip the new flooring under them. Run a trowel over the floor, and remove or drive down any protruding fasteners that you locate. Walk over the floor to identify any squeaks, and drive screws to eliminate them.

apply roofing felt Roll 20-pound roofing felt (tar paper) onto the floor, and cut it carefully to fit. Spread it flat, so there are no waves or bubbles. Staple it at 12-inch intervals. A roofer's stapler (shown at right), which drives the fasteners as quickly as you can hammer, is easier to use than a standard stapler.

acclimatize the boards Consult with a Lowe's flooring expert and check the manufacturer's instructions to see how long the flooring should lie in the room prior to installation so it can become acclimatized. This is an important step. Installing the boards too early can result in shrinkage and gaps, or boards that swell and buckle. You may need to remove packaging so the flooring can breathe. If so, stack the boards carefully so they do not warp as they dry out.

LOWE'S QUICK TIP

You can use rosin paper (also called kraft paper or construction paper) but many installers say that tar paper is better at reducing squeaks.

LEVELING A FLOOR WITH SLEEPERS

In older homes, hardwood flooring is often installed atop "sleepers"—1-by boards laid flat on top of the subflooring, spaced about 12 inches apart. If your floor is uneven or out of level, sleepers can straighten it out. You'll need materials of several thicknesses, as well as a bundle or two of shims. Make sure that the strip flooring will be solidly supported at least every 10 inches or so. Use a carpenter's level to test that the sleepers are at the correct height, and drive screws to attach them firmly to the floor.

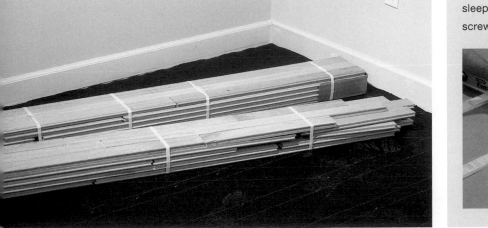

PROJECT CONTINUES ➡

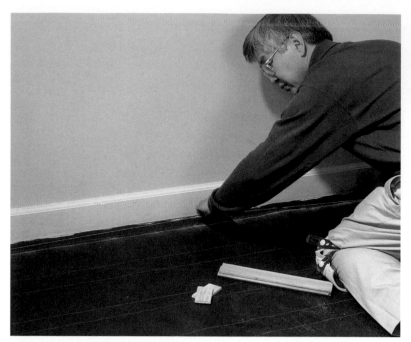

1 Start your layout on a long wall in the most visible part of the room. At each end of the wall, measure out the width of a board plus ¼ inch and make a mark. Snap a chalk line between the two marks. Measure to see that the line is a fairly consistent distance from the wall at all points and make sure that the first board will be close enough to the wall so the base moulding will cover it. Also measure from the opposite wall to the chalkline. If the opposite wall is not parallel to the line, the flooring will not be parallel to the wall when you get there with your installation. You may be able to adjust the chalk line slightly to improve the outcome or plan so that any non-parallel flooring will be covered by a sofa or other furniture.

2 Set up your cutting station to be comfortable and easy to use. A power miter box is ideal, but you can also cut using a circular saw and a square. For long boards, be sure to support both ends to avoid binding. For consistently smooth cuts, equip your power saw with a carbide-tipped blade with at least 20 teeth. Always let the saw come to full speed before cutting. Also, make sure the blade stops completely before removing the board.

SPACER

3 Choose very straight boards for the first row. Match the tongue and groove when installing the second and later boards. When you reach the end of the row, and only then, cut the last board; be sure it is ½ inch short of the end wall to allow for expansion of the flooring.

4 Fit the last board in place, carefully aligning it with the chalk line. Maintain the expansion gap by inserting a ½-inch-thick spacer. Check the joints for a tight fit. Drill pilot holes in the face of each board, every 12 inches or so. If possible, drill some holes into the joists below.

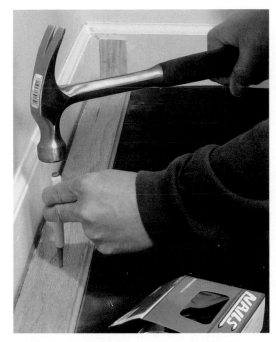

5 Working from one end of the row to the other, drive finish nails or hard trim nails into the holes. Use a nail set to drive the nail heads at least ¼ inch below the surface. (If a nail is not driven deep enough, it will rip the sandpaper when you sand the floor.)

6 Lay out the next seven or eight rows of boards in the order you want to install them—a process called "racking." Keep in mind the "1½-inch rule" (see Step 8) for staggering joints, and aim for an even distribution of various colors and grain shapes in the pieces you select.

7 When the tool will fit, start using a flooring stapler instead of face nailing. The manual flooring stapler (shown) drives a staple when you hit it with a mallet. The head of the staple should be slightly sunk into the wood. Adjust the tool if it is driving the staples too shallow or too deep.

8 As you continue to lay the flooring strips, make sure that no joint is closer than 1½ inches to a joint in either of the two adjoining rows. This time-tested rule makes for a professional appearance; closely spaced joints simply don't look right.

LOWE'S QUICK TIP

Early on, open all the bundles of flooring and check that the colors are fairly consistent from bundle to bundle. If not, mix the boards from several bundles as you rack.

PROJECT CONTINUES ➡

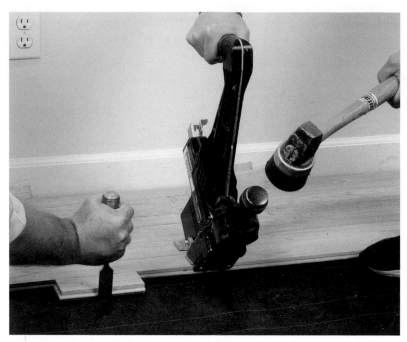

9 If a board is slightly warped, you can often straighten it out by whacking the stapler hard when you drive the staple; you may need to drive several staples very close to each other. For extra bending power, place a narrow scrap with a groove against the piece, drive a chisel into the subfloor next to it, and have a helper pry while you drive the staple. Straighten a board by driving several staples only if you are confident of success; if you fail to fix it, you will have to pry out a bunch of staples.

10 At a doorway or an outside corner, most if not all of the cuts will be covered with moulding, but the cut must be exact where it meets the jamb. Usually, it works best to measure for the rip cut (along the length of the board) using a tape measure, and for the crosscut (at a right angle to the board) by holding the piece in place and marking. Once the board is cut, fit it against its neighbor and tap it into position.

FLOORING AROUND A HEARTH

At a hearth or other decorative obstruction, a frame made of mitered flooring pieces looks better than flooring simply cut to fit. Whenever possible, position the frame pieces so that the flooring will fit onto a tongue or into a groove. In some cases, you may need to cut off the tongue of a frame board.

When you butt flooring pieces to the mitered frame, you'll probably need to rip-cut some of the pieces using a circular saw or a table saw. Wherever the frame and flooring pieces meet with no mitered joint, drill pilot holes and drive face nails to secure the boards.

ADDING A SPLINE

If you are installing continuous flooring in two adjoining rooms, or in a room and a hallway, you may come to a point where you need to turn the boards so that the tongues face in the opposite direction. Two boards will then meet groove to groove. To make the floor strong at this point, rip-cut a spline—a thin strip of wood that simulates a tongue. Once you are sure the spline will fit, squirt glue into one of the grooves and tap the spline in. Fit it into the adjacent groove and fasten.

11 In addition to small rip cuts to fit flooring against jambs (see Step 10), unless you are very lucky, you will also need to rip-cut the final row of strips. Be sure to allow for a ½-inch expansion space between the flooring and the wall. A table saw is the ideal tool for this, but a circular saw with a ripping fence is not difficult to use. (You may want to practice a few such rip cuts on scraps of flooring.) When all the boards are fastened in place, don't be surprised if some strips are slightly higher or lower than the pieces they abut. This will be smoothed out when the floor is sanded (see page 185).

12 When you get too close to the wall to use the stapler, drill holes and drive face nails as shown in Steps 4 and 5 on pages 174–175. Use a pry bar and scraps of wood of various sizes to pry the boards tight against their neighbors while you drill and drive.

13 Once the floor is sanded, stained, and finished, install the base shoe or the base moulding. Attach all mouldings with nails driven into the wall only—not into the flooring or the subflooring—to allow the flooring to expand and contract with changes of humidity.

installing wood baseboard

ONCE A NEW FLOOR IS INSTALLED, THE OLD BASEBOARD will likely look a bit nicked and worn by comparison. If a painted wood baseboard is free of dents, you can simply re-paint it, or you may wish to replace it. If the moulding has base shoe, you may choose to replace the shoe only, as shown on the facing page. To replace the entire base moulding, see pages 180–183. If you have installed tile or sheet flooring, you may choose to add ceramic base or vinyl base cove; see pages 134–135.

trim options

The purpose of baseboard and base shoe moulding is essentially to create interesting architectural shadows while covering the gap between flooring and the wall. Low-profile baseboard painted to match the wall (right) offers a contemporary look; deeper profile moulding (below) suits a more traditional style.

At Lowe's you can find four basic trim materials: plain softwood moulding, primed softwood moulding, foam moulding, and hardwood moulding (see pages 50–51). Primed trim saves time. Softwood is the easiest to work with.

For the bottom piece of base moulding, choose between quarter round, which has a pronounced profile, and the less obtrusive base shoe, which is a bit taller than it is wide. Ranch moulding has a sleek appearance that tends to recede visually; colonial base is the most common of several more elaborate mouldings that evoke a period style. For a more ornate appearance, choose three-part base or a fluted base that is used in conjunction with corner blocks. This last option is actually the easiest to install (page 183).

Measure each wall, and buy pieces of moulding of various sizes to minimize waste. To avoid having to splice moulding you may have to buy some very long pieces.

Make sure that your base moulding is tall enough to cover any paint lines or other imperfections in the wall. Also be sure that the base or base shoe is thick enough to cover the gap between the flooring and the wall.

installing base shoe

Base shoe can be stained to match the floor, or it can be stained or painted to match the base moulding. Apply the finish to the pieces before you cut and install them; then you'll need only touch up the finish after installation.

LOWE'S QUICK TIP

If your old base shoe is in good condition, remove it carefully (see page 104). Pull the nails from the back, and number each piece on the back so you can replace them in the correct order.

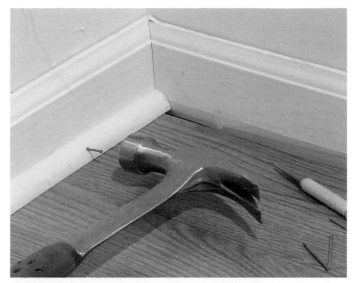

1 Start by installing a long piece of base shoe that runs from inside corner to inside corner. Measure the distance using a tape measure. Cut the base shoe about ⅛ inch longer than the measurement. Ideally, you will need to bend the piece slightly to get it to fit. If it is not easy to push the piece flush against the wall, cut it a bit shorter. Every 16 inches, or wherever there is a gap between the shoe and the base mould, drill a pilot hole and drive a 6-penny (6d) finish nail. Nails should be driven nearly horizontal to ensure that they do not contact the flooring. If the nails are not grabbing and pulling the shoe tight against the moulding, try using longer nails, or driving them at a different angle.

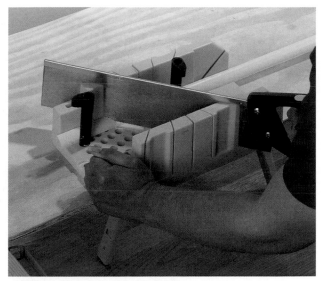

2 At an inside corner, you may be able to cut each piece at 45 degrees—especially if you can caulk and paint the joint. Test by cutting two scrap pieces at 45 degrees and seeing if the fit is tight enough. If it is not, install the first piece cut straight (as shown in Step 1) and make a coped cut (see Step 3) on the second piece. When possible, cut the coped end of the second piece first, then hold it in place to mark the other end for cutting. If you cannot do that (for instance, if the piece runs from inside corner to inside corner), measure the wall and cut the piece ⅛ inch too long. To begin making a coped cut, use a miter saw or power miter saw to cut the end at 45 degrees as shown—cutting more from the face of the board than the back.

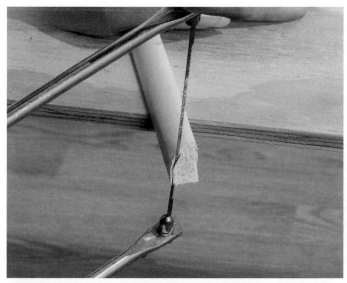

3 Lightly trace the cut line with a pencil, so you can see it easily. Cut along the line using a coping saw. Hold the saw blade at an angle so it slightly undercuts the board—it should cut more from the back of the board than from the front. Work carefully to stay precisely on the cut line at all points. Test the fit; you may need to modify the cut using a knife (see page 181).

4 At an outside corner, cut both pieces at 45 degrees. If the fit is not tight, you may need to undercut one or both pieces with a utility knife. If the corner is badly out of square, use the technique shown on page 182. Once all the pieces are installed, set the nails, fill the holes with putty, and touch up with stain and clear finish or with paint.

installing **baseboard**

Baseboard can be installed by itself, if it is thick enough. Most often, however, you will need to install base shoe to cover the expansion gap. Wherever possible, plan so that you make the complicated cut—a miter or a coped joint—first. Then hold the baseboard in place to measure for cutting the other end to length.

LOWE'S QUICK TIP

A power nailer, which works with a compressor, makes it fast and easy to install moulding, and creates fewer dents in the wood than hand-nailing. If you do not own one, it may be worth your while to rent one.

1 Base moulding is typically installed using pairs of nails, the lower one driven into the base plate (which runs all around the room) and the upper one driven into a stud. Usually, but certainly not always, studs are spaced 16 inches apart from each other. Using a stud finder, mark the locations of the studs with a light pencil line that will be visible after the moulding is in place.

2 Usually, it is best to start with a long piece that runs from inside corner to inside corner. Measure the wall using a tape measure, and cut the board about ⅛ inch longer. When cutting with either a hand miter saw or a power miter saw, be sure the board is held firmly by using a clamp while you cut. Always cut to the waste side of the cut line.

3 Bend the board into place. See that both ends are resting on the floor or are only slightly above the floor. If you cannot easily push it flush against the wall, remove it and cut it slightly shorter.

4 At each stud, drill a pilot hole and drive a 6-penny (6d) or 8-penny (8d) finish nail. Take care that you do not dent the wood with the last blow of the hammer; use a nail set to ensure against this.

cope-cutting an **inside** corner

If an inside corner were perfectly square, you could simply cut each piece of moulding at 45 degrees to produce a tight joint. Unfortunately, corners are seldom exactly square. If you are going to paint the moulding, you can cut the boards at 45 degrees and then caulk the resulting gaps. However, for a really tight, professional-looking joint, cope-cutting is the quickest and most reliable technique.

1 Cut the first piece straight and install it as shown in Step 3 on the facing page. Cut the second piece at a 45-degree angle as shown, so that you remove more from the face of the board than from the back. Once this cut has been made, the cut edge on the face of the baseboard will be in the shape of the moulding profile.

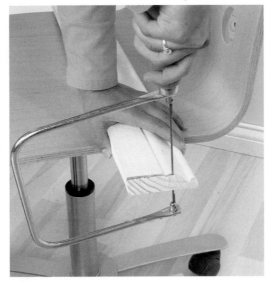

2 Use a pencil to emphasize the line cut on the face of the board. Cut along the line using a coping saw. Hold the saw blade at an angle so it slightly undercuts the board—that is, it should cut more from the back of the board than from the front. Work carefully, so you stay precisely on the cut line at all points.

3 Hold the coped cut against the already-installed board to test whether it fits tightly enough. Chances are, you will need to slightly enlarge the cut at one or two spots; mark these spots lightly with a pencil.

4 To modify a coped cut, you may need to trim the profile or trim away the back of the cut (which will not be visible when the board is installed). Cut the moulding with a sharp utility knife, or use a file.

LOWE'S QUICK TIP
Small gaps caused by cutting mistakes can sometimes be filled with wood putty or caulk colored the same as the board's stain. However, if the gap is so large that it will be an eyesore, remove the board and cut again.

mitering an **outside** corner

Before you follow the steps on this page, cut two scraps of base moulding, at least 16 inches long, at 45 degrees, and hold them together at the corner. If you are lucky, they will produce a tight joint, and you can simply cut the real pieces in the same way. Often, however, an outside corner is out of square, so you must take the time to produce cuts that are slightly more or less than 45 degrees.

1 Hold a scrap of base moulding against the wall on one side of the corner, and scribe a line on the floor that extends an inch or so past the corner. Hold the scrap against the other wall and scribe a line that intersects with the first line.

2 Hold the first board to be cut in place. Mark the top where it meets the corner of the wall, and mark the bottom where it meets the intersection of the two lines on the floor.

3 Turn the board over. Using a square, draw two lines on the back of the board: one that connects to the upper mark and one that connects to the lower mark (see Step 2). On the board's bottom edge, draw a line that connects the two lines. Use a T bevel to capture this angle. Set the miter saw to cut at this angle. (On a power miter saw you can simply adjust the angle of the blade. On a hand miter box, you may need to brace the board at a slight angle to the miter box, using shims.) Cut the board, and repeat the process for the other board.

THREE-PART BASE MOULDING

A pleasingly complex effect is achieved by using a moulding in three pieces. First install the baseboard, which is typically a straight-forward board. Install the base shoe and the cap using the mitering and coping techniques shown on this and the previous page.

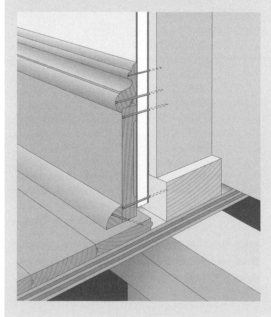

using **corner blocks**

Corner blocks not only add an ornamental touch to baseboard, they eliminate the need for miter and cope-cut joints, making it easier to install the baseboard. They're especially useful if you are inexperienced making precise miter cuts or if your walls are out of square. Purchase corner blocks for both inside and outside corners. You may need to cut down the corner blocks to make them compatible with the base moulding you have chosen.

Once the moulding is cut and fastened to the wall, filling and sanding will probably be the last task you will perform in the room you have floored. No doubt you are eager to get the job over with, but take the time to work carefully. Using a hammer and nail set, drive all the nail heads so they are $\frac{1}{8}$ to $\frac{1}{4}$ inch below the surface of the wood.

1 At each corner, hold a corner block firmly in place and drill two pilot holes. Drive 8-penny (8d) finish nails, and set their heads slightly below the surface of the wood. Measure from block to block to find the length of the moulding pieces.

2 Square-cut a scrap piece of moulding, at least 2 feet long. Hold the scrap against a block to see if a square cut will fit tightly. If not, use a straightedge to scribe a cut line. Cut the moulding a bit long, bend it into place, and attach with nails, as shown on page 180.

3 Use a putty knife or your finger to apply wood filler to each of the holes. Slightly overfill the holes.

4 Once the filler has dried (typically in less than a half hour), you can sand it flush with the surrounding wood and apply primer.

creating a striped floor

IF YOU WANT TO DECORATE A FLOOR, YOU CAN USE MANY of the faux techniques that are used on walls—stenciling, rag-rolling, trompe l'oeil, to name a few. Be sure to cover the floor with a durable finish that is compatible with the materials you used for decorating. With the stripe technique shown below, painted boards combine with the finished wood for a handsome, informal finish that is easy to apply.

LOWE'S QUICK TIP

If the paint bleeds under the tape and produces a ragged edge, lightly sand away the offending paint using a hand sander.

1 After sanding and thoroughly vacuuming the floor, lay out the design. Measure the width of three boards and mark that distance from the baseboard on the ends of the boards. Where the boards run parallel to the baseboard, simply count three boards out and make your mark.

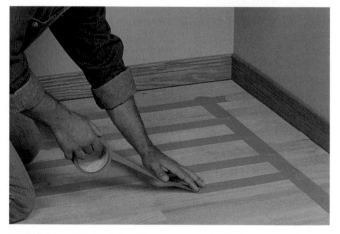

2 Using low-tack masking tape, mark off the outer edges of the border and the sets of boards to be painted. Press the tape down firmly along its entire length to ensure a good seal. Overlap the ends. To avoid mistakes, tape an X on each area to be left unpainted.

3 Use a roller to apply paint to the floorboards. To reduce the risk of bleeding under the tape, roll off excess paint on the roller pan before applying paint to the floor. Roll directly along the edges of the tape to ensure crisp painted edges. Let the paint dry to the touch, then immediately peel off the tape. (If you wait too long, the tape may lift paint along the edges.)

4 When the paint is thoroughly dry, apply clear finish to the entire floor (see page 205). Use a paintbrush to apply the finish around the edges of the room, and a lamb's-wool applicator for the remainder of the floor. Allow the finish to dry, then apply a second and perhaps a third coat.

finishing options

BARE WOOD IS VERY POROUS, SO ANY SPILLS OR RUBBED-IN DIRT COULD RESULT in stains that sink deep into the wood fibers. Therefore, once an unfinished hardwood floor is installed, waste no time sanding and finishing it.

sanding and finishing

For a first-rate final finish, you (or a professional floor finisher) should sand the floor three times, using progressively finer grits of sandpaper. The sanded floor should form a continuous, smooth surface with no board that is higher than an adjacent one.

choosing stains and finishes

The stain and finish you select largely determine the look of the floor, so choose carefully. To get an accurate impression of how the floor will look, apply both stain and finish to some scrap pieces of flooring, and set the pieces in the room. (A stained board can change color dramatically after the finish is applied, especially if you use oil-based polyurethane.) Check how the boards look both in daylight and by artificial light.

stain If you want to keep the floor light in color, you may choose to go right to the finish. However, even a light stain can enhance the beauty of wood grain. If you will be applying oil-based polyurethane, you may want to apply a light stain first to offset its yellowing effect. Use oil-based stain if you will apply an oil-based finish, and water-based stain if you will apply a water-based finish.

oil-based polyurethane Polyurethane adds plastic coating to the wood, providing a strong surface that won't flake off. Oil-based poly is the most durable; two coats should last for five years of normal use. It tends to turn yellow after a few years, lending an attractive appearance much like older hardwood floors. You can buy polyurethane in dull, satin, or high-gloss finishes. Be aware that oil-based poly is outlawed in some areas of the country for environmental reasons and therefore may not be available.

water-based polyurethane This is not as wear-resistant as oil-based poly, but it does not yellow and is more environmentally friendly. Like the oil-based version, it grips the wood firmly and will not flake off. Three coats of water-based poly will usually last three or four years, after which you should lightly sand the surface and apply another coat or two.

varnish This finish is less popular than polyurethane because it doesn't last as long and is more easily scratched. Varnish does not penetrate deeply into wood, so it must be applied carefully to prevent flaking. However, it produces a deep luster topped by a glossy finish, and it will darken in time—an effect that many people like. Both water-based and oil-based varnish are available. For extra protection, you can apply wax over a varnished floor.

alcohol-based finish Some professionals apply an alcohol-based floor finish that does not yellow and is fairly durable. It is generally not available to homeowners.

wax Floor wax must be reapplied once every year or so. On the upside, it imparts a low-gloss, mellow look and is easy to apply, making it easy to fix scratches.

LOWE'S QUICK TIP

No flooring job is perfect, so examine your floor closely after the second sanding and vacuuming. If you see a gap greater than 1/16 inch between boards, fill it with wood putty.

engineered flooring options

LOWE'S CARRIES A LARGE VARIETY OF WOOD OR WOOD-TONED ENGINEERED flooring products that are easy to install as well as to maintain. Unlike hardwood flooring, which is simply milled lumber, these products are assembled in a factory and are composed of several plies, or layers, that are tightly bonded together. This makes engineered flooring more stable—less likely to warp or shrink—than hardwood flooring. (For more on the color and design possibilities of these products, see pages 38–39.)

Other types of manufactured flooring include wood parquet, bamboo, cork, and laminate strip flooring (pages 39–43, 168–171, and 194–197). All are made by laminating or gluing together numerous pieces or plies, which gives them stability similar to that of engineered wood flooring.

LOWE'S QUICK TIP

Don't be put off by a high-gloss urethane finish on an engineered wood floor. Though the finish will remain durable, it will settle down to a semi-gloss or satin sheen after the floor has been walked on for a while.

features to look for

On a high-quality product, the top ply is made of hardwood that has been stained and covered with a hard finish. Usually, the top ply is about ¼ inch thick, so that it can be resanded once or twice if the floor develops scratches.

Today, almost all wood-veneer engineered flooring comes with a urethane finish that is guaranteed against wearing through or separating from the wood. High-end flooring comes with a 25-year guarantee; you can also buy flooring that is guaranteed for 15 or 10 years.

The hardwood veneer of engineered flooring (left and far right) gives it the warm tones of solid hardwood. The manufactured product is available in a variety of tones, finishes, and widths (above).

The most common products are either 3 or 5 inches wide, and come in random lengths. These can be either stapled or glued in place. Homeowners often find the wider strips are an attractive choice for a larger room.

Many of these products have a shallow groove where two strips meet. Because of the hard finish, this does not present cleaning problems, but you may prefer a floor with no grooves.

For an easy installation, consider engineered wood flooring that is designed to be "floated" rather than glued or stapled. This product is about 7 inches wide and comes in pieces all the same length. For extra stability, it has five (rather than the usual three) plies. There are no grooves where the pieces meet each other.

FINISHED SOLID HARDWOOD FLOORING

If you love the look of solid hardwood flooring but want to avoid the sanding and finishing, consider buying prefinished hardwood strips. These are ¾ inch thick and 2¼ inches wide, just like standard hardwood flooring, but have an attractive stain and a hard urethane finish. Because natural hardwood is more likely to shrink or swell than manufactured flooring, this product has a groove where the pieces meet each other.

trim pieces

While you're choosing the flooring, check to see that you can buy trim pieces, such as transition strips and base shoe, that have been stained and finished to match. If you don't see the trim or the finish you need on display, chances are good that a Lowe's flooring expert can order the items you need. Otherwise, you may need to buy hardwood trim and stain it to match; a Lowe's paint expert can help you choose the right stain.

stapling an engineered wood floor

IN MOST CASES, ENGINEERED FLOORING PLANKS THAT ARE 3 INCHES WIDE OR LESS should be stapled; wider planks should be either glued down (pages 191–193) or floated (pages 194–197). Check the flooring's packaging for installation requirements.

Stapling an engineered floor is much like applying a solid strip floor; see pages 172–177 for tips on laying out the job, and cutting pieces to fit. Engineered planks are easier to install than solid strips, because they are far less likely to warp.

preparing the subsurface

See pages 98–109 for instructions on preparing the floor and removing obstructions. The subsurface should be reasonably firm and free of squeaks. Remove any obstructions, as well as the base shoe or the baseboard. Undercut the door casing, using a jamb saw with a scrap of the new flooring as a guide, so the flooring can slip under the casing (see page 158).

For the firmest installation, run the flooring perpendicular or at a 45-degree angle to the floor joists, and drive long staples into the joists. If that is not possible, you can drive 1-inch staples into the subfloor, as long as it is made of plywood or planks that are in good condition and at least $\frac{5}{8}$ inch thick.

laying the floor

Scatter packages of the flooring in the room, and wait at least 3 days before you install them, so the planks can adjust to the ambient temperature and humidity.

Plan to leave a $\frac{1}{4}$-inch gap between the flooring and the wall (or the baseboard); it will be covered by baseboard (or base shoe). Drive exploratory nails or screws to locate the joists under the subfloor, and make marks on the walls to indicate joist centers.

LOWE'S QUICK TIP

If the subfloor may be subject to some moisture, staple down plastic sheeting before you install the roofing felt or rosin paper.

1 Cover the floor with 15-pound roofing felt (tar paper) or rosin paper (also called kraft paper). Roll and spread the paper neatly, so there are no bubbles or waves. Attach the paper with staples every 16 inches or so. Overlap the edges by about 4 inches. Snap chalklines between the joist marks, so you can drive staples into joists when you install the planks.

Install a test plank along a long, highly visible wall. At either end of the wall, measure out from the wall the width of a flooring plank, including its tongue, plus $\frac{1}{4}$ inch (or the gap recommended by the manufacturer), and make a mark.

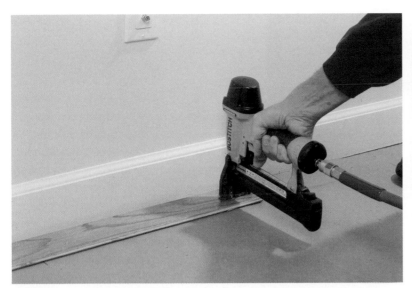

2 Snap a chalkline between the two marks. Measure from each end of this line to the opposite wall. If the measurements differ by more than ½ inch, the final piece on that wall will be visibly narrower at one end than the other. You may choose to "split the difference" and make the first row slightly out of parallel with its wall.

Align the first plank so that its tongue is directly over the chalkline. If the wall is wavy, you may need to trim the plank to maintain a gap of at least ¼ inch at all points; or you may choose to snap another line a bit farther out from the wall. Some staplers can be adjusted to shoot staples through the face of the plank; otherwise, drill pilot holes and face-nail and set 6-penny (6d) or 8-penny (8d) finish nails.

3 When you come to the end of a row, measure and cut a piece to fit, allowing for a ¼-inch gap between the board end and the wall. You will need to cut plenty of planks, so consider renting or buying a power miter saw. If you cut with a circular saw (shown), use a small square for a guide and cut the planks upside down, to prevent splintering.

4 Slip the end piece into place. Use shims or a pry bar to hold it tightly against its neighbor as you drill pilot holes and drive nails. Walls are easily damaged by pry bars, so always protect the wall with a scrap of wood before you use a pry bar.

5 Add the second row using a scrap of flooring to tap the planks together. It is normal for a plank to be slightly warped lengthwise; you may have to kneel on one end as you tap the other end into place. Then work your way down the plank to set the groove onto the tongue.

LOWE'S QUICK TIP

The staple's head should sink slightly below the wood surface. If it is not buried in the wood, the next piece will not be able to fit tightly; if it sinks more than ¼ inch or so, it will not hold the board securely. Adjust the nailer's air pressure until you get it just right.

PROJECT CONTINUES ➡

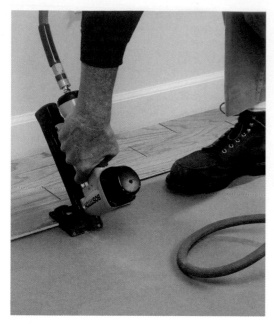

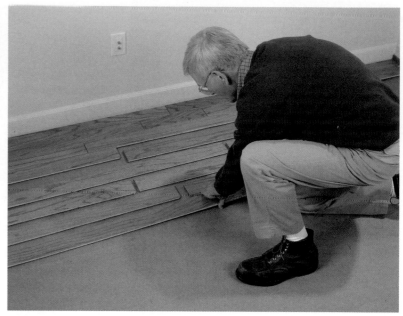

6 Once you are two or three rows away from the wall, you can stop face-nailing and adjust the stapler to fasten at an angle through the tongue of each plank. Drive staples into joists whenever possible.

7 To save time, "rack" three or four rows of planks before stapling and cutting them to fit. Lay them out in the order you will install them. Check joint spacing as you work. If planks are 3 inches wide, joints should be no closer than 2 inches to an adjoining joint—or a joint that is one board away. If planks are 5 inches wide, joints should be at least 3 inches apart.

8 Pieces in the last row will probably need to be rip-cut (cut to width). To measure, place spacers against the wall, lay a plank upside down and pressed against the spacers, and mark. If the wall is not wavy, you can simply adjust the rip guide of a table saw or a circular saw and cut all the pieces to the same width. If the wall waves, or if the planks are not parallel to the wall, you will need to measure and cut each piece individually.

9 You will probably need to face-nail the last two or three rows, because the stapler will not fit against the wall. Use shims and a spacer (shown) or a pry bar to press each plank firmly against its neighbor before driving nails. Set the nails and fill the holes with colored putty.

gluing down
engineered flooring

BECAUSE IT IS ALWAYS STRAIGHT AND UNIFORM, ENGINEERED flooring can be glued rather than nailed or stapled. Gluing can be done on any clean, firm substrate. However, the adhesive is so messy to work with, it is usually reserved for concrete, where nailing or stapling is not possible.

preparing the surface

If moisture is a slight problem, glue down sheets of pressure-treated plywood as the underlayment, then glue the flooring to the plywood (which is not thick enough for nails or staples). If the floor might actually get wet from time to time, install ceramic or stone tile rather than wood or laminate flooring.

Beware: a concrete floor that feels dry may actually be moist enough to ruin a wood floor. Perform a test during the most humid part of the year using duct tape to attach pieces of plastic sheeting to the floor in several places. Make sure the tape seals completely all around the plastic. Wait several days, and then remove the plastic. If the floor or the underside

of the plastic is wet, then the floor is too moist for a wood floor. For a more precise test, purchase a calcium chloride moisture tester and follow the manufacturer's instructions.

Examine the floor and repair any cracks, protrusions, or dips—see pages 114–115 for instructions on inspecting and patching a concrete floor.

If the floor is finished with paint, wax, or any other product, the adhesive will stick to the finish—not to the concrete. Unless the finish is strongly bonded to the concrete, it may be necessary to remove it before installing new flooring. Use paint stripper or a muriatic acid solution, then degloss the surface by sanding it or by cleaning and rinsing thoroughly.

1 Start at the most visible wall. At either end of it, measure out from the wall the width of a flooring plank, including its tongue, plus ¼ inch (or the gap recommended by the manufacturer), and make a mark. Snap a chalkline between the two marks. Place a straightedge—you can use the factory edge of a piece of plywood—along the line, and use shims (shown) or masonry screws to hold it firm, so you can press against it when installing the flooring.

LOWE'S QUICK TIP

Before you attach the straightedge, measure from each end of the chalkline to the opposite wall. If the measurements differ by more than ½ inch, the final piece on that wall will be visibly narrower at one end than the other. You may choose to "split the difference" and make the first row slightly out of parallel with its wall.

PROJECT CONTINUES ➡

LOWE'S QUICK TIP

Keep the work site, the flooring, and your clothing free of errant adhesive. Otherwise, you will have a cleaning headache after the floor is laid. If adhesive gets on your hands, wash them immediately.

2 Use the flooring adhesive and the notched trowel recommended by the manufacturer. Spread a line of adhesive wide enough for two or three planks, either pouring out dollops of adhesive, or scooping the adhesive out of the bucket using the trowel. To maintain a consistent thickness of application, keep the trowel at an angle of 45 degrees. Comb away any thick areas, which could ooze up through the planks.

3 Press the first piece into the adhesive and sandwich a spacer between the end of the plank and the wall to maintain an expansion gap of about ¼ inch. Then pull up the piece and examine its underside. If the adhesive does not cover at least 80 percent of the surface, spread the adhesive thicker. However, if the adhesive is so thick that it oozes out the sides of the plank, spread it thinner.

4 If the amount to be cut off from the last plank is more than 1 foot, save the piece to be the first plank of the second or another row. Use spacers to keep the end of the last plank ¼ inch or so from the wall.

To install the next row without creating a mess, hold the plank at a 45-degree angle to the floor, and press its groove slightly into the tongue of the preceding plank all along its edge. Then lay it down onto the adhesive and press it against the preceding plank until the seam is fairly tight.

5 For planks that are 3 inches wide, see that no joint is closer than 2 inches from an adjoining joint—or from a joint that is one board away. If the planks are 5 inches wide, see that the joints are no closer than 3 inches apart. Every few rows, use a plastic tapping tool or a scrap of the flooring to tap the pieces tightly together. Use a rag dampened with either water or mineral spirits (depending on the type of adhesive) to wipe up any spills or oozed-out adhesive.

6 To make sure that the end joints—which also attach via a tongue and groove—are tight, pry either end using a flat pry bar, with a scrap of wood to protect the wall.

7 Every three or four rows, check all the previous rows to make sure they have not spread apart. If they have, tap all the planks tight and use pieces of masking tape to hold the joints together.

8 You will likely need to rip-cut the last row. Make sure that the last row will be at least ¼ inch away from the wall. Firmly clamp the strip you are ripping. One method is to clamp the end of the strip farthest from where you begin your cut. Halfway through the cut, move the clamp to the opposite end of the plank.

9 After installing the last row, use a flat pry bar to tighten all the joints. Then tap in shims to hold the seams tight.

The following day, return to the opposite wall where you began the installation. Remove the straightedge and shims and glue in place strips of flooring to complete the job.

LOWE'S QUICK TIP
Some manufacturers recommend that you run a flooring roller (see page 163) over the flooring to ensure good adhesion. However, simply walking all over the floor does nearly the same job.

floating engineered or laminate flooring

THESE FLOORS ARE NOT ATTACHED TO THE SUBSTRATE. INSTEAD, THEY FLOAT above it on a sheet of foam underlayment. Flooring that floats must be extremely stable and resistant to warping. At Lowe's you will find two types of strip flooring that can be floated. Engineered flooring (with a veneer of actual hardwood) is typically installed by gluing together tongues and grooves. Laminate flooring (which has a hard surface that imitates the look of wood) simply snaps together for extreme ease of installation (see page 197). (Older types of laminate flooring needed to be glued, but better products are available now.)

In addition to the flooring, the manufacturer may offer an installation kit, which includes glue, a plastic tapping tool, and a pry bar. These are worth the modest cost.

preparing the room

See pages 98–109 for instructions on how to prepare the subfloor and the room. The subfloor must be reasonably strong, level, and free of squeaks, but it need not be rock solid. Remove all obstructions, undercut the casing moulding at doors, and remove either the base moulding or the base shoe.

mapping the layout

On a floating floor, it is important that all the planks be at least 2 inches wide; a narrower piece is likely to buckle. Measure the width of the room at several places—taking into account the ¼-inch expansion gap you need to leave between the flooring and the wall—then make some careful calculations. Divide the width of the room by the width of your planks. If the remainder is less than 2 inches, you will need to rip-cut the first piece.

For example, if the room is 120 inches wide and the planks are 7 inches wide, the room will hold 17 pieces, with 1 inch left over ($17 \times 7 = 119$). In that case, you should plan on using only 16 full-width

pieces, which will leave you with 8 inches of leftover space ($16 \times 7 = 112$). Rip-cut both the first and last pieces at 4 inches.

Install the first board at a long wall that is highly visible. At each end of the wall, measure out from the wall the width of the first plank plus ¼ inch, and make a mark. Working with a helper, snap a chalk line between the two marks. Measure to see that the line is a fairly consistent distance from the wall at all points. Make sure the first board will be close enough to the wall so the base moulding will cover the gap.

installing the flooring

These instructions show how to install a glue-together laminate floor. If you are installing a snap-together laminate floor, ignore the instructions for applying and wiping glue; see page 197 to see how the pieces join together.

Like other flooring types, engineered and laminate flooring should sit in the room for several days prior to installation, so it can adjust to the room's temperature and humidity.

1 Roll out the foam underlayment that is recommended for your flooring. Some manufacturers recommend that you overlap the seams of the underlayment, while others say you should not overlap. Follow your manufacturer's instructions. Staple the material firmly in place and mark your layout.

2 Install a starter strip that aligns with the layout chalkline. A strip of plywood works well, as long as you place the factory edge (or an edge that has been very carefully cut with a table saw) against the chalkline. Drive screws to hold the starter strip very firm; you will be tapping boards against it, so it is important that it not move.

3 Install the first row with the tongue facing out. Use spacers to keep the end of the first plank ¼ inch away from the wall. Glue the pieces together by applying a smooth bead of glue to the top side of the end tongues only. Press the pieces together to form a fairly tight seal; use the tapping tool if needed.

4 Measure for cutting the last piece in the row, taking into account the ¼-inch space you must have between the floor and the wall to allow for expansion. Cut the plank using a power miter saw, table saw, or circular saw (shown). Cutting a plank upside down ensures against splintering the top surface.

LOWE'S QUICK TIP

If you are installing over a concrete floor, test it for moisture (see page 191). The manufacturer of the flooring may recommend that you lay plastic sheeting over the concrete before you spread the underlayment. Both the plastic and the underlayment should be installed so they overlap the walls about 4 inches. It is easiest to trim the underlayment after you have installed the base moulding.

PROJECT CONTINUES ➡

5 Use a tapping tool (shown) or a pry bar to tighten each row. Slip one end over the end of the last board, and tap on the rear of the tool. Then insert a spacer and tap in a shim to hold the joints tight.

6 Rack a couple of rows. If the cutoff from the first row is at least 12 inches long, you can use it as the first piece of the second row, but you must start from the opposite end of the room. Apply glue and tap the rows into place.

LOWE'S QUICK TIP

As you continue to lay strips, make sure that no joint is closer than 1½ inches from an adjoining joint— or from a joint that is one board away. While closely spaced joints don't affect the integrity of the installation, they look unprofessional.

7 Install the next rows of planks. Work systematically: set spacers against the end wall, make sure that the joints are offset, and then apply the glue and press the planks together. Press the planks against each other to produce tight joints, using the tapping tool as needed.

8 Have several damp rags on hand, as well as a bucket of clean water, so you can quickly rinse the rags. Wipe up squeezed-up glue after installing each row of planks.

9 Every few rows, check the entire floor to make sure that no joints have separated. In most cases, you can tighten joints several rows away by firmly tapping. If a joint is widely separated, ask a helper to stand on one or both planks while you tap.

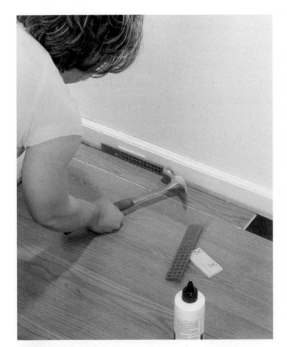

11 Install the last row and use spacers and shims to wedge it tight. Remove the starter strip and install the first row in the same way. Avoid walking on the floor for 8 hours or so before removing the spacers and shims. Now you can install baseboard (pages 178–183) and thresholds (pages 140–141).

LOWE'S QUICK TIP

When installing baseboard over a floating floor, never drive nails into the flooring. Drive them into the wall only. Install base shoe by driving nails into the baseboard only. That way, the floor will be able to move slightly as it expands and contracts with changes in humidity.

10 For the last row, if the wall is not wavy or out of parallel with the flooring, you can simply adjust the rip guide of a table saw or a circular saw and cut all the pieces to the same width. If the wall has waves, or if the planks are not parallel to the wall, measure the pieces individually. For a precise measurement, place the piece to be cut upside down and against the wall. Cut a scrap of wood to the width of the opening minus $3/8$ inch, and use it to scribe a cut line.

SNAP-TOGETHER LAMINATE FLOORING

Lay out and install a snap-together laminate floor in much the same way as you would a floating engineered floor. To attach a piece, hold it at an angle, slide its groove against the tongue of an installed board, make sure that it is tight all along its length, and push down. Double-check that the joint is tight before moving on to the next piece.

In an area that will get wet, such as a bathroom, it is recommended that you apply a bead of glue or silicone caulk to the top edge of the tongues, just as you would for an engineered floor.

combining wood with tile

WOOD GRAIN, WHETHER SIMPLY COATED WITH POLYURETHANE OR stained to a rich color, is nicely complemented by other flooring materials such as ceramic tile, stone tile, or even vinyl tile.

A tile section can function as a permanent area rug, both visually and practically. Ceramic or stone tiles are less likely to get scratched than a wood floor, so you may want to place them in an area that receives heavy foot traffic—an entry, for instance.

Incorporating a tile section into a hardwood floor requires no special skills, but you must plan and lay the floor out carefully. In most cases, it looks best if you use all full-sized tiles that are placed symmetrically in your room. Ceramic or stone tiles should be installed $\frac{1}{16}$ inch higher than the wood for ease of cleaning; vinyl or wood parquet tiles should be at exactly the same height.

Make sure that the subfloor is strong enough for the tiles you will install (see pages 100–101, 110–111). If you fear it is not up to the task, consider installing porcelain tiles, which are extra-strong and only $\frac{1}{4}$ inch thick, allowing you to beef up the subfloor a bit more.

To install each type of flooring, see the pertinent sections of the book for full instructions.

Abundant light in this living room puts a spotlight on a luxurious floor made from hardwood planks and cork tiles. This is just one example of how different types of flooring can be combined to make a stunning floor. The trick is installing each type of flooring correctly, starting with the underlayment.

installing a tile and hardwood
entryway

A strip of stone or ceramic tiles, two or three tiles wide, creates a handsome and practical feature for an entryway. This project uses tiles that are $\frac{3}{8}$ inch thick; the mortar is $\frac{1}{8}$ inch thick, for a total thickness of $\frac{1}{2}$ inch. Since the wood flooring is $\frac{3}{4}$ inch thick, $\frac{1}{4}$-inch concrete backerboard is installed under the tiles, to bring them to the height of the wood flooring.

install backerboard Prepare the floor for hardwood flooring; the subfloor should have at least $\frac{3}{4}$ inch of plywood, and it should feel solid. Lay out for a section of full-sized tiles that will be in the center of the room, or directly in front of the entry door. For appearance's sake, the flooring

LOWE'S QUICK TIP
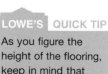

As you figure the height of the flooring, keep in mind that new or damaged hardwood flooring will be sanded, which removes $\frac{1}{16}$ to $\frac{1}{8}$ inch of thickness.

boards should be full width, so you will probably need to fudge with the size of the grout joints to make the layout work. In this example, the tile section is two 12-inch tiles wide, and the wood planks are 2¼ inches wide. The opening is 11 planks wide, for a total width of 24¾ inches. This means that the grout lines (one running down the middle and one on either side, where the tiles meet the wood) will each be ¼ inch wide.

Install the wood flooring, taking care that the opening be the correct size and have square corners. Sand and finish it if necessary. Cut and install ¼-inch concrete backerboard in the opening.

tile, caulk, and grout Set the tiles in thinset mortar so they are very slightly above the height of the wood floor. If necessary, back-butter the tiles to increase the height. Allow the mortar to harden, then apply caulk to the perimeter joints—wherever a tile abuts wood flooring. Allow a day for the caulk to fully harden, then apply grout to the joints.

possible **combinations**

To make sure that the two flooring materials will come out at the same height, place tiles against pieces of wood flooring on a flat surface and experiment until you get the height right. Keep in mind that thinset mortar will add at least ⅛ inch of height. You can build the mortar up to ⅜ inch of thickness if needed; doing so will actually increase the strength of the subflooring.

Here are some examples of ways you can combine different materials. Because flooring materials vary in thickness, you may need to modify your installation.

parquet and engineered flooring
Test to be sure that the tongues and grooves of the two materials are compatible. Typically, the engineered flooring is ⅜ inch thick and the parquet is ¼ inch thick. To build a slightly higher base for the parquet, spread the parquet adhesive with a square-notched trowel rather than a point-notched one. If you need more height, spread adhesive, lay down 20-pound roofing felt, then spread another coat of adhesive as shown and lay the parquet tiles.

engineered wood and floating ceramic tiles
Floating tiles (see pages 136–139) have a total thickness—including the tile and its integral backerboard—of ½ inch. To install floating tiles against ⅜-inch-thick engineered flooring, install three layers of 20-pound roofing felt under the engineered flooring. To install floating tiles that will abut ¾-inch-thick wood flooring, install ¼-inch backerboard.

vinyl tile and engineered flooring
Both commercial and good-quality surface-printed vinyl are ⅛ inch thick (cheap self-adhesive vinyl tiles are only 1/16 inch thick). To make the tile match the height of ⅜-inch engineered flooring, simply install ¼-inch plywood underlayment in the opening where the tiles will go.

ceramic or stone tile with hardwood
If the tiles you use are only ¼ inch thick, either use ⅜-inch backerboard or back-butter the tiles with additional thinset mortar to make them high enough.

PARQUET AND ENGINEERED FLOORING

ENGINEERED WOOD AND FLOATING CERAMIC TILES

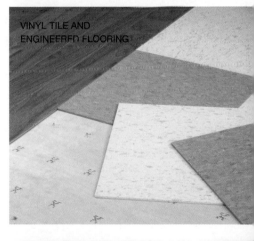

VINYL TILE AND ENGINEERED FLOORING

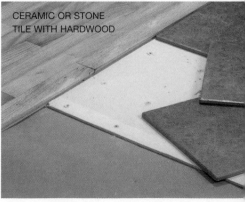

CERAMIC OR STONE TILE WITH HARDWOOD

repairs and maintenance

PROPERLY INSTALLED, MOST WALL TILE AND FLOORING will last for decades with minimal care. However, porous ceramic and stone tiles are vulnerable to staining and need to be sealed regularly. Wood and laminate flooring are not as durable and require more attention, but they, too, can last a lifetime if properly maintained.

A wood floor that receives only light foot traffic will typically need just surface refinishing every five years or so. Scratches from children's play and pets may require that you first sand the floor, then refinish.

When damage is localized—a single cracked ceramic tile, a gouge in wood flooring, or a cut in vinyl flooring—it makes sense to repair the damaged section only. Most problems with tiled areas arise not because of damage to the tiles themselves, but because the grout or caulk fails. Once a gap develops, moisture can penetrate behind the tiles where it may weaken the adhesive, damage the substrate, or even compromise the wall framing. A small amount of time spent maintaining grout can spare you major repairs down the road.

General damage may have a deeper cause. If large areas of tiles are coming loose, or if a wood floor has squeaks and gaps, the substrate may have been installed incorrectly. In such cases, the solution is usually to remove all of the flooring or wall tiles, and start over again, following the methods in this book.

Lowe's repair services can arrange for professional repair of many of the types of wall tile and flooring shown in this chapter. Once you request professional services, a Lowe's-approved contractor comes to your home, takes measurements, and presents an all-inclusive bid for the work and materials. There is a modest charge for this bid; this charge will be deducted from the repair cost if you decide to hire the contractor. The bid is binding: the contractor will not add extra costs unless you agree. Lowe's guarantees that the work will be done to your satisfaction and in a timely manner.

sanding and refinishing a hardwood floor

A DAMAGED OR DINGY HARDWOOD FLOOR CAN BE REJUVENATED BY SANDING AND REFINISHING. A medium-sized room can be sanded and stained in a day; allow several more days to apply coats of protective finish. This is a job often tackled by homeowners, but be aware that you will need to work carefully—especially when using a drum sander with heavy-grit paper—to ensure against gouging the floor.

when to sand

Make sure your floor is a valid candidate for a thoroughgoing sanding, which typically removes up to ⅛ inch of thickness from the flooring. If the floor has only surface damage, consider the alternatives to drum sanding (see box below).

LOWE'S QUICK TIP

Carefully examine the entire floor, and countersink all fastener heads at least ¼ inch below the surface of the board. A single nail head that is not adequately sunk can catch the sanding belt and quickly destroy it.

- Solid, ¾-inch-thick flooring can usually be sanded up to three times. In an older home, the floor may have already been sanded once or twice. To check for this, examine the top of the flooring in several places in the room. (It may be visible in a damaged section, or at the end of a board.) If you have less than ⅛ inch of thickness above the tongue (or the groove), there is not enough left to sand with a drum sander.

- High-quality engineered flooring can be sanded once, and no more. Consider using a random-vibrating sander (see box below) instead of a drum sander.

- If a portion of the floor is unfinished (that is, lacking in a glossy coat) and is water stained—or worse, stained by pet urine—then the stain is likely to be too deep to be sanded away. You can try sanding, but you may need to replace the flooring.

- If a hardwood floor was covered with underlayment and another flooring material, removing the underlayment will reveal a grid of nail or staple holes. These holes are likely to remain somewhat visible after the floor has been sanded and finished.

ALTERNATIVES TO DRUM SANDING

If the damage to your floor is not too severe, or if you do not need to remove a floor's stain, consider this pair of options.

To remove a floor's finish and perhaps some shallow scratches as well, rent a janitor-type **flooring buffer** (left). Buy some flooring screens, as well as a pad to hold them in place. Start with a heavy screen, such as 60-grit, and finish with a lighter 80- or 100-grit one. You may find it takes 15 minutes or so to get the hang of operating the buffer. Replace a screen once it stops removing material from the floor surface.

A **random-vibrating sander** (right) removes shallow scratches as well as the finish. It is safer to use than a drum sander, because there is no danger of gouging the floor. Begin with 60-grit paper, then use 80-grit, then 100-grit.

what you'll **need**

Rent a drum sander designed for finishing floors. A machine that runs on 220-volt current will work quickly, but you will need to be extra careful not to pit the floor and your home will have to have a 220-volt receptacle. (An electric stove and older window air conditioners require such a receptacle.)

A sander that runs on standard 120-volt current is slower—and safer. Buy drum sanding belts of three grits—typically, 40, 60, and 80 (or 100).

You'll also need an edge sander to get near the wall, and a pull-type paint scraper for tight spots and corners. It's important to repeatedly clean up the dust, so have a shop vacuum on hand. To apply the stain and finish, use a lamb's-wool applicator (a paintbrush is also handy for hard-to-reach areas). A pole sander equipped with 100-grit sandpaper speeds the job of sanding the finish between coats.

EDGE SANDER

DRUM SANDER

PAINT SCRAPER

SHOP VACUUM

LAMB'S-WOOL APPLICATOR

POLE SANDER

1 Make any necessary repairs to the floor. (If some boards are damaged and need to be replaced, see pages 206–207 for how to patch them.) To silence squeaky boards, drill pilot holes and drive trimhead screws or nails. Fill holes with wood putty that is either stainable or close to the desired finish color of the floor.

2 Remove the base shoe or, if absolutely necessary, the baseboard. Sanding can create an immense quantity of fine dust that can work its way through even small openings. Open a window and point a fan out, to expel the dust and make the air breathable. Seal doors using masking tape and plastic.

PROJECT CONTINUES ➡

3 Ask at the rental store for detailed instructions on the use of the drum sander. To load a drum sander with a sanding belt, unplug the machine and tip it up so you can get at the underside. Loosen one or two mounting nuts, then slip the sanding belt onto the rollers, and tighten the nut(s). For serious sanding, start with very coarse paper such as 36-, or even 20-grit. Begin sanding in an inconspicuous place—where a sofa will cover the floor, for example.

4 Tip the sander up so the sanding belt is off the floor, and turn the sander on. Slowly lower the belt onto the floor and allow the machine to pull forward; do not allow the sander to stay in one place for even a second or the belt will dig into the floor. Depending on the type of machine you rent, you may need to work the sander both forward and back. Overlap your passes by several inches. When the sander no longer removes material effectively, change sanding belts.

LOWE'S QUICK TIP

Some professionals start by sanding at a 45-degree angle, but sanding along the grain is a safer method. However, if you find that the machine is not removing enough material, you may want to try angle-sanding—but for the first sanding only. For the second and third sandings, sand in the direction of the grain.

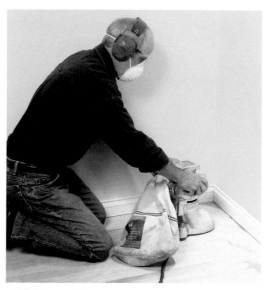

5 Vacuum the floor thoroughly after doing each sanding. After vacuuming, examine the floor for any fastener heads that may have become exposed. Countersink them to prevent damaging a sanding belt. Resist the temptation to skip one of the sandings. If you omit the medium- or fine-grit sanding, the floor will probably show visible sanding marks. Sand the surface a second time using a medium-grit paper.

6 Use an edge sander to reach most of the areas not covered by the drum sander. Wear a face mask and ear protectors when using an edge sander; this tool creates a lot of dust and is very noisy. Equip the sander with 60-grit sanding disks for the first sanding. It will take a few minutes to get the knack of keeping the machine flat and steady as you work—it can run away from you if you aren't careful.

7 Where the edger cannot reach, use a pull-type paint scraper equipped with a very sharp blade. Apply strong downward pressure as you pull the scraper toward you; it helps to push down on the knob with the heel of your hand. Whenever possible, scrape with the grain, not across it. When you must go against the grain, bear down less to avoid splintering the wood. Change the blade (or rotate the blade if you have a four-sided blade) as soon as you find that the going gets tough.

8 After the second sanding, vacuum the whole floor thoroughly. Fill any holes with wood putty, removing as much excess putty as possible with the blade. Choose putty that is stainable and close to the desired finish color of the floor or, if you won't apply stain, close to the color of the raw wood. When the putty is dry, sand the floor a final time using 80- or 100-grit paper. At corners where you used the scraper, smooth the floor using a hand sander.

9 The floor must be dust-free. Vacuum thoroughly, wait a bit, and vacuum again. Run your hand over the surface; if you pick up dust, vacuum again. If you choose to apply stain, mix it thoroughly. Apply with a paintbrush or applicator (shown) to an area of about 10 square feet. Wipe away any excess with a rag. Work quickly and systematically, so that you never apply stain abutting an area where stain has dried.

10 After the stain has dried, apply two or three coats of polyurethane finish. (See page 185 for the various products to choose from.) Apply the finish carefully, using smooth strokes, to avoid creating bubbles. A lamb's-wool applicator is the best tool for this job. Allow the finish to dry, then sand lightly using 220-grit sandpaper. (A pole sander makes the job easier.) Vacuum thoroughly. Apply one or two additional coats of finish.

repairing
tongue-and-groove flooring

TOO OFTEN, A REPAIR TO DAMAGED TONGUE-AND-GROOVE FLOORING RESULTS in a rectangular patch that stands out like a sore thumb because its joints are not staggered as all the others are. A better approach is to remove boards or portions of boards so that their ends are staggered in a way that blends in with the surrounding floor (see Step 5 on the facing page). However, because the pieces interlock, removing and patching a tongue-and-groove floor in this way is a time-consuming task that requires some skill.

preparing for the repair

Buy replacement boards that match the existing flooring in size and color. These pages show how to repair a floor made of ¾-inch-thick solid oak planking, but essentially the same techniques can be used to repair engineered wood flooring. On a solid hardwood floor, strip the finish off a piece of the removed flooring to determine what sort of wood to buy.

On a solid hardwood floor, staining and finishing may require more work and time than the actual repair. You can try to finish the new boards before installing them, but it is difficult to achieve an exact match. It may be necessary to sand and refinish the entire floor (see pages 202–205).

To repair squeaks, or to prepare the floor for installation of a new type of flooring on top, see pages 98–101. If you need to replace more than one board, plan the complete patch so that you will end up with staggered joints. You may choose to remove full-length boards only. If a damaged board is very long, however, you may choose to replace only a portion of it.

1 Use a square and a knife to mark the cut line; this will prevent splintering when you cut the board. If you are skilled with a circular saw, make a plunge cut, taking care not to cut into the adjacent boards. This cut will not be very deep. You'll need to complete the cut using a hammer and a sharp chisel. If you are not confident making plunge cuts, make the cut with a hammer and chisel. Hold the chisel with the bevel facing the area to be removed.

2 Bore a series of ⅜- or ½-inch holes across the width of the board in two places near the center of the damaged plank, spaced 4 to 6 inches apart. Be careful to avoid adjacent flooring. These rows of holes will enable you to remove a section from the middle of the board.

3 Split the area between the holes and pry out the pieces. With a hammer and chisel, slide both end pieces toward the middle to disengage the tongues and grooves on the ends. Split and remove the end pieces with the chisel.

4 Cut replacement boards. Use a scrap of flooring to protect the replacement board's tongue or groove as you tap it into place. Drill pilot holes and then drive screws or nails at an angle through the tongue to fasten to the subfloor.

5 Many times, you will need to cut off the end tongue of a replacement board. For the last replacement board, you will likely also need to remove the lower lip on the grooved side. You can chisel this lower lip off as shown, or cut it with a table saw or a circular saw.

6 Tap the last piece in place. Drill pilot holes and drive nails or trimhead screws through the face of the board. Set the fastener heads and fill them with putty. Use a power sander or a hand sander to bring the patch even with the level of the surrounding floor.

ALTERNATIVE METHOD

If only a single piece of flooring is damaged, here is an easy way to remove it. Using a circular saw, make two lengthwise plunge cuts in the middle of the damaged board, cutting from one end of the board to the other. (Be careful not to cut into adjacent boards.) Chisel down far enough to release each end. Pry out the central cut-out section using the chisel. Now you can carefully pry out the grooved side and the tongue side.

caring for flooring and tile surfaces

ONCE YOU HAVE EXPENDED THE TIME, EFFORT, AND MONEY TO INSTALL A NEW floor, don't neglect the simple steps required to keep it in top shape. Wood, tile, and stone have different maintenance requirements. Lowe's stocks a good selection of products that will keep all of your floors and tile surfaces gleaming and well protected.

protecting
surfaces

In most cases, applying a protective finish once or twice a year will keep your floors looking new and make cleaning a snap.

■ Glazed ceramic tile usually has a hard surface that requires no protective finish. However, grout should be sealed regularly using a grout sealer.

■ Unglazed ceramic tile, as well as stone tile, should be sealed regularly with a masonry or tile sealer. Even shiny stone tile can be surprisingly easy to stain.

■ Surface-printed vinyl tiles and sheet flooring have a "no wax" surface that will wear out in time. When the floor no longer shines after you clean it, apply a product designed to rejuvenate no-wax flooring.

■ Vinyl tile should be kept covered with two or more coats of floor wax or acrylic floor sealer.

■ Wood floors without a factory-applied finish require serious protection. Apply at least two coats of oil-based polyurethane or three coats of water-based polyurethane. Alternatively, you can use paste wax, which produces a warmer look. However, you will need to re-apply the wax regularly, especially in high-traffic areas. Cleaning products that contain wax to "shine as you clean" are mostly cosmetic; they do not add significant protection. Instead of using such a product, once a year or so, when the wax starts to yellow, strip the floor and apply a new coat.

■ Prefinished wood floors have a surface that can last a long time. However, the joints between strips or parquet tiles may not be tight enough to seal out moisture, so it is a good idea to apply a coat of polyurethane as recommended by the manufacturer.

cleaning

Most of the time, simple cleaning is all that's needed to maintain a floor adequately. Regularly vacuuming or sweeping not only keeps it clean but also removes lingering grit that when walked on can permanently scratch the floor. The brush attachment on a vacuum can scratch or dull the floor. Use a vacuum without a brush attachment, or raise the brush up.

Whenever possible, avoid using a lot of water, especially when cleaning a wood or porous tile floor. Instead, use a dampened mop or cloth. If you do need to wet these surfaces, wipe them dry quickly.

At Lowe's you will find standard household cleaners and also products used by cleaning professionals. Most households should have the following on hand.

- An absorber, in powder form, is good to have in case of emergencies. Sprinkle it onto spilled paint, oil, solvent, or alcohol to quickly soak up the liquid.

- Professional floor buffing liquid, available in a spray bottle, quickly removes tough surface grime such as heel marks and leaves a glossy finish.

- One-step clean-and-shine liquid quickly restores the glow to a dulled no-wax vinyl floor.

- A dust-mop treatment quickly rejuvenates a dull wood floor. After cleaning the floor, spray it onto the floor or the dust mop and wipe.

- Use a wood-floor cleaner made to clean the type of finish you have. Some products are designed specifically to clean and polish polyurethane finishes. Oil-based soaps are also a good choice.

stain removal

If grout or porous tiles are stained, first try scrubbing with a standard cleaning product; proceed to harsher methods only if that does not work. Apply the recommended product, then scrub with a bristle brush or a fiberglass mesh pad. Be sure to rinse the area afterwards; cleaner residue can cause damage if left in place.

To remove oil-based stains, paint, or tar, first try mineral spirits. If that doesn't work, use paint remover, taking care to rinse it with mineral spirits immediately. For dried latex paint, use a product made specifically to remove latex paint.

For white mineral deposits or reddish rust stains, use a product that's designed to remove either lime or rust.

In some cases, soaked-in ink, food stains, or drink stains (including coffee) can be cleaned using either hydrogen peroxide or laundry bleach.

If you have a stubborn stain in a small area, try making a poultice. Mix dry ingredients (such as laundry detergent) with just enough water to make a paste. Scrub the area with the paste, and cover it with a damp cloth for a day or two, then rinse away the paste with clean water.

acid cleaning

As a last resort, clean badly stained tiles or concrete using muriatic acid. Take care: muriatic acid will not burn you severely, but it can damage clothing and cause serious discomfort if it gets on your skin. Also, the fumes can make you sick. Work in a well-ventilated area, and wear long clothing and heavy-duty rubber gloves. Wear knee pads to keep your knees dry. If you do spill acid on your skin, rinse repeatedly with clean water.

Clean the surface, and rinse thoroughly. Wet the surface lightly—just so it is damp but without any puddles. Mix a solution of 10 parts water to one part muriatic acid. Always add acid to water; never add water to acid. Carefully pour or wipe the acid solution onto the surface and gently scrub it with a brush. A light bubbling indicates that the acid is working. Once the bubbling has stopped, rinse the surface thoroughly.

If this does not do the trick, follow the same procedure using a progressively stronger solution—five or even three parts water to one part acid.

LOWE'S QUICK TIP

If grout is not rinsed completely from porous tiles during installation, a stubborn haze will result. To remove the haze, first try scrubbing with household cleaner, then with full-strength white vinegar, which is actually a weak acid. If that doesn't do the trick, perform an acid cleaning as described at left.

replacing tiles

IF MORE THAN ONE OR TWO CERAMIC OR STONE TILES ARE BROKEN, LOOK FOR an underlying problem. Jump on a floor, or push on a wall with the heel of your hand. If you feel any flex, the substrate needs to be shored up; see pages 98–101 for suggestions. Should tiles come loose, remove them and check the substrate for damage. If you find damage in the floor plywood or wall substrate, remove as many tiles as necessary to repair the subsurface and, if necessary, the framing. Install a patch of new cement backerboard or underlayment before reinstalling the tiles.

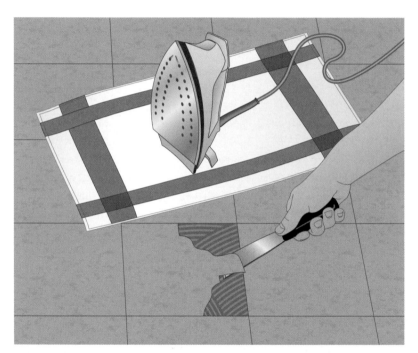

vinyl tile

If you cannot find an exact replacement for a damaged resilient tile, remove a tile from under the refrigerator or some other inconspicuous place.

If the damaged tile has started to curl up, or if there is a crack in it, use a putty knife to pry up the tile. If there is no easy point of entry, or the tile is difficult to remove, heat it with a clothes iron to soften the mastic, keeping a cloth between the iron and the tile to avoid dirtying the face of the iron. Keep the iron moving, and stop if you smell burning.

Scrape the area absolutely clean, then vacuum away all dust; even a small particle will show through most resilient tiles. Test to make sure the new tile will fit. Apply mastic to the floor, allow it to dry, and set the tile. Use a kitchen rolling pin to press the tile firmly into the mastic.

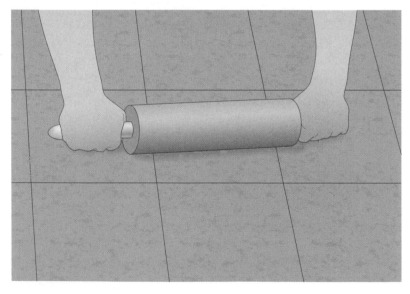

PAINTING TILE

If you find it will be difficult to replace a damaged wall tile, consider painting it. Take a tile to a paint dealer, who should be able to produce oil-based gloss paint that nearly matches the color. Dull the tile's finish by rubbing it with sandpaper, then paint the tile with alcohol-based primer (also known as white shellac), which bonds firmly with glossy surfaces. Then apply two coats of paint. The resulting surface will stand up to cleaning and scrubbing as long as you do not use an abrasive cleaner.

ceramic or stone floor tile

Removing and replacing a ceramic or stone tile is not usually difficult, but finding replacement tile and grout to match can be time-consuming. One manufacturer's teal-colored tile will be subtly different from that of another. The difference will be even more pronounced once the tile has been installed. Even "white" tiles come in many different hues.

If the manufacturer's name is printed on the back of the damaged tile, you can conduct most of your search by telephoning suppliers. If not, you'll have to drive to tile dealers with the old tile in hand to check for one that matches.

Grout can be even more difficult to match. Even if you get the correct brand and color, chances are your existing grout has slightly darkened after years of use. Clean the old grout using grout cleaner. Chip off a piece of the cleaned grout and take it to a tile dealer. Look for a grout sample that comes closest to matching the chip.

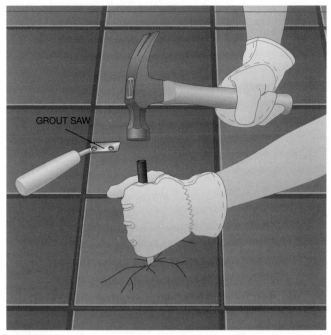

1 All around the damaged tile, scrape out the grout using a grout saw. With a hammer and cold chisel, strike the center of the tile until it cracks. Pry out the tile shards.

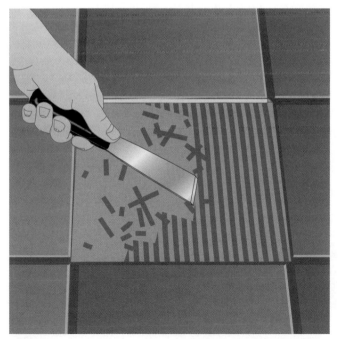

2 Use a putty knife or margin trowel to pry away the mortar. Scrape out all the remaining remnants of mortar. Use the putty knife and perhaps a hammer to gently chip remaining grout from around the area. Vacuum away the debris, and clean the area thoroughly with a damp cloth.

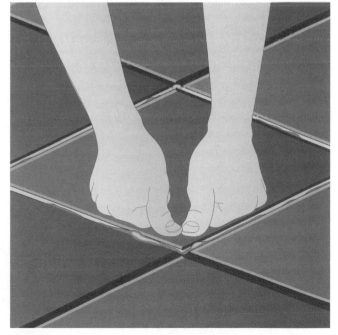

3 Back-butter the tile and press it into place. Check that it is level with the surrounding tiles, and wipe away any mortar that oozes out along the sides. Make sure all the grout lines are the same width. Allow the mortar to set overnight, then grout around the new tile.

wood parquet tiles

LOWE'S QUICK TIP
Parquet tiles may change in color over the years. To find a correct replacement, match a tile that has been hidden under the refrigerator or a cabinet.

If part of a parquet tile is damaged, it's usually easier to replace the whole tile, rather than one or two of the component strips. See pages 168–171 for instructions on installing wood parquet tiles.

Set the blade of a circular saw to cut just through the thickness of the parquet tile. Make several cuts across the tile; take care not to cut an adjacent tile. Now you can pry the tile out piece by piece. Scrape away all the adhesive from the floor.

Before installing a replacement tile, you must cut away the bottom portion of its groove on two sides, as well as one of the tongues. Set the circular saw for a very shallow cut, and remove the sections with the tile upside down.

Lay the new tile in place without adhesive to test that it will fit. Apply parquet tile adhesive to the floor using a notched trowel, or use a caulking gun to squirt squiggles of construction adhesive rated for use on floors. Slip the tile into place, press down until its top is flush with the adjacent tiles, and wipe away any excess adhesive that oozes out. Place a heavy weight on the tile and leave it there for a day or so.

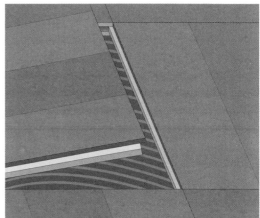

wall tile

If a wall tile was installed using organic mastic, you probably can remove the entire tile. The tile may simply come loose from the mastic, or the mastic and part of the wall may come along with it. If the paper covering of drywall or greenboard tears off, the wall will be weakened; replace the substrate if a large area of paper is missing.

Use a grout saw to remove the grout all around the tile. Keep sawing until you have reached the underlying wall. Insert a putty knife or scraper behind the tile, position a small piece of wood on the adjacent tile to protect it, and pry the damaged tile out.

If it does not come out whole, break it and then remove the shards.

Back-butter the replacement tile, press it into place, and wipe away the excess mastic. To make sure the tile does not slide down while the mastic is setting, insert nails as spacers along the bottom and secure the tile in position with pieces of masking tape.

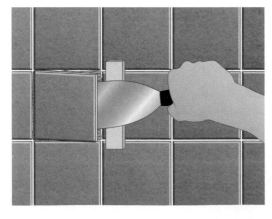

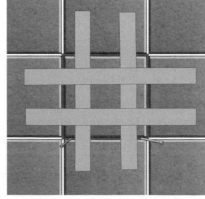

repairing grout

OFTEN A TILED SURFACE THAT LOOKS OLD AND DINGY CAN BE MADE ATTRACTIVE and new-looking by refurbishing the grout. If there are only a few holes, chances are the grout is strong but the installer missed a few spots, so patching makes sense. If grout is coming loose generally, it probably is not latex-reinforced; the grout should be removed and the area regrouted. If the grout is stained in spots or is a dingy color, try cleaning it. If you see even a small hole in the grout, patch it before moisture has a chance to work its way behind the tiles. Mix a small batch of latex-reinforced grout (use sanded grout for grout lines ⅛ inch or wider, and unsanded grout for narrower grout lines). Press it in with your finger. Wipe away the excess, allow it to dry, and clean with a wet sponge.

regrouting

If grout is recessed below the surface of the tiles, applying a thin coat of grout on top is risky; there's a good chance that the new grout will flake off eventually. It's safer to remove all the grout with a grout saw before regrouting.

Removing grout from a wall or floor is painstaking work, but well worth the effort. Saw with slow, deliberate strokes to avoid damaging any tiles. Apply only moderate pressure; let the grout saw do most of the work. If the going starts to get slow, the saw may have become dull. Buy another one.

Vacuum away all dust, and wipe the area with a wet sponge. For complete instructions on applying new grout to floors, see pages 132–133; for walls, see pages 86–87.

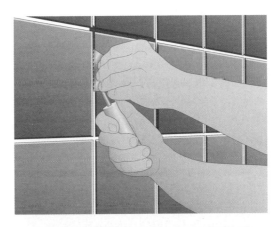

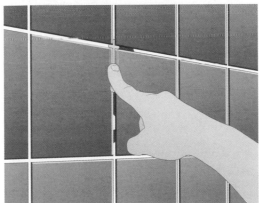

CLEANING GROUT

A good grout cleaning can dramatically improve the appearance of a tiled surface. If your tile is dull and your grout is dingy, first try cleaning it. Use a special tile and grout cleaner, available at Lowe's.

LOWE'S QUICK TIP

If you need to remove a large area of grout, consider buying a power tool attachment made for the purpose. Some can be attached to a drill, while others attach to a small rotary power tool.

re-caulking

MANY BATHROOM TILE INSTALLATIONS ARE MARRED BY A POOR CAULKING JOB, or by caulking that is stained or peeling. Applying a clean-looking bead of caulk that sticks firmly in place is not easy. Practice on scrap pieces of tile or in an inconspicuous location before you attempt the real thing.

choosing caulk

Don't be tempted to scrimp when buying caulk. Inexpensive latex or a latex/silicone type will be difficult to keep clean. And although silicone caulk is durable and easy to clean, it has a tendency to come loose if the surface is not perfectly clean and dry when you apply it, or if it gets repeatedly scrubbed. High-quality "tub and tile" caulk may be the best choice; it adheres well, and is scrubbable.

removing old caulk

It is imperative that you remove all the old caulk before re-caulking. Use a scraping tool that holds a straight razor blade. First scrape down the surface of the tiles near the tub, then scrape along the bathtub rim.

Next, scrub with an abrasive pad. The tile and the tub should feel smooth.

Some varieties of caulk can be softened with heat, greatly easing the work of removal. Aim a heat gun or hair dryer set on high at the caulk until you see it start to change shape, then scrape it away.

the tape method

You can apply caulk using a wadded rag, as shown on page 78. Or try this method, for a very neat appearance.

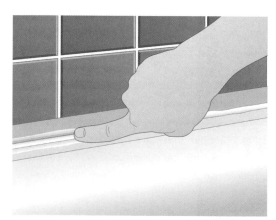

1 Apply a piece of masking tape along either side of the joint, taking care that the two pieces are straight and parallel. Apply caulk to the joint, then smooth the caulk with your finger.

2 Before the caulk has a chance to dry, pry up one end of a piece of tape and pull it away, taking care not to smear caulk as you do so. Do the same for the other piece of tape.

laminate floor repair

LAMINATE FLOORING IS NOT EASILY SCRATCHED, BUT ONCE SCRATCHES DEVELOP, you cannot completely erase them. To prevent scratches, keep the floor well vacuumed and place rugs in heavy-traffic areas.

patching a puncture

Small areas of damage can be filled with patching putty. If possible, bring a scrap of flooring to Lowe's so you can choose the right color putty. Use a utility knife and chisel to cut the hole at least ¼ inch deep and square up its edges. Squeeze putty into the hole, then use a putty knife to force it into the hole and to scrape the surface (right). Wait for an hour or so, then wipe the area with a damp cloth.

replacing a strip

Laminate strips are very long, so you will likely want to replace only part of a strip.

Because of the tight-fitting tongue and groove on a piece of laminate, you need to follow the method shown in the steps below to remove a damaged section and replace it with new laminate.

1 Mark the section you want to remove, then use a circular saw to cut out a portion from the middle that is about 1 inch away from all four edges. Pry this middle piece out. Cut the end lines with a circular saw, and complete the cuts with a sharp chisel. Make four short angled cuts running from the cutout area to each of the corners; complete the cuts using a chisel. First, pry out the end scraps, then remove the tongued strip and the grooved strip.

2 Cut a new piece of laminate flooring to fit snugly into the cut-out area. Turn the piece upside down and use a circular saw or a table saw to cut off the lip below the groove. Test that the patch will fit, then remove it. Apply glue to the top of the patch's tongue, as well as to the top of the tongue that is exposed in the floor. Also apply glue to the ends of the opening in the floor. Slip the patch into place and weight it down for a day before walking on it.

LOWE'S QUICK TIP

Because laminate flooring has a slippery surface, take extra care when cutting with a circular saw to make sure the saw doesn't skate away and damage an adjacent strip.

carpet maintenance

ALL FLOORING PRODUCTS REQUIRE CLEANING AND MAINTENANCE, BUT CARPET calls for a special vigilance to retain its fluffed-up and clean appeal. Though most good-quality carpeting is stain-resistant—meaning it has been treated with chemicals to repel soil and liquids—carpet fibers naturally collect dust, dirt, and other particles that over time cause matting and general deterioration.

- suction that is strong enough to reach the carpet's backing.

- a filtration bag that will effectively contain dirt so that it won't re-circulate in the house.

spot cleaning

The second line of defense is readiness for the inevitable spots and spills—a quick reaction will best remove the offending substance. Lowe's carries a spray-on product that adds an extra layer of protection to keep stains from soaking through to the bottom of the carpet. There are also a variety of spray-on spot removers that contain detergent and solvent to remove both oil- and water-based stains, as well as pet stains, blood, oil, lipstick, grease, tar, and other offenders. Lowe's also carries a kit that uses dry particles (not steam or shampoo) to remove stains. The particles are activated with misting and brushing, and then removed with a vacuum.

vacuuming

The first line of defense is regular vacuuming—it's an easy way to extend the life of carpet. Lowe's has a good selection of vacuum cleaners. Look for one with:

- a beater bar with adjustable rotating brushes to loosen the dirt. (Electric brooms and canister models don't have a beater bar.)

steam extraction

For heavy-duty cleaning, steam extraction is recommended over carpet shampoo, which leaves a residue. Steam extractors loosen dirt by first applying a high-pressure solution of hot water and detergent, then extracting (suctioning) it. Confirm whether the steamer is recommended for the type of carpeting you have. For instance, some commercial models are recommended for use with low-level loop and commercial glue-down carpet.

Lowe's carries steam extractors for rental or for purchase. The lighter-weight models for purchase are effective for maintaining heavy traffic areas. For a thorough job of cleaning an expanse of carpeting—which should be done once per year or every other year—it's a good idea to rent a commercial machine or hire a professional cleaner.

There are a few pitfalls to avoid with steam extractors.

■ Don't over-wet the carpet lest the backing or seams separate.

■ Let the carpet dry completely before walking on it, usually at least 12 hours.

■ Keep the house well ventilated so that odor from the cleaning solution doesn't get trapped indoors.

replacing damaged carpet

If a section of carpet needs to be replaced, it's often possible to remove a piece from a closet or other obscure location to create a patch. The hole in the closet can then be filled by a swatch from a carpet store or home center.

You'll need a sharp utility knife, carpet seaming tape, and an iron if the tape is heat sensitive. If it's tacky tape, you won't need the iron.

First, clean the affected area; this will produce the best color match. Cleaning will also cause any worn fibers to stand up straight, which will make it easier to create a seam.

Create a paper template a little bigger than the area that needs to be replaced. Use the template to mark the damaged section for removal. If the carpet has long fibers, push them to the side to make a clean cut with a utility knife at the base of the carpet.

When you choose the piece of carpet that will be your patch, take care to match the pattern, if there is one. Use the template to cut two patches—one to repair the damaged section, and one from the swatch to replace the piece removed from the closet.

Tuck seaming tape into the cutout so that half is under the carpet and half visible. Apply heat from the iron if needed—only on the tape that is visible. Carefully position the patch within the cutout, so that it tightly abuts the edges of the hole. Press it into place, then fluff the carpet fibers. Follow the same steps to install the replacement patch in the closet.

HIRING A PRO TO CLEAN CARPET

If your carpet is heavily stained, it may make sense to hire professional cleaners. Call around to compare prices and cleaning methods. Many companies charge by the square foot, so measure the rooms in your home—multiplying length by width to get each room's square footage.

Be sure the company uses steam-cleaning or extraction. A truck-mounted unit has more powerful suction than a portable unit. Ask whether the company will move your furniture and if there is an extra charge for this. Choose a company that is insured, in case your carpet—or anything else in the house—is damaged.

glossary

back-buttering The technique of troweling thinset mortar onto the back of a tile. It is recommended if the backs of tiles are uneven, or when it is not feasible to apply mortar to the wall or floor.

backsplash The area, usually about 4 inches wide, on the wall behind a counter; it may be covered with tile.

base shoe A small, rounded piece of moulding that is often attached at the bottom of a baseboard, where it meets the floor.

baseboard Moulding that runs along the bottom of a wall. Baseboard covers both the gap at the bottom of the wall and the gap between the flooring and the wall.

batten A straight board or metal piece used to temporarily hold tiles in alignment during installation.

beater board A short, flat board or piece of plywood, also called a beating block. Used with a mallet to firmly embed tiles in adhesive and to ensure they are at a uniform height.

blind nailing Driving a nail at an angle through the top of a flooring board's tongue. The nail head is completely hidden by the next installed board.

border Perimeter pieces, either wood or tile, usually in a color that contrasts with the central material.

bullnose tile A trim tile with one rounded edge, applied wherever a tile edge will be visible.

casing Trim used to cover the gap between a door or window jamb and the wall. The bottoms of vertical door casing pieces are typically undercut prior to installing a new floor, so the flooring material can slip under them.

caulk A sealant made of a flexible material such as silicone, used to fill a joint that may move slightly due to expansion and contraction. It comes in tubes and is applied with a caulk gun.

ceramic tile Tile made from non-metallic minerals (such as are found in clay), fired in a kiln at a high temperature. Ceramic tiles may be glazed or unglazed.

concrete backerboard Also called cement board or cement backerboard. Underlayment for tile—both wall and floor—that comes in large sheets; made primarily of Portland cement and sand.

cove base Also known as base cove. A flexible vinyl baseboard that is adhered to the wall with cove base adhesive.

cross cut A cut made perpendicular to the length of a board.

curing The process by which an adhesive not only dries, but also achieves full strength.

down-angle tile A tile with two rounded bullnose edges, used at a corner.

embossing leveler A pourable form of cement applied over a subfloor to smooth out minor imperfections.

engineered flooring Tongue-and-groove flooring made of several plies, like plywood. The top ply is hardwood, usually coated with a durable urethane finish.

expansion joint A gap between ceramic or stone tiles on a large floor. The gap is filled with caulk or another flexible material to accommodate expansion and contraction of the floor.

face nailing Driving a nail through the top (the face) of a piece of flooring (as opposed to blind nailing). A face nail should be countersunk and the hole filled.

field tile A tile in the main part of a tiled area; all four edges are unfinished. Most tiles are field tiles.

flooring adhesive A bonding agent used to affix tile or other floor coverings to the subsurface. The two basic types are thinset mortar and mastic.

glaze A glasslike coating that is affixed to ceramic tile by baking.

grout A mortarlike substance used to fill the joints between ceramic or stone tiles. Gaps larger than $1/8$ inch call for sanded grout; narrower gaps require unsanded grout.

hardwood A species such as oak or maple, typically used for flooring because it resists denting.

impervious tile Tile fired at a very high temperature, making it nearly waterproof and suitable for outdoor use in freezing climates.

isolation membrane A sheet of fabric or plastic, set in adhesive, that allows a flooring substructure to move without damaging the tiles set on top.

jamb The framing to which a door or window is attached.

joist A framing member, typically made of 2-by lumber, that supports a subfloor. Joists are usually spaced 16 inches apart.

laminate flooring Tongue-and-groove flooring with a thin, hard top layer made of polymer or resin rather than wood.

latex or polymer additive A liquid or powder used to increase the flexibility and strength of thinset mortar or grout.

mastic Also called organic mastic. An adhesive that is extremely sticky and that retains flexibility after it cures, making it well suited for vinyl, wood, and other flexible materials.

miter cut An angle cut. Materials that have been miter-cut at 45 degrees can be joined to produce a 90-degree corner.

mortar A mixture of sand and Portland cement, and sometimes a latex or polymer additive, that serves as an adhesive. See thinset mortar.

mosaic tile Small tiles (usually 2 inches square or smaller) mounted on a sheet for ease of installation.

parquet tile A tile made of many small pieces of hardwood. Parquet tiles join together with tongues and grooves, and are affixed using adhesive rather than nails.

paver A general term for a type of ceramic tile that is fairly thick, natural in color, and porous because it was fired at a low temperature.

plunge cut A cut made by lowering a circular saw blade into a board.

rip cut A cut along the length of a board.

score To cut a very shallow line. On tile, a tile-cutting tool with a scoring wheel is used. Once scored, the tile can be snapped apart, making a fairly straight cut.

sealer A liquid agent that partly penetrates a tile and/or grout and partly remains on the surface, providing protection against dirt and freezing.

self-spacing tile A ceramic tile that has small nubs (called lugs) at each corner; they create perfect spacing when the tiles are pressed together.

spacer A small piece of plastic, often cross-shaped, used to maintain even spacing between tiles during installation.

thinset mortar Mortar that is extra-sticky and that can be applied as thinly as $1/8$ inch, making it an ideal material for installing ceramic or stone tile.

threshold A strip of moulding that is applied to a floor to bridge the gap between two adjacent floor surfaces.

tongue-and-groove flooring Wood, engineered, parquet, or laminate flooring that has grooves running along two sides and protruding tongues along the other two. The tongue of one piece fits snugly into the groove of an adjacent piece.

underlayment A surface, often made of plywood, that is attached over a subfloor before setting vinyl tiles or other products that require a very smooth subsurface.

V-cap A trim tile that wraps around the front edge of a countertop.

working lines Guidelines, usually made with a chalk line, that show where tiles or flooring should go for an accurate installation.

credits

DESIGN

10: Mark Hutker & Associates, Architects; **11 top:** Bill Bauhs, Architect; **12 top:** Paul Janicki, Architect; **13 top left and bottom, 14:** Dave McFadden/Past Basket; **17 top left:** Carol R. Knott, ASID; **19 bottom:** Carol Glasser Design; **24 bottom right:** Tile: Walker Zanger; **25 top:** Jean Stoffer, Designs for the Kitchen; **25 bottom:** Eve Robinson Associates; **27 bottom left:** EJR Architects/Ellen Roché; **29 top:** Jim and Jean Wagner, WoodFellows; **29 bottom:** Marilynn Davis; **31 bottom right:** Noel Jeffrey; **33 bottom:** courtesy of Blackstock Leather, Inc.; **39 bottom:** courtesy of Timber-Grass Fine Bamboo Flooring & Panels; **40:** Lisa Melone; **41 top:** Daniel DuBay; **41 bottom:** Brit Carter; **47 bottom:** McDonald & Moore; **48 left:** Kelly Hutchinson; **51 top:** Susan Churcher; **51 bottom:** Plan One, William Gottlieb; **53 top:** Deborah Oertle; **54:** Stephen Blatt, Architects; **72 right:** Raino-Ogden Architects; **79 top:** Talon Architects; **88 bottom:** Thomas Bollay, Architect; **89:** Interior design: Linda Applewhite & Associates. Architects: Halperin & Christ; **93 bottom right:** Brett Design; **95 top:** Stone-Wood Design; **96 row 1, col 2:** Morningstar Marble and Granite; **96 row 2, col 4:** Siemasko & Verbridge, Architects; **118 row 1, col 2:** courtesy of Hearst Publications; **118 row 4, col 3:** Steve Knutson, Knutson Designs; **142 top right:** Terra Designs/Anna Salibelo; **146:** Michael Trahan Interior Design; **150 row 2, col 3:** Miller-Hull Architects; **167 top:** Lisa Melone; **167 bottom:** Brian Murphy, Architect; **200 row 3, col 1:** courtesy of TimberGrass Fine Bamboo Flooring & Panels; **200 row 3, col 3:** Jim Davis; **200 row 4, col 4:** IDT/Stuart Narofsky; **216:** Linda Applewhite & Associates.

PHOTOGRAPHY

Aged Woods, Inc.: 164 row 1, col 1; **Armstrong/Bruce Hardwood Floors:** 1; **Armstrong World Industries, Inc.:** 8 row 4, col 1, 8 row 4, col 2, 31 bottom left, 32, 33 top, 34 both, 35 both, 36, 37 both, 38, 39 top, 42, 43 top left, 186 left, 191 top; **Bomanite Corporation:** 44, 45 both; **Marion Brenner:** 147, 148 all, 149; **Bruce Hardwood Floors:** 5 top middle left, 164 row 2, col 2, 166 bottom, 168, 172; **Caroline Bureau, Robert Chartier, Michel Thibaut:** 184 all; **Wayne Cable:** 5 top left, 60 middle right, 60 upper right, 60 lower right, 60 bottom left, 60 bottom middle, 61 top left, 61 middle left, 61 bottom left, 61 top right, 61 middle right, 61 bottom right, 62 top right, 62 middle, 62 middle right, 62 middle left, 62 bottom, 63 top, 63 middle left, 63 middle right, 64 top left, 74 all, 75 top, 75 bottom, 76 all, 77 all, 78 all, 80, 81 all, 83, 85 all, 86 all, 90, 91 all, 93 top left, 93 middle left, 94 all, 105 all, 110 both, 111 top left, 111 top right, 118 row 4, col 2, 121 all, 123, 126 both, 127 all, 129 all, 130 all, 131 top left, 131 top right, 131 bottom left, 132 all, 133 all, 154 both, 155 all, 156 top right, 156 bottom right, 157 all, 169 all, 170 top left, 170 top right, 170 bottom right, 171 all; **James Carrier:** 20 right, 66 row 3, col 3, 143 bottom, 200 row 2, col 3; **Congoleum Corporation:** 96 row 3, col 2, 150 row 3, col 2, 150 row 3, col 4, 158 top left; **Coronet Carpet Images:** 48 right, 49 both; **DalTile:** 8 row 4, col 3, 28; **DeWalt:** 63 bottom left, 65 bottom left; **Chris Eden:** 150 row 2, col 3; **Edge Flooring:** 136 right; **Engelmann, Inc., Contractors:** 166 top; **Phillip Ennis:** 142 top right, 200 row 4, col 4; **Cheryl Fenton:** 178 bottom; **Scott Fitzgerrell:** 50; **Forbo Linoleum, Inc.:** 150 row 1, col 1; **Jay Graham:** 89; **John Granen:** 51 bottom; **Art Grice:** 39 bottom, 200 row 3, col 1; **Ken Gutmaker:** 216; **Doug Hall:** 33 bottom; **Margot Hartford:** 95 top; **Douglas Johnson:** 79 top, 146; **Muffy Kibbey:** 24 bottom right, 47 bottom; **Dennis Krukowski:** 17 bottom right, 31 bottom right, 93 bottom right; **Laticrete:** 20 left, 27 bottom right; **David Duncan Livingston:** 95 bottom; **Peter Malinowski/ InSite:** 88 bottom; **E. Andrew McKinney:** 15 top left; **Melabee M. Miller:** 40, 167 top; **Nafco by Domco Tarkett:** 152; **Eric O'Connell:** 51 top; **Pergo:** 43 top right, 43 bottom, 187 bottom right; **David Phelps:** 200 row 3, col 3, 88 top; **Porter-Cable:** 64 bottom right; **Eric Roth:** 17 top right, 19 top, 23 bottom; **Ann Sacks:** 73 all, 118 row 3, col 4; **Mark Samu:** 27 bottom left, 118 row 1, col 2; **Shaw Carpet:** 47 top; **Michael Skott:** 19 bottom; **Thomas J. Story:** 24 bottom left; **Tim Street-Porter:** 75 middle; **Tim Street-Porter/beateworks.com:** 167 bottom; **Valspar:** 178 top; **Brian Vanden Brink:** 10, 11 bottom, 16, 18, 31 top, 54, 55, 96 row 1, col 2, 96 row 2, col 4, 96 row 4, col 1; **Dominique Vorillon:** 2, 25 bottom; **Jessie Walker:** 11 top, 12 both, 13 all, 14, 15 top right, 15 bottom left, 17 top left, 17 middle, 21, 22, 23 top, 24 top right, 25 top, 29 both, 30, 41 both, 48 left, 52, 53 top, 72, 118 row 2, col 1, 118 row 4, col 3; **Westminster Ceramics:** 26, 27 top left, 79 bottom; **Wicanders Cork Flooring:** 53 bottom, 198 top left

index

A

Adhesive, 54, 77, 84, 153, 155, 192. *See also* Organic mastic; Thinset mortar
Air quality, 54
Asbestos warning, 107

B

Backerboard, 81, 110–111
Backsplash, 89, 91, 94, 95
Bamboo flooring, 39, 56
Baseboard, 51, 86, 104, 135, 178–183
Base shoe, 104, 178–179
Base tile, 134
Bathroom accessories, 69, 73, 76, 82
Bathtub surround, 74, 80–87
Batten, 72, 92, 123
Beater block, 62, 76, 130, 143
Blades, 61, 71, 127, 136, 174
Bluestone tile, 29
Borders and trim, 50, 73, 167, 178, 187. *See also* Bullnose tile; Moulding
Brick or block, 70, 83, 87, 147
Bullnose tile, 80, 91, 147, 148

C

Cabinets, 88, 95, 102, 103
Carpet, 46–49, 107, 140, 216–217
Caulk and caulking, 78, 214
Caulking gun, 63, 78

Ceramic tile
    about, 14–17, 52, 56
    caring for, 208–209
    floating, 136–137, 199
    removal and replacement, 106, 211, 212
Chalk line, 61, 121
Chisel, 207
Cleanability, 53, 136, 155
Cleaning, 147, 208–209, 216–217
Commercial tile, 30–31, 151, 152
Concrete, 44–45, 70, 114–115, 117, 146, 209
Cork tile, 39, 53, 57, 198
Cost considerations, 52–53
Countertops, 26, 27, 67, 88–95
Cutter, vinyl tile, 64, 156
Cutting
    curves, 86
    45 degree or corner, 93, 127, 170, 179, 181, 182
    holes for pipes, 84, 128
    notches, 125, 127, 171
    rip, 176–177, 197
Cutting guides, 85, 126, 127, 177, 197

D

Design elements, 13, 29, 44, 72
Doorways, 105, 158, 160, 176. *See also* Thresholds
Drill, 60
Drywall, 68. *See also* Greenboard
Drywall square, 60, 70
Durability and hardness, 14, 22, 23, 31, 42, 53

E

Electrical outlets and switches, 69, 73, 78, 95
Embossing leveler, 109, 152
Engineered or laminate flooring
    about, 38–39, 42–43, 55, 57
    floating, 43, 187, 194–197
    installation, 187–197
    with other floorings, 198–199
    repair, 206, 215
    snap-together, 197
Entryways, 53, 55, 198
Expansion joint or gap, 116, 174, 189, 192
Eye protection, 137

F

Finishes
    about, 37, 45, 167, 185
    masonry or tile sealer, 147, 149, 208
    no-wax, 32, 208
    paint, 184, 209, 210
    polyurethane, 37, 171, 185, 205, 208
    prefinished products, 187, 208
    stain, 37, 45, 166, 185, 205
    varnish, 185
    wax, 19, 37, 185, 208
Fireplace surround, 146–149
Flange, pipe, 80, 128, 157, 159, 161

Floor
concrete, 44–45, 70, 114–115,
117, 191, 195
finished height, 97, 98, 119,
151, 165, 198
firming, 100–101
flooring over existing, 172, 173,
191, 195
inspection, 98–99
leveling, 109, 115, 130, 137
patching, 99, 113, 114–115, 215
patterned, 17, 32, 144–145, 160,
163, 166–167, 184
preparation of substrate,
98–111, 152–154, 173
removing obstacles, 102–108
squeaks, 99, 172, 201, 203
strength, 98, 114, 119, 120
Flooring
choices of materials, 10–11
vinyl (*See* Vinyl sheet flooring)
wood (*See* Engineered or laminate flooring; Parquet wood
flooring; Strip flooring)
Floor tile. *See also* specific tile types
about, 16
adjustment of, 131, 155, 162,
169
combination of types, 198–199
cutting, 126–128, 145
installation, 130–135, 138–139,
144–145
removal or replacement,
106–107, 210–212
scale of, 12
tiling over existing, 153

G
Glass products, 24, 83, 87
Granite tile, 11, 22, 79, 143
Graphs or scale drawings, 83, 88,
122, 144, 153
Greenboard, 70–71, 80
Grinders, 61, 115, 148

Grout
aerosol, 136, 139
application, 77, 86–87, 132, 139
cleaning and repair, 209, 213
color, 17, 120, 142, 211
removal of excess, 77, 86–87,
131, 139, 209
selection, 17, 77, 79, 86, 213
on tile-wood interface, 199
Grout float, laminated, 62, 77, 86,
132
Grout lines. *See also* Spacers
adjacent to wood flooring, 199
with self-spacing tile, 16, 75
straightness, 131
width, 17, 120 (*See also* Grout,
selection)

H
Hardwood, 36–37
Health protection, 107, 108, 137,
203, 204
Hearth, 146, 147, 167, 176
Heat gun, 104, 106, 134

I
Installation
electrical outlets, 78
guide for, 72, 92, 123
minimization of disruption
during, 55
order of work, 123, 129, 153
Irregular tiles, 75, 85, 122, 123,
142

J
Jointing, 77, 86, 133
Joists, 98, 99, 100, 188
Jury stick, 60, 73

K
Knee pads, 59
Knives, 60, 64, 110

L
Laminate flooring. *See* Engineered
or laminate flooring
Laminate tile, 43, 57
Laying out
bathtub surround, 83
countertop, 92–93
flooring, 168, 174, 175,
188–189, 194
jury stick for, 73, 121
tiles, 72–73, 120–123, 144, 1
53, 168
tools for, 60–61
Leather tile, 33
Level, 60, 130, 148
Limestone tile, 28, 79
Linoleum, 10, 35, 57, 153

M
Mallet, rubber, 62
Mantles, 149
Marble tile, 13, 15, 22–23, 26, 79,
131, 141
Medium-density fiberboard
(MDF), 50
Membranes, isolation, 70, 105, 117
Metal tile, 24
Mixing paddle, 62, 84, 129
Moisture, 81, 87, 131, 191.
See also Membranes
Mortar, 84, 86, 129, 211.
See also Thinset mortar
Mosaic tile
about, 16, 17, 24–25, 26, 57
borders, 24, 72, 79
cutting, 128
installation, 76, 143
Moulding, 50, 104–105, 121, 178,
182

N
Nailer, power, 64, 180
Nail set, 64, 65, 175, 180
Nibbling tool, 61, 85, 126, 143
Nonvitreous tile, 15

O

Onyx tile, 23
Organic mastic, 69, 74, 76, 77, 80, 84, 212

P

Parquet wood flooring, 40–41, 167, 168–171, 199, 208, 212
Plaster, 68, 81
Plumbing
    expansion gap for, 116
    removal, 80–81, 90, 102–103
    sheet flooring around, 159, 161
    in a sink installation, 95
    tiling around, 84, 85, 128, 157, 159
Plumb line, 69, 71, 83
Plywood, 112, 120, 121, 129, 141, 145
Porcelain pavers or tile, 20, 56, 129
Porosity, 15
Practical considerations, 52–53
Preparation of substrate
    for bathtub surround, 80–81
    concrete, 70
    countertop, 90–91
    for fireplace surround, 147
    floor
        for engineered flooring, 188, 191, 198–199
        for refinishing, 205
        for tile, 98–111, 136, 143, 152–154, 198–199
        for wood flooring, 168, 172–173, 198–199
    to tile over existing tile, 69
    walls, 70
Protective clothing and gear, 108, 137
Pry bar, 60

Q

Quarry tile, 21, 56, 129, 131
Quartzite tile, 23

R

Racking technique, 175, 190, 196
Radiant heat, 53, 117
Radiator, removal, 102
Ratings for tile, 14
Repair. *See also* Cleaning
    carpet, 56, 216–217
    ceramic or stone floor tile, 56, 58, 201, 211, 212
    concrete slab, 114–115
    grout, 213
    laminate flooring, 57, 215
    re-caulking, 214
    strip flooring, 57, 202–207
    subfloor, 99
    vinyl tile, 58, 210
    wall, 71, 75
    window, 87
    wood parquet tile, 212
Resilient flooring. *See* Vinyl sheet flooring; Vinyl tile
Roller, floor, 64
Rubber tile, 31

S

Safety. *See* Health protection; Slip resistance
Saltillo tile, 18, 75
Sandblasted stone, 29
Sanders, 65, 202–204
Saws
    circular, 59, 108, 136, 215
    coping, 65
    hacksaw with rod saw blade, 61, 75
    hole, 61, 128
    jamb, 59, 158
    jigsaw or saber, 63, 136, 138
    miter, 65, 180
    radial-arm, 170
    reciprocating, 59
    wet or tub, 62, 127
Scrapers, 60, 203, 205, 214
Sealer
    for grout, 17, 87
    for porous stone, 15, 132, 142, 147, 149, 208
    seam, 153, 163

Self-spacing tiles, 16, 75, 84
Self-stick tile, 32, 33, 58, 152, 154, 157
Setting tiles
    bathtub surround, 84–86
    bullnose, 148
    countertop, 94
    fireplace surround, 147, 148, 149
    floor, 130–131, 138, 154–155, 168–170, 199
    "on point," 12, 40, 93, 122, 145
    tools for, 62–63, 74, 153
    wall, 74, 75, 76
Sheet flooring. *See* Vinyl sheet flooring
Showers, 82
Sinks, 88–89, 90, 91, 95, 102
Slate tile, 10, 28, 29, 53, 79
Sleepers, 173, 206
Slip resistance, 16, 21, 24, 26, 27, 54
Snap cutter, 61, 126
Sound considerations, 53, 55
Spacers, 75, 81, 84, 124, 132
Sponge, 63
Square (tool), 60, 61, 70, 71
Square, checking for, 120
Stain removal, 209
Staplers, 63, 64, 173, 175, 176, 189–190
Steam extraction cleaning, 216–217
Stencils, 11
Stone tile
    about, 14–15, 22–23, 58, 79
    agglomerated, 22
    installation, 79, 116, 130–135, 142–145
    polished, 22–23, 58, 79, 143
    replacement, 211
    rough, 15, 28–29, 58, 142
    tumbled, 13, 15, 26–27, 58, 142
    with wood, 10, 11, 199
Straightedge, 61, 94

Strip flooring. *See also* Engineered or laminate flooring; Parquet wood flooring
about, 57, 165–167, 172, 173, 175
installation, 172–177, 206
repair, 206–207
sanding and finishes for, 201, 202–203, 208
straightening, 176, 189
with tile, 198–199
Style, 11–12, 31
Subfloor, 98–101, 165, 172, 188
Substrate. *See* Preparation of substrate

T

Tape
fiberglass mesh, 71, 111
masking, 82, 87, 94, 184, 193, 212, 214
Tape measure, 61
Templates, 145, 153, 158–161, 163
Terra-cotta tile, 15, 18–19, 55, 56, 129, 131
Texture, 13, 16, 26, 41, 54
Thinset mortar. *See also* Mortar
application, 130–131, 143
mixing and set time, 74, 84, 110, 129
"3-4-5" method, 120, 122
Thresholds, 51, 117, 136, 139–141
Tile cutter, hand, 126, 128
Tile nippers (nibbling tool), 61, 85, 126, 143
Tile stone, 62, 84, 110
Toilet, removal, 103
Tools
for baseboard, 65
cutting ceramic or stone (*See* Nibbling tool; Saws; Snap cutter)
cutting vinyl and linoleum, 64, 134, 153, 154, 156, 157
demolition, 60
finishing, 65, 77, 115, 133, 203
grouting, 77, 86, 95, 132
layout, 60–61, 72, 73, 121, 125

mixing, 62, 84, 129
nailing, 64, 65
for plumbing removal, 80, 81, 103
setting, 62–63, 74, 153
for spacers removal, 132
stapling (*See* Staplers)
substrate preparation, 59–60
wiping, 63
Traffic considerations, 14
Travertine tile, 23
Trim. *See* Borders and trim
Trowels
margin, 62
notched, 63, 64, 74, 94, 130, 154

U

Underlayment. *See also* Backerboard; Greenboard
about, 105
for carpet, 49
for countertop, 90
foam, 32, 55, 194–195
installation, 112–113, 137, 194–195
removal, 108
for strip or engineered flooring, 172, 191, 194–195, 202
for tile, 105, 136, 137, 152, 210

V

Vacuums, 203, 204, 216
V-caps, 88, 91, 92, 94
Vinyl cove base, 51, 104, 135
Vinyl sheet flooring, 34–35, 58, 107, 158–163
Vinyl tile
commercial, 30–31, 58, 151, 152
installation, 152–157
maintenance, 205, 209
removal, 106, 210
surface-printed self-stick, 32, 33, 58, 152, 154, 157
Vitreous tile, 15
Volatile organic compounds (VOC), 54

W

Wall
backsplash, 95
laying out for tiling, 72–73, 83
patching, 68, 212
plumb, 69, 71, 83
preparation for tiling, 68–71
removing obstacles, 69, 80–81
Wallpaper, removal, 70
Wall tile. *See also* specific tile types
about, 16, 67
expansion joints, 116
installation, 74–87, 148
removal, 81
replacement, 212
tiling over existing, 69, 146
Water. *See* Moisture
Windows, 72, 73, 83, 87
Wood flooring, 36–37, 166. *See also* Engineered or laminate flooring; Parquet wood flooring; Strip flooring
Wood paneling, removal, 70
Working lines
for countertop tile, 92
on the floor, 121, 188
for wall tile, 72, 73, 74, 83